Summer of
the Bass

Summer of
the Bass

My Love Affair with America's Greatest Fish

For John —
who loves Bass,
as much as I do!

W. D. WETHERELL

enjoy + all Best

wishes!

WD Wetherell
Agust 2017

Skyhorse Publishing

Skyhorse Publishing books may be purchased in bulk at special discounts for sales promotion, corporate gifts, fund-raising, or educational purposes. Special editions can also be created to specifications. For details, contact the Special Sales Department, Skyhorse Publishing, 307 West 36th Street, 11th Floor, New York, NY 10018 or info@skyhorsepublishing.com.

Skyhorse® and Skyhorse Publishing® are registered trademarks of Skyhorse Publishing, Inc.®, a Delaware corporation.

Visit our website at www.skyhorsepublishing.com.

10 9 8 7 6 5 4 3 2 1

Library of Congress Cataloging-in-Publication Data is available on file.

Cover design by Tom Lau
Cover photo credit: "Bass" by Winslow Homer c. 1900

ISBN: 9781634503952
Ebook ISBN: 9781510701083

Printed in the United States

Contents

For Ray Chapin

One

Fishing is about rival tugs, or that's what I used to think. For a bass, it's a tug on the jaw, a tug on its complacency, a tug on its notion of how the world operates. For the fisher, it's a tug on the wrist, a tug on the forearm, a tug, if you're receptive, on the heart. That my tug can overcome a bass's tug doesn't prove mine is any finer or nobler—it means that the fly rod, in the hands of an experienced angler, is a wondrous equalizer. But I never think I've vanquished a fish or defeated it or whupped it when I bring it to hand. Call our struggle even—and if I add up all those bass I've caught over the years, think of their power, vibrancy, and beauty, the advantage is all on their side, and it's me who's been hooked, played, landed, and never yet released.

Today, on a perfect May morning of copious sunshine, extravagant greenery, a choir festival of birds, I'm taking the canoe up to Smarts Pond, a five-mile drive into the hills from our home near the river, tugged there by my fascination with this most quintessential of North American creatures, the bass—the All-American fish, the one you want on your side if muscle, courage, and pluck are needed for a win. I'm in love with them, have been for a long time. It was the fish I lusted after as a kid, abandoned for trout when I was in my twenties, rediscovered when I moved north and found that the waters hereabouts were full of them—the fish I want to pursue and study and celebrate in what remains of my fishing life.

We used to live in Lyme Center, the uphill, older part of town, in a red gambrel-roofed house built in 1910 and hardly improved upon until the day we moved in. One electrical outlet upstairs, one outlet downstairs, an unreliable spring for water, a septic system far from systematic, a barn the nether parts of which no one had entered in the last sixty years. The price was $55,000, so we didn't ask many questions, not even with a mortgage of thirteen percent.

It was the house we brought our daughter to from the hospital when she was born. Four years later, it was the house we brought our son to after the same happy drive. My mother, long gone now, helped us strip five layers of wallpaper off the walls, and we signed our names on the plaster before putting up the new paper, so generations in the future would know who did the grunt work. My father, squinting with bad eyes, helped me plant lilacs along the front porch. We had birthday parties on the patch of front lawn—Matt, age one, presented with a big slice of cake, stuck his finger in the candle and cried. On the little slope that led down from the barn we took the kids sledding—and then, in summer, set up a sprinkler so Erin could run laughing through the spray.

I wrote four books in the extra bedroom upstairs. Cooked many meals in what passed for our kitchen. Practiced fly casting in the back yard, learning to lay my line across a fallen maple leaf five times out of five. Explored the surrounding hills, sometimes on skis, often pushing a baby carriage to places baby carriages had never gone before. Learned what it takes to make a marriage that lasts.

No wonder that, passing it on the road, I slow down and draw the mental equivalent of a deep breath.

Never for long—no, not for long. Sunset moods are to be avoided at my age, so I'm wary of what I'm feeling as I drive up to fish Smarts. If you start getting nostalgic for your youth, it can easily get away from you, thicken into nostalgia for a time, an America, you think actually existed but probably never did. It's a tug, a really hard tug, balanced by a tug that becomes stronger the nearer I get to the pond—the tug, the anticipation, of playing with those bass. The past has got me by the ankles, but the present yanks hard on my ears—the anticipation of fishing has pulled me out of deeper moods than this.

Where have the years gone? is something worth thinking about, but not today, not up against the brighter, more insistent question, the classic question, the one whose answer we fishers never know in advance: *Will I catch one?*

Nostalgia is a slippery slope—I have to put the car into third to get up the long forested hill that leads to the town landing. These New Hampshire hills have stories a lot older than mine. The Appalachian Trail crosses the road, and then climbs Lambert Ridge past stone walls built by settlers who farmed rocky, high, and lonely. If they didn't escape west to Iowa or Nebraska, they were buried in the overgrown Beal Cemetery where the road levels off; little brass shields mark the graves of those who fought in the Revolution. Loggers stripped the hills after the farmers gave up, men named George Mousely, Arthur Chesley, or Chester Pike, and, tougher than any of them, Ruth Park, a Vassar grad who our oldest old-timers can remember driving her team into Lyme village for her mail.

Sixteen schoolhouses, one-roomed or two, were spaced across these hills, when snow and mud kept youngsters near home; my daughter attended kindergarten in the last one surviving before it too was finally closed down. Houses burned to the foundation, or collapsed under snow, became nothing but cellar holes choked with briars. Lilacs had been planted by kitchen windows so their perfume could waft in on the May breeze—and they can still be found in the deepest woods, heavy with blossoms when even the cellar holes have disappeared.

These settlers were plucky, strong, freedom loving, indomitable— traits shared, as it happens, by the American black bass. They would not have recognized the name, of course; the oldest, remembering fish stories told them by Puritan grandfathers, might have heard of the sea bass of Europe, but that's it. Smarts Pond didn't exist in their day—its flowage was damned after the Civil War to store a head of water for the factories springing up on the Mascoma River fifteen miles downstream. The first bass was stocked in 1875, brought in a wagon from Hanover Reservoir twelve miles south of here, a key distribution point in the smallmouth's great migration eastward from the Great Lakes.

So the first generation of settlers would have known nothing about bass—and, if you explained that the motive force behind their migration was sport, not food . . . that the reason bass were now living in these New England hills was because they pulled hard on the end of a fishing line . . . they would have looked at you like you were mad.

"Eat 'em?" they might grunt.

"Sure. Well, sometimes. Actually, hardly ever. I throw them all back."

Mad, crazy—and that proved it. My settler would squint in the sun, spit, and then go back to building his stone wall or reading brochures about free land in Kansas.

Theirs is a New Hampshire, a New England, an America that is gone now, and no wishing will ever bring it back—and yet many people do wish, and their wishing, in the time I'm writing in, can often turn sour.

And maybe that's the first thing I've discovered as I start in writing; it's hard to discuss bass without talking about American traits, American virtues, the battering they're taking these days in what seems, in its bitter divisions, a second Civil War. What's anthropomorphism called on a national scale? Americamorphism? Bald eagles suffer from this, grizzlies, wild mustangs—all the iconic American creatures we like to think tell us something about who we are. I'm sometimes guilty of this—often guilty, now that I think of it. But there's something about bass fishing that gets you thinking along those lines.

If I were going to fish for trout, I could be nostalgic, regretful, and bittersweet all I wanted. Our native brook trout are mostly gone, the shy remnants I can count on my hand, but our bass are flourishing, and their golden age is now. Fishing for trout, I sometimes feel I'm fishing for the past; fishing for bass, I'm smack-dab in the present, playing with youth, being a boy again, so it's no wonder they fascinate me. I even dress differently when I fish for bass. No expensive fabrics weigh me down, no $700 waders or high-tech vests. I'm wearing gray work pants, gray work shirt, a head net to keep away the blackflies, held down by a thirty-year-old porkpie hat—dressed honestly, to meet this honest creature without blushing.

There's a mile where the trees touch tops over the road, and then a beaver pond, and then the big pond itself comes into sight, with the green bulk of Smarts Mountain sweeping upward from the wild northern shore. The town owns a small patch of land here, just big enough to launch canoes. In the Depression, the last farms having gone bust, Lyme took the land for unpaid taxes, this lot being one of the few it still retains.

Some idiot has left his bob-house here after a winter's ice fishing (later, when I complain about this to our constable, he nods, says "That's my son"), so there is hardly room to park. I slap sunscreen on my face, spike it with bug juice, slide the canoe off the car, and drag it to the water, and then—having had just peripheral flashes until now—for the first time really look out over the pond.

I would describe Smarts as being typical bass water, if there was any such thing. Typical bass water? It would have to be a blend, a montage, a bouillabaisse, a stew. Mix mossy sloughs hidden away in the Florida backcountry with big suburban lakes outside San Diego with farm ponds in Ohio and rivers in the Ozarks with clear rocky lakes in the Quetico-Superior and water hazards on Texas golf courses and brackish inlets in North Carolina and 2,500 miles of the Mississippi with limestone quarries in Pennsylvania and shaded stretches of the Shenandoah and dammed impoundments in Montana and TVA lakes in Kentucky and huge reservoirs in Oklahoma and ranch ponds in the high desert and ponds on sugarcane land in Hawaii along with skating ponds in big cities and lakes in Minnesota where the wild rice grows, the outflow of nuclear power plants, mudholes behind your garage, Walden Pond, and all five Great Lakes—six if you count Lake Champlain . . . Mix these and dozens of other styles of lakes, rivers, sloughs, millstreams, impoundments, bayous, oxbows, lagoons, creeks, tarns, and ponds across forty-nine states and Puerto Rico, and you would get your "typical" bass water.

Smarts is a good example of one of the subdivisions within this huge variety—your classic North Woods smallmouth lake, rocky, clear, ringed with spruce and scented by sphagnum, the kind of water you find in Maine or Northern Michigan. It's a lake that looks like it should have a moose swimming across it—and yes, I saw one once, its black-brown body undulating like a sea serpent's, its head arched back to keep its antlers dry, so it gave off an impression of extreme power and great fastidiousness. It also looks like the kind of pond where loons will cavort beneath your canoe, and that's happened to me, too—loons, two of them, submerging right under me to come up on the other side, the water so transparent they could have been flying there, not swimming.

There are a few summer homes along the eastern shore—"camps" they're called, though one or two are Adirondack-style elaborate. There are a few too many docks and powerboats for a lake so small—when the weather warms, I don't revisit Smarts. Still, I've been fishing it in May for more than thirty years now, and if the hills in which it sits are heavy with remembrance, then the lake is, too; there's not a rock along the shore-line that doesn't carry with it an other memory, not a weed bed that doesn't get me reminiscing. Slowly, laboriously, rowing myself around the pond in the tiny inflatable rowboat that was all we had in the early years, the *Bismarck*. Bringing my kids here on picnics to catch yellow perch. Telling a friend, "There's a one-eye bass behind that rock," and having him on his first cast catch it. Sheltering in the woods with my fishing pal Ray Chapin during thunderstorms, the great peals of sound being tossed between ridges and magnified, the lightning close enough to smell, nothing to defend ourselves with but the spruce overhead and a half-empty bottle of Wild Turkey.

There are more specific memories, tactical memories, that I draw upon when I fish; nostalgia here is one of my weapons. Thirty years of fishing has taught me not only which rocks shelter bass and which ones don't, but at which stage of the season a particular rock is liable to have a bass near it—and this cycle, this bassy calibration, never seems to vary. The roundish rocks in the southeastern cove near the Dart-mouth Outing Club cabin? Late season rocks. The sharper ones, drag-on's teeth, leading to the bay with the old stone dam? Mid-season rocks. The sunken stone wall, a ghostly six feet under, left from an early settler's farm? Early rocks—and where they emerge from the water in three porcelain-smooth boulders . . . salt-shaker, pepper-shaker, sugar bowl . . . is where I always catch my sixth, seventh, and eighth bass of the year.

Why the cycle should be so precise here is anyone's guess. Some rocks are closer to deep water than other rocks; some catch more sun and act as reflector ovens; some are close to weed beds . . . but I can't draw any direct causal link between which rocks are fishing hot, which ones cold, and any of these variations. On this trip, I focused on the early rocks, the ones that the bass will seek out when the water is still chilly. We had record warmth back in March, and, with the ice going out so early, I worried that I may have timed the spawning cycle wrong, and might be too late to find bass on their nests.

It used to be easier to get this right. Memorial Day always represented peak spawning on Smarts. I'd go for the first time on May twentieth, catch an early bird or two, move in close to examine the shallows, and, not seeing any beds, know I had a few days yet before things got exciting. Then, after ten years of perfect predictability in this respect, I found, going out on Memorial Day, that most of the spawning was already over, and the male bass, faithful guardians of the nest, had moved out to deep water.

I adjusted my schedule accordingly—went out scouting on May sixteenth, found them on the beds on the twentieth. This is a surprisingly quick response to a change that must surely be coming even faster than climatologists predict. We shared the hottest spring in the history of record keeping with thirty-one other states. Those bayous, farm ponds, creeks, and Great Lakes are heating up fast; the bass, whose judgment is centered in their reproductive instincts, not their political ones, are getting the message before we do.

If I were more scientifically minded, I'd have been sticking a thermometer in the pond all these years, taking temperatures, keeping records—water in the mid sixties is what the bass are waiting or. But I prefer more impressionistic methods. It's time to start bass fishing, my inner clock says, when mockingbirds start singing in our maples; when little kids jump in the water, and, screaming in shock at the chill, jump right out again; when girls start wearing summer skirts; when the lilacs blossom, the blueberries blossom, the honeysuckle blossoms, the black-flies get bad, high schools hold prom night, the dandelions take over the lawn, and the NBA playoffs go to the second round—*that's* the time to go bass fishing, water temperature be damned.

On the way to the pond, I passed a girl out running—and she was dressed in a fleecy warm sweatsuit, not shorts, a very bad sign. When I got out of the car at the landing, instead of immediately being mugged by blackflies, only a lonely one or two buzzed down—another bad sign. Or were these good signs? I want to be a bit early on this first trip, it's part of my strategy. Catching only ten-inch bass will assure me I'm not too late to catch eighteen-inch bass next time out.

I slide the canoe in, decide to round the lake counterclockwise, which will bring me to the best "early" spots last. A beautiful stillness, this time of morning. The rocks sticking up from the water accept the sun before the water does, thanks to their verticality, so, for a few minutes, bronze plinths seem planted in a field of gray—and then the bronze bleeds into the water and everything shines with the same golden brilliance. The shore is lined with white pines, their reflections plunge into the depths just as straight and green as they tower into the sky, so I can't see their tops looking down, just as I can't see their tops looking up; which is the real tree, which the reflected, is not easy to determine.

I start casting when I come to the first rocks—late season rocks, but I try them anyway. I've been fishing for trout for the two months prior to this, and going from a three-ounce fly rod to a four-ounce fly rod seems like a much more dramatic change than the difference in weight can account for. Power becomes the emphasis in using a bass rod, not finesse; fine motor skills are replaced by brawn—which is an exaggeration, but you get my point. When I fish for trout, I feel like a member of a craft guild or artist's colony, someone who wields a brush; fishing for bass, I feel like a member of a union, and the beefier tool feels good in my hand.

No one is out on the pond besides me. A weekday morning, bugs starting to bite, the water too cold yet for swimming, bass under catch-and-release regulations so the meat fishermen aren't interested. It's always that way in May. In all my years of coming here, I've never seen another person fly fishing for bass. Not a few. Not a handful. None.

Solitude can seem like an entitlement if you're not careful. Sometimes I fight down the urge to be possessive of Smarts, but sometimes I play around with it. If I were king of the pond, the first thing I would do (well, the second—the first would be banning motorboats) is issue birth control pills to the pickerel. For many years, they thrashed out a rough equilibrium with the bass—the pond seemed seventy percent smallmouth, thirty percent pickerel—but now through some invisible coup or demographic explosion, the pickerel seem to have reversed the equation, so you catch two pickerel for every bass rather than the other way around.

I have nothing against pickerel—they weren't Thoreau's favorite fish for nothing. They were here before the bass were, just like the Mouselys were here before the Wetherells and the Abenakis were here before the Mouselys, so they have right of precedence—only their teeth are murder on leaders, and it gets expensive losing those flies.

I use my second-string poppers fishing Smarts, so if the pickerel loot them I don't much care. Don't ask me how, but poppers and bugs seem to reproduce in your box over the winter, propagating weird mutants that resemble no popper you ever actually purchased. Stubby rubber legs instead of long floppy ones; mullets of deer hair rather than crew cuts; marabou that's molting; hooks that were born rusty and brittle. They appear in my box out of nowhere, but are perfect for fishing Smarts, where the bass seem to like them just fine and the pickerel, if they rip one off, are doing you a favor.

I shouldn't be fishing top water anyway—this early in the season, with few insects on the surface yet, flies that sink are much more likely to catch fish. But the pond's surface is so tranquil and still it seems wrong to break the surface film; I'm using a popper for aesthetic reasons, not tactical ones, which has always been one of my weaknesses.

I try some casts in the cove that leads to the old stone dam, and then paddle along the western shore past one or two of the oldest cabins. These rocks are early rocks, so I'm more alert now, more expectant. For thirty years this is where I've caught my first bass of the year. There's one rock in particular five yards out from shore, its top half exposed—it's as round as a granite dartboard and makes a good target. My no-name popper hits the bull's-eye and drops near a patch of weed. Nothing. I strip it back for another cast so fast that its convex lip makes it dive underwater, and the moment it submerges a welling surge of water blows it back up to the surface where it spins as if dazed.

Big pickerel? Big bass? Big *something* anyway. I paddle just far enough to get out of the danger zone, take the popper off, put on a black Wooly Bugger, a sinking fly that looks like a stubby combination salamander, leech, grub, crayfish, and worm—a Tootsie Roll with feelers. We hear about the omnivore's dilemma when it comes to what we humans eat, but the bass has no dilemmas about its own unfastidious carnivorousness—it clobbers anything that might taste meaty, and a Wooly Bugger triggers this reflex better than almost anything.

(Trout are picky eaters in comparison. Trout are the ones that at a restaurant ask the waiter if the bread is gluten free, if the chicken is free range, if the sauce has MSG.)

Wooly Buggers are buggers to cast—I have to do it with a lobbing, straight-armed motion like a bowler in cricket. The second it lands, the water surges toward it again, only this time the wave has a mouth attached, and that mouth, clamping down on the bubbles, takes hold.

Viciously takes hold. The bass is protecting its spawning nest and/ or trying to kill, and the fury of this, the pure savagery, is transmitted through the leader up the fly line along my arm. I've caught thousands of bass, but that initial jolt always surprises me. I'm never prepared for it, and it could be the first smallmouth I've ever caught, so astonished am I at being plugged so suddenly into all that power.

Fishing for trout, you feel like you're up against a con artist or a pickpocket or a white-collar criminal; fishing for bass, you're up against gangsters, and they favor direct methods like sticking a revolver deep into your ribs. But I quickly have to change analogies—the bass jumps now, not like a trout with a graceful pirouette, but like a jitterbugger from the old days, thrown high by an invisible partner, tossing their hair back in exuberance as Artie Shaw and his band thunder on.

Anthropomorphism? You bet. There is no more anthropomorphic creature than the American black bass, which is half the fun of catching them.

This bass turns out to be a bruiser from the old school, follows the classic kind of smallmouth battle plan. Up with that first jump, a fast run toward the canoe while I frantically try to gather in line, then up again in a higher jump, then down, down, down, a fast run back toward shore, a power surge sideways, another plunge, back up toward the surface again, a last wistful, slow-mo jump, and then repeated resentful tuggings—*no, no, no*—as it comes reluctantly toward the canoe.

But wait—I spoke too soon. The bass seems to gain new strength when it sees my waiting hand, runs back out again, tail walking across the surface with a whisking kind of "f" sound. *Fight, fight, fight* it could be saying, like a cheerleader urging itself on. *Fun, fun, fun* it could be saying, like a giddy kid. Or *Fuck, fuck, fuck*—it could be saying that, too.

Again, I come to this after weeks of trout fishing, so let me stick with my comparisons. The rainbows I've caught sip when they eat, zip when they run, fly when they jump; the bass gorge when they eat, barge when they run, somersault when they jump. If a trout on the end of a line had a caption over its head it would read *whoosh;* if a bass had a caption, it would be *kapowie!* They're break-dancers, not ballerinas, and I never get tired of their playground moves.

This bass is eighteen inches long and probably weighs three pounds—almost certainly, a bass guarding its nest. Unlike a trout, who will wiggle like crazy, it behaves itself once you actually hold it in your hand (thumb in lower lip, that old bassin' trick)—a club fighter, it seems to know from experience when to accept defeat. (As an old-time fishing writer put it, once landed "bass do not indulge in distracted, unreasoning spasms of fright as do members of the *salmo* family.") Releasing a trout, you have to carefully restore it to the water, even swim it back and forth to encourage it to breathe, but I've never had to do that with a bass, never had one turn belly up no matter how long the fight has lasted. The second they're released, all their vibrancy comes back and they swim off, not defeated, not even weary—but pissed, plenty pissed.

But let me hesitate here before releasing this one. Let me try and look at it like a person who has never held a bass before, never even seen one.

I think your first impression . . . first gut impression, without focusing too much on what prompts it . . . would be that this is indeed a creature of great strength and power, despite its relatively modest size. Strong squarish tail (black on the narrowest part, fanning out into lighter black ribbing), gills as wide and prominent as shoulders, mouth fixed in an uncompromising frown, torso of compact muscularity. This is a form, even at rest, that radiates explosive potentiality, like a howitzer shell, so, in handling it, inspecting it, admiring it, you proceed gingerly, afraid that it might go off.

A piscine athlete—that might be the other analogy you'd come up with. This is an animal in superb shape, without an inch of wasted flesh. Sport? Football. Position? Fullback, linebacker, tight end.

An art student, drawing a bass, might be tempted to make its silhouette sleeker and slimmer than it is in fact. A little kid could do it better—a ten-year-old, enjoying roundness better than squareness, would be sensitive to the curvature under the torso back from the gills, and then upward toward the tail. A kid might have fun with the fins, too—winglike and filmy on the bottom, fan-like (fore) and rounded (aft) on top, a notch where the two shapes meet. This upper fin, the dorsal, features an imposing row of sharp spines, though they're easy enough to smooth down over its back if you're careful.

Color? Bronze—greenish bronze, brownish bronze, silver bronze, but *something* bronze. Blackish marbled stripes shimmer vertically down the flanks since it's a smallmouth we're inspecting; if it was a largemouth, this shimmy would be horizontal; on both bass, the striping is more intricate and crowded on top of the fish than it is toward the bottom. The bottom is a conspicuous white, like the zone of demarcation on a nude with a good tan.

There are scales back of the gills, set in rows, though they're not very noticeable—it's a subtle art deco pattern, and it feels good to slide your hand along it, enjoying the way they overlap. (Crazy, but when I visit New York, look up at the Chrysler Building, I always think of bass.)

You've been avoiding the eyes until now—your first glimpse of them probably made you nervous. It's hard to say what would hit you hardest when you finally take a look: the utter blackness of the pupils, the wine-dark red of the irises, or maybe, if you're a detail person, the rim of whitish orange that separates one from the other like a circular fence. They're the kind of eyes you can read a lot into—*a lot*—but, again, it would be adjectives associated with power, strength, and aggressiveness you would end up using. Angry eyes. Militant eyes. Predator eyes. Voracious eyes. Eyes of an anarchist.

There are no eyelids to soften this, of course. A bass faces life without blinking.

Pugnacity. It's there in the mouth, too—a Churchillian kind of resolution and defiance, so it's easy to picture those lips chomped down on a cigar. A smallmouth bass mouth is far from small—*smaller*mouth might be a better name, since it's only in comparison with a largemouth that this mouth would seem small. As the late great Red Smith put it, "Smallmouth black bass—so named because he is not black and his mouth is suitable for storing oranges."

If you examine the mouth closely, you'll notice the bottom of the jaw forms a conspicuous horizontal V-shape; the hinge, the apex of the triangle, is directly below a smallmouth's eyes; in largemouth, the hinge extends beyond the eye—which is one way you can tell the two apart, though color (largemouth look like they've been dipped in a lemon-green wash) and striping will usually tell you first. You can also count the scales from the gill cover to the tail. Around fourteen rows and it's a smallmouth; eight to twelve and it's a largemouth. The mouths on both bass are expansive and flexible, and always put me in mind of one of those anvil-opening bags that doctors or plumbers once carried, spreading wide on top and able to hold anything.

(Experienced anglers don't have to count scales or measure jaw angles to tell the difference between the two fish. Fishing writer John Alden Knight wrote: "For some reason not clear to me, a great many bass fisherman have trouble distinguishing Largemouth bass from Smallmouth bass. Personally, I don't think a Largemouth looks any more like a Smallmouth than an Irishman looks like a Chinaman.")

Kiss my bass! . . . those lips seem to indicate when you pry out the fly, like the slogan tough guys put on their bumpers—only these are the genuine article when it comes to toughness, and they don't need slogans. Americans love gangsters, which goes a long way to explaining why we love bass. (My pal Nick Lyons calls them "one-punch knockout artists with bad intentions.") They're not beautiful like trout are, not beautiful *beautiful* or pretty *pretty*. Handsome, interesting, full of character—we're talking Cagney or Kate Hepburn, De Niro or Streep, though if I had to cast an actor as a bass, it could only be Edward G. Robinson.

A person who has never held one before, never really studied one, might still come up with its name. "Bass!" someone from the South or Midwest would call out, since it's part of the iconography there, seen on billboards, bumper stickers, and postcards. New Englanders probably wouldn't get the name quite as fast. "Billy Bass!" they might shout, remembering the wall ornament that was a craze in the 1990s, the flexible bass that sang. Others might remember having to read the story "The Bass, the River and Sheila Mant" back in middle school or high school English, wherein a fourteen-year-old boy has to choose between the fish of his dreams and the girl of his dreams (a decision I've been faced with many times in my life).

Someone erudite, a philologist ringer, might try to impress us by rattling off all the names it's been called over the years, paying tribute to its regional variables. Marsh bass, southern chub, jumping perch, achigan, bigmouth, linesides, trout-perch, green trout, jumper, Oswego, Kentuckies, slough bass, reed bass, moss bass, Roanoke bass, Erie bass, Carolina trout, Henshall bass, Welshman, Straw bass, Neosho bass, and—for many years—Large-mouth and Small-mouth, capitalized with conspicuous hyphens.

A scientist might know the Latin terms, *Micropterus salmonides* for the largemouth, *Micropterus dolomieu* for the smallmouth—and might even tell us why our great American fish is named after a French mineralogist.

My own favorite nickname for the smallmouth is bronzeback. A gladiator's name, a warrior's, a hero out of Tolkien. Not rustback or mossback, but *bronze*back. Perfect!

"Catch any?" Celeste will ask when I return from a morning on Smarts.

"Six bronzebacks," I'll say—and I can't tell you how good those syllables feel coming out.

But we've been admiring our bass long enough. Back into the water he goes, with an encouraging push, which he hardly needs. And, following him in toward shore with the canoe, it becomes clear that it is indeed a male we've been studying. They come in before females to sweep out beds in the shallows—and there it is three feet down, a light sandy circle in what otherwise seems a bottom of layered rocks, like one of those small beaches you find tucked into the ironbound coast of Maine. Paddling along shore, I don't see any other such patches in the cobble, get no more takes, so it's apparent the bass I caught was an eager beaver, getting the evolutionary jump on the competition. The good news is that I'm right on schedule with my calendar, I haven't missed anything, the real excitement is yet to come.

Back at the car, muscling the canoe onto the roof, I notice something too mundane to ordinarily notice. I've taken off my sweater, unbuttoned my work shirt, and yet I'm still sweating. Humid! Where did *that* come from? It was spring when I woke up in the morning, the air still had a bite, but sometime out on the pond, probably when I was playing that smallmouth, summer moved in, though we have a month yet before the solstice. Meteorologists will smile, but for me that's linkage. Summer starts, not when I see girls with tans, not when ice-cream stands and movie drive-ins reopen, not when softball leagues start play or strawberries ripen or kids get out of school. Summer starts when I catch my first bass of the year, the summer fish, the one that bears on that beautifully bronzed back warmth and sunshine and life at its fullest.

Just as many memories wait for me driving down the hill from Smarts as awaited me driving up. I only slow down once though, and it's passing the house where we once lived. The lilacs are higher now than when we planted them, I can just barely make out the window of the spare bedroom where I wrote my books, but it's enough to bring on that old imaginative itch, when an idea seems, not just a remote possibility anymore, not just a vague, easily-resisted temptation, but something that grabs me, holds me, tugs me hard.

Hooked, by god! And I thought I was the one doing the fishing.

So. Let me explain.

The bass is the great American gamefish, the most widely distributed, the most characteristic, bringing fun to the millions, hard to catch but not impossible, a perfect fish for beginners and a worthy challenge for experts, one that can be enjoyed on all kinds of tackle, with traits that seem typically American in the best sense of the word, the old sense, brave, freedom-loving, indefatigable.

"With all his machismo," writer Pat Smith puts it,

[T]his underwater pug with the two-sized mouth is also our most pervasive and endearing symbol of all that is still wild across a national landscape that grows a little tamer, a little more predict-able with each passing season. As his more delicate brethren shrink before the crunch of time, the black bass, God bless him, stays to slug it out with dams, bridges, highways, irrigation canals, too many second homes and too many people. No matter how we batter, shackle and poison his world, he somehow survives and in doing so invests the world with a whisper of wilderness. The black bass is the ultimate holdover—our past living in the present. He's the guts and soul of American angling.

This is well said. All the sadder to realize there's never been a great book written about the bass, hardly even a good one, and this stands in need of rectification. A minor classic on bass would fill a great void—and, until someone steps up to write it, I'll try my best to create a bridge between the mediocre ones of the past and the future classic that will eventually say it all.

Trout get the literary respect. Izaak Walton started it off in 1653, writing about English trout fishing with the emphasis on the why, not just the how. His followers have enriched that tradition ever since; when you write about trout, you're free to be as sensitive as you want, search your soul if you're inclined that way, wax poetical, write as lyrically as your prose style can manage. Many books of permanent value have resulted from this impulse, which is alive and well today, with writers taking the humble fishing essay in imaginative and even startling directions, while staying true to Walton's legacy of quizzically gentle self-reflection.

It has been otherwise with the bass. Its literary godfather, Dr. James Henshall, a man I'll have more to say about later, published his landmark work in 1881, *Book of the Black Bass,* and on its cover had embossed in gold his famous slogan, "Inch for Inch, and Pound for Pound, the Gamest Fish that Swims." It established the American tradition of bass fishing in 451 firmly didactic pages (or, the truth is, accomplished this in just twelve pithy words), and made sure, right from the start, that in writing about bass the emphasis would always be on the how not the why—that technocrats, boosters, and bass killers would be the ones writing about our great fish, not poets, dreamers, or bums.

Dr. Henshall also started another tradition—the bass was going to be used to *sell* stuff. He designed rods to catch them, shorter than what was then popular, the famous "Henshall rods," and actively boomed them through his writings and sold them through the mail. It's as if Father Walton went into business selling the willow poles he used on the banks of the Itchen—"Walton wands," he might have called them, turning many a tuppence in the bargain.

Someone who thinks there may be more to bass fishing than the mere catching, someone who is made uncomfortable by all the commercialism, will always feel like an outsider when it comes to writing about bass—and have to deal with many contradictions. The bass is the fish of the American masses, yet I'm almost always alone while fishing for them. Bass fishing makes lots of people lots of money, yet takes a deep bite out of my savings account. Fishing for bass is about fancy reels, gang-hooked lures, overpowered bass boats, magic scents and creams, but I fish from an old leaky canoe, and when one of those boats speeds past, almost drowning me, feel like a dissident, a rebel, a fisher with a chip on his shoulder, a basser with an attitude . . . and, lonely as it is sometimes, it's a feeling I rather enjoy.

(I'm not a young turk anymore, but not quite an old fart either, not in my fishing life, when the boy in you still puts up a fight. The bass police, after perusing what follows, will find I don't go quietly.)

I'm writing at a time when all is not well with our great American basses. Physically, environmentally, they're doing fine; long gone are the days when commercial netting in Lake Erie killed 600,000 pounds of bass a year. Trout would lose half their range if the government didn't spend enormous amounts of money raising them in concrete tanks, trucking them to rivers, dumping them in, but the bass require no such welfare—every bass you catch in a river, lake, or pond was almost certainly born there. Yes, global warming is a threat, particularly to smallmouth; yes, invasive species like the Asiatic carp have to be watched carefully; but bass seem positioned well short of the environmental tipping point that threatens so many American creatures.

It's culturally that they're threatened. Over the past forty years, they've been taken hostage by yahoos, flimflammers, and Mad Men, turned into slaves to serve corporate empires that care for little but profit—even their very name has been appropriated and copyrighted.

Now a little commercialism has never hurt the bass; a little commercialism has always been part of the fun. Your River Runt Spooks, Hula Poppers, De-Liars, Onawa Bass Lodges, Bill's Bait Shops, Pfleuger Supremes, *Outdoor Lifes*, Popperackles, Hawaiian Wigglers, and Tack-L-Aprons all made money of course, but no one ever got rich off them, and they were just the harmless accoutrements that any pastime or hobby brings in its wake.

But, like so much in America, it's a matter of scale. Bass bringing in a few hundred badly needed dollars for a gal and guy running a bait stand down at the dock is one thing; but for corporations fronted by retired presidents, ass-kissing politicians, and "bass pro" TV celebrities it is quite another.

Competitive fishing—bass tournaments modeled on PGA golf tourneys and NASCAR racing—is beyond the power of irony to describe, so I'll have little to say about it after this paragraph. But that bass have been captured by this empire, tracked on sonar, chased down by the bass boys in their overpowered speedboats, clubbed on the head with high-tech plastics, leads me to my second motive in writing this book: to reclaim the American black bass as something more than just a moneymaking jester, rescue it from captivity, remind people that it's a creature of the quiet lonely places, the beautiful wild places, and not just flat-screen TVs.

I'm not the first writer on bass to feel a crusading zeal. Ray Bergman was one of the better old-time fishing writers, someone who eschewed the usual machismo in favor of a gentler, more nuanced approach. Having written a classic called *Trout* in 1938, he felt compelled to follow it up with *Bass* in 1942, feeling, he admits, "heart-stricken by the blasphemy against bass so often expressed by the rabid trout fisherman I challenge this blasphemy."

I challenge this blasphemy—and yes, when it comes to this greater blasphemy, the enslavement and commercialization of the bass, then I do, too.

"All right, we are two Americas," a famous novelist declared in the 1920s when the country seemed split in half. We're at another of these divisions, when almost any activity you can think of seems to fall into warring, heavily politicized camps. Red State versus Blue State, liberals versus conservatives, Northeast and Northwest versus South and Midwest. Bass fishing hasn't escaped this, and I feel I must stage a raid to bring it back—not to my side of the border, but to the old-fashioned, barely existent middle ground. When I take into account all the waters it's found in across the continent, the bayous, lakes, sloughs, rivers, creeks, and ponds, I think of linkage, not division—but there you are. Hard angry times are hard angry times. Even Doc Henshall found bass fishing to be an excellent way to sit out the Civil War.

In writing about bass, I'm going to take my cue from the fish itself, favor brashness, feistiness, unpredictability, over sensitivity and introspection. If I manage to find some balm for my soul, I'll gladly take it (in our time, restoring our souls seems less important than merely preserving our sanity), but the emphasis here will be on having fun. Irony I'll try and stay away from, but wryness will certainly creep in. Speaking selfishly,

I welcome the added focus that writing about one of nature's creatures brings, especially at an age when powers of attention can attenuate and drift. You look differently at the natural world when you ask it questions; I enjoy fishing most when I'm writing about it.

As for my biases, prejudices, leanings, I probably have as many as you do, but only one matters here at the start—not a bias at all, but God's honest truth.

The bass is America's greatest fish.

Two

Picture a summer house overlooking a placid lake, a quiet pond, a lazy river. Picture how it looks in late May, when the world not only stirs with ripening life, but also beats with it, throbs with it, aches to the point of bursting. Think of all the springtime "re-" words, the prefix for "once more" and "anew." *Re*generation, *re*birth, *re*newal, *re*awaken, *re*juvenate, *re*fresh, *re*vitalize. Think, even, of the term wild-life biologists use to describe the newly born of a species: *re*cruitment. All those "re-" things are going on now right off the porch; nowhere else in the yearly cycle is the life force, even on our battered planet, so visibly intense.

Picture a man and woman sitting on the porch toward sunset. Make them retirement age—a little bit removed from the world's busy hubbub and, after a lifetime of hard work, ready to sit back and savor the smells, sights, and sounds of a perfect May evening. Call them Elsa and John.

That a lot is going on is something of which they're keenly aware. Bird guides lay open on the end table, binoculars are ready at hand if the mergansers swim back into the cove with their brood, or the bluebirds return to the box put out for them on the lawn. On the table opposite are vases filled with lilac blossoms and sprigs off the crabapple—no perfume in the world can match the warmth of their mingled scents. The blueberries around back are creamy with buds; the rhubarb is already worth picking. A bear with its cubs crossed the garden in the morning, and Elsa can't stop talking about it. Fawns seem to be everywhere—a pair come to the pond near twilight to take a sip.

Our couple doesn't have to leave the porch, nature's spectacle comes to them, and even the insects seem part of it tonight. On the screen appears clouds of butter-colored mayflies, innumerable, as if nature, tired of making life singly, has decided to do it in volcanic bursts.

And man is not immune to it, this May explosion of life. Ronny Balch, the boy who cuts their meadow, had a shy-looking girl riding the back of his tractor in the morning, and, judging by the way she held on to him, nestled her chin down into his shoulder, things are progressing there very nicely. And Mary Elizabeth, their youngest daughter, is expecting her baby any day now—their bags are packed just waiting for the call, and off they'll go to see their new grandchild.

They note all these things with the greatest satisfaction, pride themselves on savoring what so many people are too busy or blasé to enjoy, and yet that one of America's greatest natural rituals is taking place ten yards in front of them, right there in the shallows around their dock—taking place with considerable drama, turmoil, and excitement— is something they are completely oblivious to: the spawning season of the American black bass.

John and Elsa don't fish—they mostly stare out across the lake, rarely down into it, taking most of their beauty off the top. Sometimes they'll go out in the canoe for a paddle, and see a dark shape flushed by the bow shadow. "Turtle!" they'll yell simultaneously, thinking a shape that large couldn't possibly be a fish. And sometimes, when the sun is just right, they'll notice round sandy patches on the bottom where all else is gravel and rock. "Look at that!" they'll say—but that's the end of their investigation. They'll go back and sit on the porch, thinking, not for the first time, that May is life's richest month, even though they're missing one of the most supportive pieces of evidence.

Bass spawning is one of those spectacles that is hidden in plain sight. Brown trout and brookies spawn in late autumn, in the coldest and nastiest of weathers, when no one, not even fishermen, are out there to notice; rainbows repeat the trick in early April, but there's no one to watch then, either. And what's to watch? Trout don't stick around long when they reach a tributary's spawning grounds—the act is accomplished and back they go to the lake.

Bass spawn at a time when people are returning again to the water, opening their summer homes after a long winter, going out for the first voyage of the summer in their kayaks and canoes. The swimming is a bit chilly yet, but kids do it; the docks have to be repaired, so people wade out and start hammering; a boy walks out on a jetty and shows his sister how far he can skim a rock. This is the precise moment when bass spawn—when the whole process is potentially at its most visible and accessible—and yet only bass fishers probably know this. There are no "bass walks" like there are "bird walks," no smallmouth tours like there are garden tours, and if someone were to ask nature lovers to chart the great springtime birthings, bass would probably not make the list.

This neglect is something bass fishers rather enjoy. Everyone likes to know a secret no one else does, and so if we get puzzled, dubious looks when we tell friends that bass are on their nests, that's okay by us.

I have half a dozen bass books spread open on my desk, and, when it comes to spawning, they all agree on the basics. As water temperatures warm toward 55 degrees Fahrenheit, bass, led by the bigger males, will begin moving into shallow water searching for a suitable spawning site. For smallmouth, the critical temperature is 60 degrees. When the water warms above this, they begin scooping out the "nests" (aka, "beds" or "redds") on the lake bottom. If the weather suddenly turns cooler, they may abandon this work, even if the nest is almost completed—it's like they're going on a sexual strike because the sun won't shine. If it warms again, they will often go back—strike over!—but in the schizoid kind of warm-cold-colder-hotter spring we've had this year, this fussiness about water temperature can mean a poor year for bass recruitment. And complicating the matter further is the fact that a lake's temperature can vary significantly from shore to shore, cove to cove so spawning may well be under way on the northwest shore while the southwest one, getting less sunshine, stays nest-less.

(Humans should relate to this—we can be pretty fussy about the temperature of the water we immerse ourselves in—and while cold showers are said to calm the libido, hot tubs are reputed to increase it.)

If the temperature warms to the mid 60s and holds there, bass begin building their nests by a vigorous fanning movement of the tail fin that clears away algae, vegetation, gravel, and silt; they'll do this by assuming a vertical, broom-like position they never adopt at any other time. They'll even use their mouths to remove stubborn bits of debris; the bass, as fishing writers never tire of pointing out, is a fastidious housekeeper.

As with so much else about the bass, the date of sexual maturity varies greatly, but seems more dependent on size than it does on age. Males usually spawn beginning when they reach ten inches (females twelve inches), though bass as small as seven inches have been seen guarding a nest. The males make their nest twice their own size, so the nest of a fourteen-inch bass will have a circumference of approximately twenty-eight inches.

There are variations within this pattern, based on circumstances. While bass prefer making these nests in two to three feet of water, there have been reports of beds as deep as twenty-two feet below the surface; in rivers like the Connecticut, the levels of which fluctuate significantly due to dam releases, the bass make their nests in water three or four times deeper than they do in nearby lakes. And while smallmouth like those clean, well-swept nests, largemouth are a bit sloppier; not finding gravel, they'll settle for mud, making their nests of small twigs or leaves, or even depositing their eggs on the branches of a sunken tree.

Elsa and John, if they do peer down while canoeing, may notice these nests without understand what they represent. I'll go back to my analogy of sandy beaches set within an ironbound coast—that's the effect they give, a pleasing tropical one in north country lakes whose bottoms seem otherwise so Puritan and stern. Not knowing what they are, you still find yourself drawn to them, just as female bass are—they suggest gentleness, ease, repose, in a waterscape that is otherwise adamantine and forbidding. Who wouldn't want to deposit their eggs there! If you put on polarized sunglasses, stand up to get some perspective, you'll notice dozens of these nests spaced along the shoreline, like (changing analogies now) fine china saucers from which the teacups have been lifted and not yet set back down.

Bass like building their nests in shallow areas that have ready access to deep water; shallow coves, otherwise so bassy-looking, never seem to have any nests, while rocky shelves that jut out toward the middle of the lake will have saucers set out along their entire length, as if the entire royal family is expected for tea. In my experience, the nests will be made in exactly the same spots every year, to the point it's rare to see a bed where I've not seen one before. People who have studied their habits closely report that it can take a large male (working mainly in the morning) anywhere from four to forty-eight hours to make a nest that meets his standards, a variation that depends on whether they're building in a new, undisturbed area (where work goes slowly), or at an old site that is still relatively clean (where work goes fast).

Once the nest is ready, the female bass—which has been harried and bullied by the bass onto exactly the right spot—will deposit from 2,000 eggs to as many as 15,000, which can represent twenty-five percent of her weight. Not all of these eggs will be deposited at once—it may be over the course of four days, in intervals of thirty seconds, fifty eggs at a time. The male, after fertilizing these eggs with milt, drives the females into deeper water, then takes over the job of protecting the nest from predators.

(In all my years of observing bass, I've never seen the actual spawning act take place—or have I? I've seen, rarely, two bass on the nest together; I've seen one of these tilt over on its side—and when a fish deliberately tilts over on its side, you know something biologically important is going on.)

The eggs are glutinous, golden yellow in color, and highly adhesive, so they cling to anything they touch—females lay these in neat rows. Incubation ranges from eight to ten days, though if the water warms quickly to the 70s, this may speed it up to two or three days; if the water cools, it may take three weeks. When they hatch, the young, about fifteen millimeters long, stay on the bed, feeding on their yolk sacs, guarded by the father bass who periodically stirs the water with his tail to promote oxygenation. He continues guarding them for anywhere from a few days to an entire month, before, as perfectly formed miniature bass, the fry scatter to begin a hazardous life on their own; only about one percent of them will survive long enough to spawn.

The deserted nests, the beds, can be easily discerned through much of the summer, becoming increasingly mossy, as if the housekeeper, tired of sweeping, has up and quit—but they still shine on the bottom like oases of circumferential light.

"All this is perfectly distinct to an observant eye," Thoreau said of similar under-our-noses phenomena, "and yet could easily pass unnoticed by most."

How someone who is fascinated by bass, seeks to learn as much about them as he can without causing any harm, fits himself into this process presents an ethical dilemma that isn't at all clear. You could stay off the water entirely while they spawn, not even risk scaring them with a canoe; there are video clips you can watch of bass spawning, and you can look up all kinds of interesting factoids while you're online—a virtual experience with zero impact on the bass.

Risking a bit more, you could go out in a canoe or kayak, take a spawning tour around the lake, searching out those light patches on the bottom; with the right kind of filter, you could snap photos of the bass, giving you a guilt-free trophy to bring home. You could monitor water temperatures and see how this correlates to nest numbers, become an expert amateur as so many become with birds.

Raising the stakes, you could fish for them—carefully, considerately, putting the fish back as soon as you caught them. Or, if the stress involved with handling them makes you feel uncomfortable, you could try another approach, one I'll describe a bit further on.

Again, the ethics aren't clear. Salmon are fished for during spawning runs, as are shad and steelhead, and no one thinks the worse of you, though fishing for *salmonoids* actually in the act of spawning is illegal almost everywhere. Fishers who go after bass on the beds might split hairs on this, point to the fact that they're not fishing for spawning fish at all, but fish who have *already* spawned.

Some writers heap scorn on this view, insisting that fishing for bass during spawning season is beneath contempt. Wallace W. Gallaher, who published the still very readable *Black Bass Lore* in 1937, insists that "No thoughtful sportsman will take Bass from the spawning beds by any method of angling," though the key word here is "take" meaning "kill." Ray Bergman, writing a few years later, says, "Of course the bass fisherman will always have excellent fishing before the spawning season is over—but at what cost to future generations of bass!" Writers of that day knew nothing of catch-and-release, and it's hard to know whether this (purportedly) low-impact way of fishing would have changed their opinions.

Another old reliable bass writer, Erwin A. Bauer, describes how views began to change.

> The reason for closed seasons and limits on bass in the first place was to protect them during spawning and to assure that the waters would never be fished out. Right after World War II, it became evident to many biologists that legal fishing methods in use had little or no effect on fish populations—rod-and-reel angling simply couldn't fish out a lake—so why close seasons and limit catches at precisely the period when fishing might prove best? The number of bass in a lake, these biologists realized was determined by factors other than sport fishing. That meant that an angler could fish for bass during spawning season, and even catch them right off the spawning beds, with a clear conscience.

And that seems to be the official line today—that catch-and-release fishing for bass on the beds has little impact on the overall health of the species. I'm not one to let state government decide for me what's moral and what's not, but in this case I agree with them—that between May 15 and June 10 of every year, fishing with a single-hooked artificial lure, immediately releasing any bass you capture, is no bad thing. And so I fish during spawning season, rearrange my calendar every year to make sure I have plenty of free time the last two weeks of May, look forward to this with the keenest anticipation, so, in a very real way, my springtime cycle is geared to the bass.

I fly-fish for them, using a rod that isn't so heavy it derricks them from the water, or so light that I play them needlessly long. I can't pretend this doesn't stress the fish (biologists think it may take an hour for a bass to recover from a fight), and the longer he's off the nest or groggy the more chance there is for predators to nip in and eat the young. But my fly, my bug, is single-hooked and barbless, so I can release the fish instantly; if it's windy, I beach the canoe and fish from shore, not wanting to have the bass blown away with me during the fight and be released too far from its nest; after catching four or five, I usually quit, though I could run the number up if I wished. At no time during the season are bass so approachable; at no other time can you "sight fish" for them so readily, spotting your fish, watching it rise through the water column to strike; at no other time, truth be told, are they so easy to catch.

For better or worse, ethically speaking, I engage with this beautiful and vivacious creature via my fly rod, which functions like an antenna, allowing me to explore nature with a focus and concentration that leads to an understanding I would otherwise never achieve. That I take this one step further, not just going out to perfect the art of fly casting, or to contemplate my surroundings, but seeking to become, quite literally, *attached* to the experience, is where the ethics become trickier—and leads to the little experiment I'll be writing about below.

When bass are on the beds, I head up to Sunday Mountain Pond one town north of us. Sunday is treated more gently than the ponds in my own village. A local conservation organization protects much of the shoreline, there is only one house, and no speedboats are allowed to tear it all up. When I go to Sunday I know that even if I catch nothing I'll come away with a lot.

A shoreline of wild blueberry fringes successively higher terraces of hardwood and spruce. The north shore has a cliff that's been disintegrating for thousands of years, and, while still in no hurry, likes to drop a boulder or two every few months, scaring the kayakers. The opposite shore is shallower, softer, with pickerel weed just thick enough to hide baby ducks. It's a good place to see loons—two in the spring, four in the summer, if they've been lucky with nesting.

As beautiful as Sunday is, the day has two quirks, which affect the fishing. Often I'll drive up on a morning without even the slightest zephyr of wind, and the calm will last right up until the moment the pond comes into sight—and it will be covered in whitecaps, sheet after frothy sheet, as if some wrinkle of topography, some rogue freak of meteorology, has awaited my arrival to start blowing. There's no way to predict this ahead of time; often, I'll make the eleven-mile drive, and, seeing the wind tunnel, immediately drive home.

The other thing Sunday is famous for is boulders. These aren't the bowling balls you find in our other ponds, not the tombstones, not the old stone walls. Sunday scorns such puny stuff, boasts instead rocks the size of tanks, rocks the size of pyramids, rocks the size of Gibraltar. They were scoured from the cliffs by the last glacier and have been resting on the bottom ever since—glacial "erratics" that Picasso would have found inspirational; appropriately enough, the hill the pond faces is called Mount Cube.

If God were a smallmouth, she/he might have designed such a pond. Bass love these rocks, and will spend the summer lurking under their shadows, scoffing down crayfish and the occasional bluegill. In spawning season, rather than seek out Sunday's few sandy patches, they'll sweep the moss and silt off a flattish rock, make their nests atop granite; fry hatched there, growing to maturity, seem to carry this adamantine quality in their DNA, fight twice as hard as bass spawned in more effete ponds.

This is what I'm looking for when I fish Sunday—light patches of radiance that, rather than moving with the slant of the sun, stay fixed on the bottom as if the sunlight is glued. I stand up in the canoe to spot these better, will often paddle that way around the pond, like a Maine lobsterman sculling his dinghy. If my timing is right, I'll see male bass hovering just above the nests; if my timing is wrong, the nests will be empty. The fish you spot seem perfectly happy to be there—they could be sunbathing—and the only note of restiveness comes from the black vertical edginess of their tails.

It's odd seeing them so clearly. Fishing is often nothing more elaborate than a watery hide-and-seek—bass do their best to hide, we do our best to find them—and to have them out in plain sight means a different kind of game, one played in the open one-on-one. I slowly paddle away from the fish until it's a longish cast to reach back, drop the bug over what I can see of the radiance, then . . . if I'm lucky . . . see the darkish, black-striped shape immediately rise, and, in a jolt I never tire of, transmute all that grace into viciousness in one savage bite.

The male bass protects its nest from all comers—and these include the thumb-size intrusion of a deer-hair bass bug floating harmlessly over the top. I don't blame the bass for acting this way; two of the rare occasions in my life when I totally lost my temper, went ballistic, was on the point of slugging someone, came just after my kids were born, when my protective instincts were so strong they almost ripped me apart. It's a mammalian response—and all the stranger, then, to see it so explicit and strong in a cold-blooded fish. Never do I feel so close to them.

One of the first books ever devoted to the species, W. J. Loudon's *The Small-Mouthed Bass* of 1910, tells of an experiment in a bass-rearing pond where the nest was surrounded by a cylindrical screen shortly before the young bass were ready to leave it. The father bass was excluded—and for the next six days constantly circled around the screen, butting it again and again with his head.

Admirable—but is this *all* protective? Most experts insist that bass don't eat while guarding the nest. "It is doubtful," Gallaher asserts, "whether Black Bass take food at all while the spawning lasts. True, they strike at lures on or near the nest, but rather than to feed, the motive seems to be to punish the intruder, or drive it away from the nest."

I'm not sure of this myself. When a bass comes up and takes my bug, it seems to want to eat it, not just punish it. There's a kind of strike you get later in the summer that seems more slapping than biting, like the bass is challenging you to a duel, but that's not what you get in spawning season, when the strike seems intended to kill.

Bass, under ordinary circumstances, will rarely strike a lure twice if they miss the first time—and this rule seems to apply even in spawning season, when you would think that, having failed to drive away the intruder, they would give it another try. They don't—which makes me conclude they think it *is* food, and not a predator come to raid the nest.

If I remember one thing about caring for babies, it's this: the energy required makes you famished. I don't think less of a bass because he occasionally snacks while watching the kids (though, as far as snacking on *them* after they hatch, the less said about that the better), and this may also explain why you can cast a small size 16 caddis fly over a nest and get a hit, even though it represents no threat at all.

(When it comes to protective instinct, the bluegill . . . which nests at the same time as the bass . . . may be the champ. Smallmouth will leave the nest if my canoe's shadow crosses it; bluegills don't budge. If I were dropped naked on a nest, I'd feel safer with smallmouth than bluegills.)

Since only around twenty-five percent of the bass in a lake will be spawning during any one year, a lot of the fish I catch in May aren't guarding a nest at all, but merely hungry. They fight hard, of course, but not as hard as the father bass, which is trying not merely to escape but to get back to its parental responsibilities on the nest. This gives a different feel to our struggle—other generations are involved, and emotions I can empathize with all too readily—and makes me consider alternative ways of fishing the nests or not fishing them at all.

I've been thinking about this a lot lately. Fishing, and fly-fishing in particular, can be broken down into two almost entirely distinct halves: the challenge of fooling a fish into striking; the challenge of landing it after it does. Over the years, the emphasis has become increasingly focused on the first, particularly in trout fishing, and the second challenge has increasingly been seen as a kind of semi-embarrassing afterthought.

This wasn't always true. Back in the day, writers would go on and on about the fight, describing how the bass shot from the water like a Polaris missile, then raced toward deep water like Mario Andretti at Indianapolis, wrapping the line around a sunken log, forcing the fisherman to plunge his rod in the water and shove it to the other side, only to see the bass turn a series of perfect ten somersaults like an Olympic gymnast. Now, with animal rights activists having gotten us thinking, writers tend to say very little about the fight at all.

Tournament anglers, the ones you see on Saturday morning TV, reel in their fish as fast and joylessly as possible—no "fight" is involved whatsoever, though, theoretically, they're chasing bass because of the way they fight. In fly-fishing, the emphasis has turned to the cerebral side of the sport, not the part that involves brute strength.

But brute strength—brute force—is still part of fishing's appeal. Flyfishers go after marlin now and hundred-pound tarpon, where landing one requires real physical stamina. Bass are probably the smallest species you can catch that brings brute strength into play—a three- or four-pound spawning male will seek to detach your arms from your shoulders—and, as much as I delight intellectually in fooling them to strike, I enjoy even more the slugfest that follows.

With bass, it never comes as an anticlimax, as it does in much of trout fishing; it's an integral part of the excitement. This is particularly true in the way I choose to fish. A fly rod not only lets you feel every surge; it allows you to anticipate them, understand them, in a way the deadening stiffness of a spinning rod won't. Even your reel hand gets involved; playing a bass off a single action reel, or stripping in line, gives you a direct and vital connection, not the highly-geared remove you get using a spinning or bait-casting reel. And while when I first started fly-fishing for bass I thought "fighting butts," those three-inch extensions you brace against your belly, were for weaklings, I don't think that now; some of those four-pound Sunday males can't be landed by extended arm strength alone, or at least not *my* extended arm strength.

So I like fighting bass, but I like it less in spawning season, when guilt makes me borderline uncomfortable. Partly for my own sake, partly for the sake of the bass, I've experimented this spring with trying to separate the two halves of the process—getting them to strike; landing them after a battle—to see whether I can find satisfaction in the first challenge alone.

What I've done is very simple—taken pliers to a dozen of my bass bugs and cut off their hooks. In normal fishing, I miss a lot of strikes anyway, which vexes me no end; now, I would miss them deliberately, and hope that it made me happy.

"I'm headed out," I told Celeste Monday morning when we finished breakfast.

She had her eyes on her cell phone, barely lifted them. "Fishing?"

"Ethics lab."

It was early enough that Sunday was still calm, with the sun at an angle that revealed most of the bottom. I saw bass near the canoe launch, with nests scoured so thoroughly they were almost white, but I saved those for later and kept paddling. I've learned over the years to avoid the weedy coves, which look so bassy but are almost always fishless, and concentrate instead on the points where the shoreline starts dipping inward, then, across the other side of the cove, starts jutting back out; picture a series of rounded m's, me casting to where the bottom of the letter hits the line. This give spawners what they're looking for—shallows near depth—and the biggest males will appropriate these spots for their nests.

I had clipped the hooks off deer-hair bugs, not cork ones, figuring the bass would hold on to the softer material longer. I shook some line out through the guides, got the rod working, and dropped the bug over one of those sand-colored circles. A bass took it immediately—there was the usual exuberant splash—and I lifted my rod as I have thousands of times . . . lifted it, not to the weight of a good bass, not to its immediate tugging, but to bass-less thin air.

"Missed!" I said to myself. "Shit!" It took me a few seconds to remember that this was exactly the point.

It didn't take long for another strike. This time I remembered to mutter "Good!" when the bass came off, though the ancient hunter in me and my emotions weren't quite convinced. For fifty years, I'd been regretting every fish that got away, and old habits die hard. But I'm flexible when I have to be—I immediately decided to count each miss as a fish caught and landed, which helped a little. If nothing else, I could hook, play, and land an abstract number, a digit, and tell myself later that I'd "caught" eighteen bass.

(That's a word that should be expunged from the fishing vocabulary—caught. In one of the few bright ideas I've ever had in my fishing life, I suggested in print some years back that, as a better reflection of a fishing day, it be replaced by the word encounter, as in, "I encountered eighteen bass," including, in that tally, fish that you landed, fish you missed, fish you netted for your buddy, fish you saw in the shallows, fish that rose off in the distance, fish that, in other words, you encountered and enjoyed.)

I played around with the hookless bug until teabreak time, working my way counterclockwise around the ins and outs of Sunday's wooded shore. The longer I tried it, the more interesting it became. Some fish would spit out the bug immediately, others would gum it for a few seconds before letting go, and one—the star—took it in his mouth and kept on going right out of the water in a beautiful leap, tossing the bug like he was posing for a sporting calendar circa 1937, captioned "Off!" or "Free!"

I realized early that there was nothing I could do to influence how long the bass held on, though I still tried (because I couldn't help trying) to set the hook. I thought maybe I would get some repeat strikes, since the bass wasn't feeling any hook, but this never happened, making me wonder if it's not the disgustingly ersatz taste of the bug that bothers them, not the barb.

Halfway around my circuit, as if placed there for my convenience, comes a beautifully flat rock that acts like a miniature island. It's a perfect place to land, though it takes some maneuvering; there's a V-shaped slot between the big rock and a sharper neighbor, and you have to slide the canoe in between like a ferry nestling up to its landing, then carefully disembark. I've had some great picnics here over the years with the family, and it always makes me a bit sentimental being there alone.

But I wasn't alone, not entirely. I lay back against the slanted part of the rock with my thermos; the slant kept going down into the water, and a foot further out a bass hovered over its tropically white nest. It saw me, but didn't seem particularly ruffled—it moved from the far side of the nest to my side, not so much threatening me, but as if asking for a handout. I tossed a piece of hermit bar toward him, but he watched it dribble by without moving.

While I rested, I thought about my experiment. It was early days yet, I'd have to try longer, but I was on the point of deciding that it was all rather silly. As someone who takes fly-fishing seriously, not just the stalking/hunting part but the ethical big picture, I'm always trying to lessen my impact on the fish I'm trying so hard to catch. Certainly, not hooking bass, merely getting them to show themselves, lessens the strain on them, lessens the risk of their not being able to find their way back to their nests. From their standpoint, a momentary bad taste in the mouth is much to be preferred over a prolonged tug-of-war.

From my point of view, it's a bit murkier. Certainly, the best way to protect bass while they guard their nests is not to fish for them at all, while the most satisfying way to fish for them, if you do fish for them, is to fight it out with one on the end of your line . . . and it's hard to see a middle expedient that satisfies both my environmental conscience and my caveman lust. Getting them to attack hookless poppers doesn't quite do it for me—and so I'll either have to give up bass fishing the last few weeks of May, or continue as usual—hooking, playing, and landing them as gently as I can.

(It's worth noting that in some parts of Europe, where animal rights activists are more militant, catch-and-release fishing is considered crueler than killing them; why play a fish and stress it just for fun? In North America, it's exactly the opposite—catch-and-release is seen to be much kinder than killing a fish for food.)

Most of the ethical debates about fishing revolve around trout—interesting, that the bass seem left out. While you have to be careful about blaming the victim, you do have to wonder if maybe the bass's personality is somewhat responsible for this. (Pat Smith: "He's a fierce-eyed, foul-mouthed, tobacco-chewing redneck, paying his way and giving no quarter.") Trout, thanks to the literary tradition that enshrines them, seem so much more philosophical; it's almost as if, in fishing for them, we're trying to enter into whispered conversations with Hegel or Kant, whereas, fishing for bass, we're trying to collar Whitey Bulger or Al Capone.

Last year, fishing Sunday, I brought along my daughter Erin, home from grad school for the summer. Spawning was over for the season, but I wanted her to see the nests—and maybe fish a little while we were at it. As a girl, she liked dangling a worm, but now she expressed interest in learning how to fly-fish, and of course I was excited to try and teach her. I set her up with one of my extra rods and a bright wet fly, since there are plenty of bluegills in Sunday and they're the perfect fish to learn on.

It was difficult for her, at least at first, because the ones that hit were so tiny they didn't tug on her line, but just nibbled. "You'll find it easier with a big one," I said, and right on cue, a fat bluegill took hold. She was playing it nicely, laughing at the mad circles it described in the water, when, out of nowhere, the biggest bass I'd ever encountered on Sunday came up and chomped down on the bluegill's middle. Erin screamed, I shouted . . . and for the next thirty seconds we kept shouting, as we tried desperately to cope with what was happening.

The bass, having let go the bluegill when Erin instinctively yanked back, seeing it still dangle there in the water, grabbed hold of it again. Erin pulled and the bluegill came flying into the canoe. "What shall I do!" she yelled. "Cast it back!" I ordered—and this she immediately did, having hardly ever cast a popper on a fly rod before, let alone a living bluegill.

It flew back into the water, and the bass, even more viciously now, grabbed it a third time. Erin yanked again, the bluegill came out, fell across a limb extending over the water, and as she tried disentangling it, the bass came out of the water and slashed at it again. It wouldn't give up. Drama! Violence! Nature in the raw! And it wasn't over yet, because, when the bass tried grabbing the bluegill, a huge pickerel, the biggest I'd ever seen, came up and slashed at them both.

All this time, the fly, a small one, was tucked in the bluegill's lip, so there was no chance of hooking the bigger fish. And, when it was over, the bluegill seemed fine, and swam away with even a better story to tell than ours. As for Erin and me, we felt drained and exhilarated—and, truth be told, a little bit scared. This wasn't the quiet philosophizing of professors we had witnessed. This was the hunt, the kill, as naked as I'd ever seen it, with the bass at its very center, entirely untroubled by ethical qualms.

But that was then, this was now. The bass at the base of the picnic rock, suspended above the saucer of sunlight, seemed incapable of such brutality. A few yards away above a smaller bed hovered a male bluegill with reddish fins, and the two fathers seemed at peace with each other as if they watched their children from a bench in the park. And, to both fish, I probably looked as harmless as a lumpy cloud that would soon pass; that this cloud was capable of tugging them around a lake by the lip just for fun was something too *outré* for them to entertain. I would argue in my defense that it wasn't *just* for fun—that understanding and even empathy were involved—but I'm not sure they would buy that, at least not now, when all that concerned them was the twenty-four-inch circumference onto which, into which, over which, nothing could be allowed to intrude.

The bass wouldn't be there much longer. The books say that the males will protect their nests for upward of a month, but here in New England, after doing their duty, they seem in a hurry to leave. I used to wonder why the fishing fell off so much after spawning, especially with the ponds as richly endowed with food as they ever will be . . . dragon-flies, moths, crayfish, baby fish, frogs . . . but ichthyologists say that they retreat to the depths to recuperate from the physical stress of procreation, and only return to the shallows later in June, famished, ready to tear into anything they can find.

When I do come back to fish Sunday, my understanding of bass and my appreciation for them are deepened by having fished during nesting. In the end, this is the only argument I can make for continuing to fish for them, with a hook or without one—that it doesn't just bring me pleasure, but involves me in a great seasonal cycle the non-fisher doesn't even know is taking place. Put that on the list of the bass's mer-its—that it allows us to get so close to the most important act it will ever engage in. If we tread lightly there, remember we're intruders come to learn, it might be possible to do this without causing them, in a life filled with danger, gratuitous harm.

And one last story to tell of my day on Sunday, before moving on to other waters, other themes. A remarkable incident occurred the morning I tried fishing hookless—in some respects, more surprising than the attempted murder of my daughter's bluegill.

I had company on the pond—another fisherman! I never see them on Sunday, at least not on weekday mornings in May. This wasn't just any fisherman either, but a flyfisher. He had a green canoe like mine, and he stood up in it when he cast, which I thought I was the only one foolish enough to attempt. He traveled clockwise around the shoreline, I went counterclockwise, and while we were careful to give each other lots of room, it was clear our separate circumnavigations would intersect near the canoe launch. He fished slower than I did, worked the shallows more diligently, but he looked to be about my age, my build, with my taste in fishing duds, so for a few uncanny moments it seemed like the sun had projected my image horizontally across the water and stood it up.

I beached my canoe, was starting to load the car, when his canoe came around the point twenty yards offshore.

"I've never seen anyone fly-fish this pond before," he said, with a gentle laugh of wonder.

"I've never seen anyone fly-fish this pond before," I said in return.

That's all he said—that's all I said. Nothing more was needed. He continued around for another circuit, while I lugged my canoe to the car. We were twins, at least in one respect. We were in on the secret.

Three

The only battle he was ever interested in fighting was man against bass. Brother against brother? His sympathies lay with the South, but he could see no reason to follow the lead of a few hotheaded planters committed to a policy of rule or ruin; "selfish marplots," he called them, the fiercest denunciation in his arsenal. North versus South? He was raised in Maryland, lived and worked now in Kentucky—border states, neither fully Union nor Confederate, and he felt divided that way himself, this most thoroughly American of American men.

He carefully thought the arguments through, listened to friends who were making their choice, decided that, with politicians of both sides leading an "unholy crusade against truth, right and justice," to remain neutral—to work out his own individual, highly-original separate peace.

And so on a fine September morning in 1862, while other Americans his age were busily trying to destroy each other, Doctor James Henshall, age twenty-six, decides to play hooky, not just from his medical practice, but from the entire Civil War.

This is in north-central Kentucky, the bluegrass country between Cynthiana and Frankfort, blessed with many fine rivers full to the brim with smallmouth bass. Which shall it be today? the doctor wonders. The Elkhorn, Rockcastle, or Cumberland? The Licking as it turns out—it's near home, and if he starts early he'll be able to see the neediest of his patients before fishing. He harnesses his horse, climbs up on his buggy, conceals in his umbrella a split-bamboo rod, hides in a bag with his pills a small click reel with an enameled silk line, secrets in his doctor's smock what looks to be a prescription book but is actually a book of flies.

He slides down the bank, hops from boulder to boulder until he reaches a riffle where he knows there are bass. It's shady there—elms, maples, and sycamore lean well out over the river. Behind him, the sumac-covered bank folds over into fertile bottomland, with fields of corn, clover, bluegrass, and tobacco. Upstream, the wheel of a lichen-covered mill adds a gentle plashing to go with the castanet click of water through the rocks. Downstream, he can see a weathered covered bridge, spanning the river with shadows even deeper and more promising than those cast by the trees.

Over everything drapes an atmosphere of deep, lasting, undisturbable peace. Years later, an old man at the end of an eventful and productive life, he recalls those Kentucky mornings again and again, remembering not only the sweetness of youth but the promise of a land as beautiful and unspoiled as any country was ever blessed with.

> The streams were rocky, with a never-ending succession of riffles, pools and still reaches as they went racing and circling around wooded cliffs adorned with the ornate tints of sumac, red-bud and dogwood; went meandering through pastoral scenes of meadow land and broad fields of grain and tasseled corn; went gliding along the grassy banks clothed with sedges, ferns and nodding wildflowers . . . And so, even onward, purling and gurgling over the riffles, murmuring and singing in the white water of miniature cascades, sliding over ledges and whirling in eddies as they went merrily on toward the sea, carrying messages of peace and good will yet to come to a distraught nation.

The young doctor ties two flies to his leader—a Polka and a Professor—sends them with an expert cast dancing across the riffles. Immediately, he's attached to a smallmouth that with "bristling fins and red extended jaws" leaps clear of the rocks, and then goes bouncing and skittering downstream, forcing the doctor to abandon all dignity and chase in pursuit. He lands it, a nice two-pounder, dispatches it quickly with a blow to the head, lays it in his creel atop dampened ferns. It's for dinner—not for him, but for Aunt Judy, an old slave woman who will be the last patient he'll see before driving home. He catches three more even bigger; then, filling his pipe, sits smoking on the bank, where cows come so near they almost nuzzle him, and owls, unafraid, perch on the tree in the sweet blue smoke ascending skyward from his pipe.

> And so whenever fortune favored me, I fished and dreamed and wondered. And the struggles of a hooked fish brought to my mind, somehow, the struggle of a misguided nation. Then I would attend to my fishing more zealously, concentrate my mind, and confine my efforts to the matter in hand—a fair fight and a bloodless victory.

Dr. Henshall never did go to war—the war came to him. Confederate General John Morgan led 800 cavalry troopers on a raid deep into Kentucky, which was met by a smaller Federal force in the "First Battle of Cynthiana." Henshall, a member of the local home guard, armed himself with a shotgun, but, conflicted in loyalties, intended to fire it only in self-defense. He soon had his chance. As he hid behind a tree on the town's main street, a Confederate officer wearing a red fez rides at him waving his sword, yelling "Give the damned Yankees hell!" He swings his sabre at Henshall and misses; Henshall, ducking, fires both barrels at him as he disappears.

"I saw him wince at each shot, but as he made no other sign, he probably flinched at the sound of the bullets as they whizzed by."

So. He has fired a shot in anger after all—he has taken part in a battle, albeit a small, highly forgettable one. Enough. Honor has been served. He can go back to healing his patients. He can go back to the Licking River. He can go back to battling bass.

Confederate raiders aside, central Kentucky circa 1862 was the perfect place to fall in love with bass fishing. The rivers abounded in walleye, pike, and even muskies, but the smallmouth was king, and there were devoted anglers eager to catch them using increasingly sophisticated tackle.

> The good people of the blue-grass region of Kentucky exhibit many of the distinctive traits and customs of their English and Scots-Irish ancestors, but in no feature is this heredity more pronounced than in their love for angling. With them, angling is the outward manifestation and practice of an inherent and inherited attribute, and is no sense a fad or hobby . . . Black-bass fishing, as an art, had its origin on the historic soil of Old Kentucky, in that particular portion known as "God's own country"—the blue-grass counties of Fayette, Woodford, Scott, and Harrison . . . Most of these anglers were among the best and brightest and most intelligent and cultivated men of that period.

Some of these anglers fly-fished for their bass, very much in the English tradition; others were in the process of perfecting the famous "Kentucky reel," multiplying reels that were a huge improvement over the single click reels used previously, which were little more than bobbins holding thread. In a multiplier, a small pinion on the end of the spool shaft is geared to a larger cog wheel attached to the crank, so that one revolution of the crank (the handle) produced three or four revolutions of the shaft, making it a much handier and more efficient tool for casting the minnows or minnow imitations that bass love.

George Snyder, one of Kentucky's most skilled silversmiths and watchmakers, made a multiplier as early as 1810, and by the 1840s his invention was being perfected by brothers Jonathan and Benjamin Meek of Frankfort. Henshall, fishing in 1862, would have used a reel more beautiful and jewel-like—and nearly as sophisticated in its engineering—as any used today.

And it was wading these rivers, trying hard not to think about the war, that Doctor Henshall had his idea, *the* great idea of his life, and one that forever changed how Americans viewed their most characteristic fish.

By this point in his life, Henshall had caught a lot of different fish species—stripers, bluefish, weakfish, brook trout, walleye, pike—but none of them fought like the black bass did, none gave him so much delight. And while a coterie of gentleman anglers in Kentucky thought very highly of them, in the rest of the country they were virtually ignored. Trout and salmon were the species that "proper" anglers raved about—outdoor writers, still in obsequious thrall to English traditions, poured out books and articles extolling their virtues, and implicitly dismissing those lesser species found only in America.

They never mentioned black bass. The only ichthyologists who seemed to know anything about them were Frenchmen (not surprising, since there were hardly any American ichthyologists at all), and the most basic facts about them—i.e. did they hibernate in winter?—were largely unknown. The average fisherman considered them to be little more than trash fish, a dinner to be brought home for the cat.

Trash fish! Nothing fought so hard as a bass, nothing demanded more of an angler. It made Henshall furious, to think of their neglect.

And so, "with a spirit of rank heresy in my heart," Henshall's great idea dawns. The black bass is fully a trout's equal. For that matter, allowing for the difference in weight, the bass is a salmon's equal—no, their *superior*. In American waters, their superior—the best gamefish the country possessed.

> The black bass is eminently an American fish, and is representative of his characteristics. He has the faculty of asserting himself and making himself completely at home wherever placed. He is plucky, game, brave and unyielding to the last when hooked. He has the arrowy rush and vigor of the trout, the untiring strength and bold leap of the salmon, while he has a system of fighting tactics particularly his own. That he will eventually become the leading game-fish of American is my oft-expressed opinion and firm belief.

"Game" is the key word here. Game in its old-fashioned, particularly American usage; game meaning bold and unquenchable, "have a resolute unyielding spirit." No higher praise could be heaped upon an American in Henshall's day than to say someone was game, as in "He's a little guy, but he's game—game for anything."

And so, when his famous slogan occurs to him, what he was really saying of the bass wasn't just "Inch for Inch, and Pound for Pound, the Gamest Fish that Swims," but "Inch for Inch, and Pound for Pound, *the most American Fish that Swims.*"

That's what Henshall took from the Civil War—that the bass was the greatest fish in America. And since Henshall was nothing if not game himself, he did more than just come up with the idea, he decided, now that this needless conflict was over, to make sure people understood.

In the gallery of great American characters, Dr. James Alexander Henshall deserves at least honorable mention. There's a state historical marker outside of Cynthiana near the I-27 bridge that commemorates him as "A renowned piscator," and any bass fisher at all interested in the history of their sport has at least heard the name, but in the *Webster's Dictionary of American Biography,* Henry, Patrick, is followed by Hepburn, Kate, with Henshall, James, not even mentioned.

That's a shame. Henshall was the epitome of a type of American that justified the Founders' faith in the common man. Self-educated, inquisitive, imaginative, with a sharp commercial sense, a self-deprecating sense of humor, good with mechanical tasks, a born tinkerer, a self-made man in every sense of the phrase, a pragmatic, hands-on scientist, alive to all things cultural, a good sport and good sportsman, no more egotistical than he had a right to be, bursting with energy and ideas, Henshall had that nineteenth-century can-do optimism and spirit imprinted on his genes.

Certainly, no fish species ever had anyone like him in their corner; no fish species ever had a better publicist, a firmer advocate, a better student, a greater lover and champion. He wasn't just the "Father of American bass fishing," he was its Thomas Jefferson, its Louis Agassiz, its Izaak

WRITING RULE WORTH COMMENTING ON

To The Editor: V/N 3/13

The first sentence of author W. D. Wetherell's recent article ("How Does a Writer's Talent Grow?" Feb. 23), ends with a preposition: "Writing talent is a subject you won't find much writing on."

When I was taking English Composition about 80 years ago, such syntax was to be avoided. However, over the years, such rules are being relaxed. No greater writer of English than Winston Churchill is said to have aided in the demise of this requirement. According to the story, Churchill had prepared a public statement and sent out a draft for review. One reviewer took public issue with his placement of a preposition at the end of a sentence. In one version of the story, Churchill is said to have responded: "This is the type of impertinence up with which I shall not put."

Wetherell is an accomplished writer, especially about fly-fishing, a subject for which we share a passion. I have read most of his books, and he must be aware of the rules, past or present, about prepositions placed at the end of a sentence. Perhaps he was only trying to get someone to bite on one of these little artificial lures attached to the end of a line. I bit.

JOHN E. YOCOM
Hanover

Walton, and P. T. Barnum. "Henshall bass" was once the smallmouth's nickname—and that was only the good doctor's due.

What's more, study photographs of him, and you can see this All-American quality in his very expression. It's an avuncular face, humorous, self-composed, bespectacled, with a twinkle that seems to come more from his walrus mustache than it does from his sensitive eyes. An outdoorsy Oliver Wendell Holmes Jr. is what he suggests—dignified, but ready to laugh at himself, and terrifically eager to get to the next challenge at hand.

Despite being unknown to the public at large, he has always been blessed with a faithful core of disciples devoted to preserving as much "Henshalliana" as they can. One of these, Clyde Drury, has edited a very readable edition of Henshall's autobiography, and the life outlined there takes your breath away from its sheer muscularity. Americans like to pick up stakes and move, granted, but Henshall seems to have inherited this trait at its itchiest, so merely listing all the places he lived and worked in his life can leave you winded.

He was born in Baltimore on February 29, 1836—under the sign of Pisces, he always enjoyed pointing out. In later life, he would brag about being able to remember the "Tippecanoe and Tyler, too" campaign of 1840, this man who lived long enough to see Calvin Coolidge become president. His youth was filled with fishing, hunting, crabbing, and sailing on Chesapeake Bay. He remembered riding the first train in America; he remembered seeing the first telegraph poles being erected—and remembered, most of all, an unspoiled landscape the beauty of which now seems like a dream.

It had its rowdy side, pre-bellum Baltimore, and the young Henshall became an eager participant in a proto Civil War.

On public holidays, the various up-town clans would unite for mutual defense and offence against the combined down-town contingents. On Washington's Birthday especially, the united forces of up-town and down-town would meet by custom and common consent on the commons near the Washington monument, and after the military parade was over several thousand boys would engage in a pitched battle lasting all the afternoon. My scalp still bears the scars, honorable or otherwise, the results of wounds inflicted by sharp stones, dexterously thrown, during some of these encounters.

When he was sixteen, the family moved to Cincinnati—his formal schooling was over. He began working as a typesetter, that upwardly mobile profession of so many Americans who went on to prominence, but, tiring of it, he moved back to Baltimore to be a clerk. A dead-end job, so he decided to attend medical school back in Ohio. He was soon "Doctor" Henshall, but always remained less than enthusiastic about his vocation, and later, when the time came, abandoned medicine without regret.

He saw his first black bass on July 4, 1855, fishing with a friend on the Little Miami River in Ohio. Words could hardly do justice to the intensity of the experience.

Amid a shower of water, the brave fish bounded out again and yet again, with scarcely a moment in between. My eyes seemed bulging out of my head as I tried to follow him in his eccentric course as the line went hissing through the water, now here, now there, with an audible swish as he rushed toward the rocks, then toward a patch of weeds. Finally, he lowered his crest and turned up his armored side to the summer sun in sheer desperation, and as he was slowly reeled in he seemed to exhibit his defiance and to protest against his undue defeat by slapping his broad tail on the shimmery surface. It was my first view of a black bass. His capture was a revelation.

He soon caught one himself, and, quite literally, became hooked. He began fishing for bass at every opportunity—it was now he began fashioning his own rods—but he was still a few years away from his great transformative idea. After Fort Sumter, he tried enlisting as an assistant surgeon in an Ohio regiment, but there was some unspecified difficulty with this, so perhaps his sitting out the conflict had something to do with wounded pride.

Post-war is when his life began revving up. In 1865, he moved to New York City to join a friend's medical practice. While there, he began delving into what meager scientific literature on the bass he could find. Two years later, he moved to Oconomowoc, Wisconsin, in the midst of great bass country, and soon became the first mayor of the town.

He became a valued contributor to *Forest & Stream* magazine, writing under the pen name "Oconomowoc," and booming, not only the bass as a gamefish, but the soon-to-be famous "Henshall rod," which was more flexible and sporty than the broomsticks most fishermen then used; the Henshall rod, he claimed, could "hook, play and subdue a bass in an artistic and sportsman-like manner."

(When he first approached Charles Orvis with the idea of getting the rod in his catalog, Mr. Orvis scoffed, "There is no demand for such a rod." Henshall immediately shot back, "Then I will create a demand.")

He returned to Kentucky to research more on the bass, went on a long sporting trip to Florida, which he wrote about at length (he claimed to have caught a twenty-pound largemouth on this trip), and then returned to Cincinnati in 1880 to oversee publication of the first edition of *Book of the Black Bass*, his groundbreaking classic.

This was travel and success enough for any man, but Henshall was just getting his second wind. He returned to Florida, moved back yet again to Ohio, and then spent a full year on a pleasure trip to Europe with a close male companion; this trip included a pilgrimage to the Museum of Natural History in Paris, where he examined the old dusty smallmouth specimen that had led French naturalists to coin the bass's scientific name eighty years before.

(A music lover, he managed to be in Milan for the world premier of Verdi's *Otello*, attended by the great composer himself. Henshall grumbled about the $25 ticket price and criticized the orchestra as "decidedly Wagnerian.")

He abandoned medicine, and, using his self-taught expertise, led a U.S. Fish Commission expedition to the Gulf Coast of Florida; then, working for the same organization, prepared the elaborate fisheries exhibit that was part of the White City at the 1893 Chicago World's Fair. He nearly became the U.S. Fish Commissioner, but poor political connections meant the appointment went to a lesser man. Instead, he became the superintendent of the federal fish hatchery in Bozeman, Montana, working on trout and grayling propagation; in 1901, he took a similar position back in bass country, in Tupelo, Mississippi, retiring at age eighty-one, and only then because of failing eyesight.

He kept writing in retirement, stressing the need for conservation and good sportsmanship ("The black bass was in a fair way to be exterminated by the hand line and trolling spoon in the hands of fish hogs who were taking the name of angler in vain"), and served as the honorary president of the Izaak Walton League. He updated and revised the *Book of the Black Bass* again and again—the final edition was published in 1923, more than forty years after it first came out. He died two years later in Cincinnati—and fifty years after that, when his famous book was reissued, it sold about 400,000 copies.

He had a happy and prosperous life. He married Miss Hester Stansbury Ferguson in 1863, but after admitting that fact early in his autobiography, he never in the course of 250 pages mentions her again. This can be interpreted in several ways—but let's hope that it was nothing worse than his taking for granted a patient, understanding, long-suffering wife.

How well does Henshall's famous book stand up today? Let's look at the 1904 edition, the ninth impression of which, published in 1917, shows how popular the book remained well into the new century.

It's a handsome, attractively bound book, with a wet fly engraved on the bottom of the spine and crossed fish hooks decorating the top. On the cover is a leaping bass embossed in gold—he seems to be jumping straight into the title, *Book of the Black Bass,* like a weed bed where he'll be safe. Henshall's catch slogan, "Inch for Inch, and Pound for Pound, the Gamest Fish that Swims," is printed toward the top, also in gold, and on the bottom of the cover, if anyone missed the point, the slogan is hammered home: "The Best Game Fish of America."

It's cleverly illustrated, with drawings and engravings fitted right into the text, so the paragraphs part to admit them, and then realign below. There are dignified portraits of the men who crafted pioneering rods and reels, drawings of a dapper old gent stiffly demonstrating how to cast, a copy of a wall painting from Pompey showing a bare-breasted Venus fishing in a river along with baby Cupid, and then, since Henshall was very much a man of his times, an illustration of "The Ideal Still Fisher" showing a black man sound asleep on the bank, the flies swarming unswatted around his face, his pole neglected on his lap.

As for the prose, it's fair to say that one half is completely dated and unreadable—but that means the other half *is* readable, and for a book written in the 1880s, this is a very high percentage. The how-to stuff on baits, hooks, and "miscellaneous implements" is out-of-date and skippable, but his account of how the modern bass rod and reel evolved is still worth reading; his chapters on the bass's life cycle are concise and interesting, and, while his style is often purple (he can't resist alliteration), it can sometimes be lyrical and witty.

Walton it's not—but it shows a man thinking hard and originally upon a subject that fascinates him, and this makes the book live. He wasn't simply the first to write about bass in America, he *knew* he was the first, and wanted to set the record straight when it came to the fish's history.

Nowhere is this sense of responsibility clearer than in his first long chapter wherein he tries clarifying the confused story of how the two species of black bass first came to be identified and named. Americans in 1801 were catching bass, of course, but they had no name for them, or rather, a variety of names depending on region; in South Carolina, for example, largemouth were called "trout" or "trout-perch." This was only twenty-five years after the Revolution—there were no American ichthyologists available, so some early enthusiasts, knowing they had a unique fish but confused as to what exactly it was called, appealed to the one person who might be able to help them, a Frenchman, an aristocrat, and one of the best naturalists in the world.

Bernard Germain de Lacepede was a man of many parts. Opera composer, self-taught scientist, an adroit politician (he had to be, to survive the Reign of Terror), he was one of those remarkable Europeans who, in his spare time, was busily identifying and naming species, not only in France, but—via letters, drawings, and specimens sent to him at the Jardin des Plantes in Paris—from all over the world.

In 1801, he received his first example of a black bass from America—a smallmouth as it happened, a fish completely unknown in Europe. Unfortunately, it was a mutilated specimen, with a deformed dorsal fin, several of the last rays having been bitten off when the fish was young, so it had the appearance of a separate small fin.

Lacepede, after trying out *Labrus salmonides* for its trout-like shape (and being additionally confused by a drawing he'd been sent of a largemouth, *not* the smallmouth sample right in front of him), ended up calling the new species *Micropterus dolomieu*—*Micropterus* meaning "small fin," and *dolomieu* in honor of his friend Deodat Gratet de Dolomieu, Knight of Malta, adventurer, womanizer, duelist, and the pioneering mineralogist after whom dolomite is named.

The "small fin" designation for smallmouth confused everyone back in the States, and Lacepede didn't know largemouth were different. Other scientists stepped in with their own names, rival French naturalists, and then early American ones, including the great Louis Agassiz, until there were upward of forty rival names competing to be *the* name, or, since there were two species, name*s. Lepomis flexuolaris. Grystes nigricans. Grystes nobilis. Dioplies treculli.* They all had their enthusiasts, they all had their shots.

Poor communication between scientists, misprints in scholarly journals, fuzzy drawings, mutilated specimens, the regional differences that confused everyone—these all muddied the waters. As late as 1860, the matter was still unresolved, though another Frenchman, a Dr. Valliant, took Lacepede's original designation, *salmonides,* added to it *Micropterus,* and gave the largemouth its eventual name, *Micropterus salmonides.*

Well might Henshall lament,

The scientific history of the black bass is most unsatisfactory. This representative American fish was first brought to the light of science in a foreign land, and under the most unfavorable auspices; it was born a monstrosity; its baptismal names were incongruous, and its sponsors were, most unfortunately, foreign naturalists.

It was Henshall himself who finally, grudgingly, resolved the matter once and for all in the first edition of his book. Since none of the names were perfect (and nobody was picking up on his hint to call the bass the "Henshall"), why not go back to the original?

Lacepede conferred the name *salmonides* because the drawing first sent to him was the "trout-perch" of Carolina. If we take its game qualities into consideration, there is no fish is so salmon-like as the black bass; none that exhibits so nearly the characteristic leap, the pluck, the endurance of the "king of the waters." The name is therefore not altogether inappropriate. Dolomieu being a French proper noun, might be considered objectionable; Lacepede used the name, however, not through accident, but for the sake of euphony and to perpetuate the name of his friend. Let the name of the small-mouth bass then, stand as *dolomieu*—the name of a brave man for a brave fish.

By 1880, after their slow start, the first generation of American ichthyologists had learned quite a bit about the bass, and it's remarkable that Henhsall, without academic credentials of any kind, managed to turn himself into one of the most important of these researchers, making up for his lack of schooling with devotion and patience. For hours at a time, he would peer down at spawning bass from blinds made of bushes on the bank, trying to understand and document the whole spawning cycle. By the time he wrote the biology sections of his book, he was in contact with fishermen and scientists all across the country, and he skillfully draws upon their knowledge to supplement his own.

Great stuff, concisely presented—but then comes his howler.

It's a big one, and he falls into it in two pratfalling missteps. In the course of praising the bass's virtues, Henshall writes, "There are few fish more prolific, while there is none more hardy, healthy and better able to take care of itself and none that protects or cares more tenderly for its young."

Fine, those first two clauses, but when it comes to the third, the "tenderly" business, he's on much shakier ground. Yes, the bass protects its nest after spawning, but only for a few days, and then, when the fry start milling around, the father is likely to gobble up as many as it can reach.

Just a poor word choice from an otherwise careful observer? Possibly—but a few pages later he says it again.

"The black bass being hatched with but a rudimentary umbilical vessel or yolk-sac, needs the fostering care and attention of the parent fish, who teaches it how and where to find its food, and protects it from its enemies in the same way that a hen cares for its brood."

Maybe it's to Henshall's credit, that he could be capable of such sheer sentimental nonsense. Bass, for all their virtues, do *not* teach their babies how and where to find food. The very image of this is risible—a big largemouth homeschooling its offspring in the lake, showing them crayfish and hellgrammites and other healthy choices, while warning them about bad dudes like pike. What led Henshall to say this is a mystery, since there is no possibility of his ever witnessing such behavior.

Did his affection for bass get the better of him? They not only had to pull hard on the end of a life, run, jump, and cavort, but they also had to be helicopter parents as well? It's interesting in this respect to think Doctor Henshall himself was childless—and maybe some unrequited filial sense made him go temporarily out of his head.

The science gives way to the how-to-catch-'em section, with Henshall explaining the strategies best suited to catching fish under a wide range of conditions. He was inventing the literary model that would be followed by lesser bass writers in book after book for the next century—suggesting a method of fishing, and then backing it up with an illustrative anecdote about how using a special lure or tactic once saved the day on Gogbie Lake or Big St. Germain.

The emphasis on the mechanics of it all, the "how-to," would sink many bass books to come, but not Henshall's. The reason it doesn't is that he refuses to follow his own advice.

"The book of the black bass," he writes in the introduction, "is of an entirely practical nature. It has been written more with a view to instruct than to amuse or entertain. The reader will, therefore, look in vain between its covers for those rhetorical flights, poetic descriptions, entertaining accounts and pleasing illustrations of the pleasures and vicissitudes of angling which are usually found in books of like character."

A straightforward, business-like, somewhat philistine statement of intent—but Henshall totally ignores it. His book is *full* of rhetorical flights, entertaining accounts, and pleasing illustrations—and, what's more, it's full of poetry. He quotes Wordsworth and Pope, quotes them several times, and then takes a crack at writing a poem himself.

But look!
Saw you that gleam beneath the flood? A flash—
A shadow—then a swirl upon the pool?
My hand, responsible to the sudden thrill,
Strikes in the steel—the wary bass is hooked!
And now with lightning speed he darts away
To reach his lair—his refuge 'neath the roots.
The singing reel proclaims him almost there—
I give the butt—the ever-faithful rod
In horse-shore curve now checks his headlong flight
Right lustily he tugs and pulls. Egad!
But still the barb is fast.
Another leap!
Ye Gods! How like an angry beat he shakes
His bristling mane and dives below again.

It's hardly Emily Dickinson, hardly even Eugene Field, but how many bass writers after him would ever even dare attempt this? Even his prose often strives toward poetry, and in phrase after random phrase manages to achieve it.

"I can find something beautiful or interesting in every fish that swims. I have an abiding affection for every one, from the lowly, naked bull-head to the silver-spangled king the salmon."

"Not only the fly, but every implement of the fly-fisher's outfit is a materialized poem."

"The angler wending his way by the stream, or resting upon its grassy bank, has an innate love for all his surroundings—the trees, the birds, the flowers—which become part and parcel of his pursuit; become true and tried friends and allies without whom he could no more love his art, nor practice it, then the astronomer could view the heavens with pleasure on a cloudy, starless night."

"To be a good angler depends on aesthetic and poetic features."

And poetry is not the only anomaly in Henshall. This oh-so-typical American of his era, the workaholic, the booster, the muscular Christian with his missionary zeal, could stand far enough apart from his culture to view it with a critical eye. And what he saw in the Gilded Age was a race of men becoming emasculated and deadened by the move from the country to the city, from life on a farm to life in an office.

> In the rapid race for wealth and distinction men labor night and day, with mind and muscle, especially during the seasons of business activity. But too often, alas, they labor in vain and find that the "bubble reputation" or the "wealth that sinews bought" has in a moment been swept away after years of toil and anxiety. Or, if they make their footing sure, they find, too often, that the result has only been attained at the expense of a permanent impairment of health . . . I claim that the more enlightened and civilized a nation becomes, the more it is interested in the world of nature and her laws; that the more artificial and advanced we become, the more readily we turn for rest and enjoyment to the simplicity of nature's resources.

In the end, that's Doctor James Henshall's prescription in a nutshell. For whatever ails you, go fishing. Better yet, go *bass* fishing. For all the how-to, poetry, history, and science in his book, he never strays far from his overriding message: that the bass is America's greatest fish and it's high time everyone understands this.

> The book owes its origins to a long-cherished desire to give to the black bass species their proper place among game-fishes, and to create in anglers an interest in two fishes that had never been so fully appreciated as their merits deserved. At the present day, however, the author's prediction that they would eventually become the favorite game-fish of America has been fully verified.

And then, in words that could have been written on his tombstone, he flat out says it, the great idea of his life.

"I wanted to give the sport of bass fishing a higher place in the catalog of noble sports."

Henshall, in old age, was convinced that the *Book of the Black Bass* was absolutely the last word on bass fishing and nothing more need be said. "There is not much likelihood of there being any occasion for adding anything to it during my life," he wrote in the last edition, "and it is not at all likely that anyone will add any thing to it after I am gone."

The hundreds of bass books written since would seem to put the lie to this—and yet in one respect this sense of finality was justified, since so many of them merely repeat, in more contemporary sounding ways, what he said, and slavishly follow the same pattern: a little science, a little history, and then on to the endless how-to, with illustrative anecdotes drawn from the writer's experience.

And it's interesting to speculate on what Henshall would make of it, American bass fishing of today.

The big box fishing stores would be the first place to take him. After his initial shock at how crowded, bright, and lavish it all was (*"Egad!"*), he might be pleased to find that so many of the lures, reels, and rods are only updated versions of the ones he made popular two centuries ago.

The electronics would puzzle him—cameras to spy on fish!—and the dominance of plastic. He was a shrewd businessman, so he would probably ask the manager about profit margins—but then again, maybe he wouldn't. Seeing how many items are endorsed by celebrity bass anglers might make him take pause. This is the man, after all, who could put his hand over his heart and pledge, "Though there have been rods, reels and lines named for me by enthusiastic friends, the honor has been my own and sufficient recompense, for I have never received, and would scorn to accept, any pecuniary fee for any thing devised by myself, or made prominent by my efforts for black bass fishing."

What would interest him the most would be the fly-fishing section, small as it is in such stores ("Fly-fishing is the most legitimate, scientific and gentlemanly mode of angling"), and he would be fascinated to see all the imaginative fly patterns that have evolved since his beloved Lord Baltimore.

Bass tournaments would appall him. The word "competition" doesn't appear in his writings, and the idea of catching bass on TV for huge prize money would seem to him a betrayal of everything he stood for—"Fish hogs masquerading under the name of sportsman, but taking the name of angler in vain."

Life beyond bass? The larger American scene?

He would be dismayed by our culture's emphasis on credentials, this self-taught scientist who, never having gone to college, became one of the country's leading ichthyologists. He would be saddened to learn that fewer young people take up fishing. He would be depressed by the fact that, 150 years after the Civil War, the country is embroiled in a new war, one without cavalry raids or pitched battles, but where the hate and ferocity, the brutal divisions, are almost as great as they were in the Kentucky of his youth, Confederate against Union become Red state versus Blue.

"*Ye Gods!*" he might say, slapping his forehead, disgusted yet again with the "jealousy, dishonesty, and unscrupulous selfishness exhibited by the leading politicians, the selfish marplots, who are most active in the unholy crusade against truth, and justice."

A country still divided. Yes, it would bother Henshall greatly, and then he might thank his lucky stars he was out of it, give his mustache a contemplative twirl, gather his rod, reel, and flies, and do what he always did when American life got him down—go fishing, go fishing for bass.

Four

It's always troubling when your favorite bias bumps against a cherished hope. It happened to me yesterday, and so I'll try to explain while the contradiction still hurts.

Let's start with the bias, which concerns bass-fishing tournaments. The easiest way to say it, the starkest, is to admit that I'm an elitist snob, yuppie scum, left-leaning Blue-state self-righteous fly-fishing bleeding-heart loon lover who hates NASCAR, despises golf, loathes big outboards, fish finders, and sonar, abominates commercialism and celebrity-hood, and abhors, in particular, the amalgam of all these egregious qualities that is American professional bass fishing. Competition is no bad thing, and trying to outwit a fish is something I've devoted much of my life to accomplishing, but when big bucks get involved, competition—not to put too fine a point on it—reeks all to hell.

That's on the prejudice side.

On the cherished-hope side is my wishing that high-school athletic departments would ease off on their support for traditional competitive sports like football and basketball, and turn more of their energy and budget to promoting lifetime sports like kayaking, cycling, hiking, and running. And indeed, something like this is actually happening. Football, now that the risk of brain damage is becoming understood (and litigated), might eventually disappear as a school-sanctioned sport. At the same time, sports like soccer are being privatized, to the point that elite, all-year-around travel teams are increasingly loath to release their players for a high-school season.

So maybe it's not that big a surprise that more and more states are beginning to organize high-school bass fishing teams and state championship tournaments, complete with uniforms, cheerleaders, and trophies. Illinois and Kentucky have long had teams, Missouri has joined in, and New Hampshire, I discovered in my local paper, was about to become the first state in the East to stage a high-school state bass championship of its own.

I called Scott Fitzgerald, the athletic director of Kearsage High School, and one of the organizers.

"We didn't know what to expect," he said. "We thought, well maybe we'll get five or six schools involved, but over forty have signed up. This is really catching on."

One of their motives, he explained, was to get students involved who didn't participate in traditional sports. And, judging by the kids in his own school who had signed up so far, this was proving to be the case.

"Have you had practices?" I asked.

"I had them in the science classroom practicing their flip casts into garbage cans. The state tourney is May ninth on Lake Winnipesaukee. I can get you a seat on the press boat if you'd like to come."

I'd never been on a "press boat" before—a press anything, for that matter—so I immediately said yes. I woke up yesterday morning at 4:00, drove two hours through the fog-draped hills to the Lee Mills boat launch, and spent the day trying to learn whether high-school bass fishing was a really brilliant idea or a seriously dumb one.

I got there before 7:00, but already most of the teams were waiting in their boats at the dock for the first "flight" to be sent out. Stratos, Triton, and Nitro were the bass boats favored, but there were plenty of Skeeters, too; all the boats seemed to have pixie dust mixed in with their gel coat, so they looked sleek and surprisingly feminine. B.A.S.S. (Bass Anglers Sportsman Society) stickers adorned many of them, and whether purposefully or not, their pattern resembled the logo of the NRA.

Team members fussed with their tackle, applied scent to their lures, peeked over at rival teams to see what they were tying on, or just sat there staring into the fog trying their teenage best to look chill. There were lots of hooded sweatshirts in evidence, lots of camouflage, but some teams had shirts done up in their school colors, and they seemed so proud of them they wouldn't put on rain gear, even though the mist was heavy. Each team had a captain, an adult volunteer, and a lot of these wore the bright bibs and parkas of the bass fishing pro.

One thing immediately struck me. When your son or daughter plays serious high-school sports, you become aware of other kids who, while waiting for the bus to take them home, look with envy and shyness at the athletes waltzing out to practice. Not for them the comradeship of being on a soccer team; not for them the glory of a last-minute touchdown. It's hard to describe them other than that—they come in all varieties of shapes and sizes—but I've seen that look on enough faces that I realized, walking along the dock where the bass teams waited, that these were those kids.

Good for you, I decided, with a surge of emotion. And, despite all my irony and skepticism, the feeling stayed with me all through the day.

I walked along the landing, taking in the scene. Maybe it was the mist, the hour of morning—but it was strangely quiet, even hushed, for an assemblage of 108 teenagers; I had the sense everyone was over-awed by the occasion, or trying hard not to be. One of the teams wore the green-and-white colors of Sunapee High School, which is located smack in the middle of great bass water—surely they would be among the pre-tourney favorites?

They smiled when I told them that, Chris and Matt. So many students had signed up for the bass team that there had been tryouts just like in basketball—a "fish off" on Little Sunapee Lake that Chris and Matt had won. I asked them about their fishing experience (Matt: "I fish a lot"); I asked whether they watched bass fishing tournaments on television (Chris: "All the time"); I asked if they played any other sport (simultaneously: "No"); I asked if they had a game plan (their captain this time, the adult volunteer: "Too many game plans!"); and then I wished them luck, said I'd be looking for them out on the lake.

I chatted with the next boat, the Londonderry Lancers, and then went on to Pinkerton Academy's Number One boat, with, sitting on the pedestal seat swaddled in rain gear, one of the two girls taking part in the tournament.

Elizabeth Preble was her name, a sophomore—and yes, she seemed very happy to be there in the middle of all those boys.

"Play other sports?" I asked.

"Swimming and I dance."

"Getting any grief at school about being on a fishing team?"

"People think it's cool," she said. "All my friend wish they could do it."

Sixty kids had shown up for the first meeting at her school, about twenty turned out to be seriously interested, and, after tryouts, two teams of two had been selected, and they had been practicing twice a week for the last month.

I started talking to Pinkerton's captain, something was said about fly-fishing, and this really got Elizabeth smiling. Her dad was a flyfisher, he'd taught her how, and it was spin fishing that was new to her, so she wasn't sure she would catch anything today.

"Good luck to you all," I said. "Rip their lips," and this made them laugh.

I wasn't the only one making the rounds with my notepad. There was a reporter from New Hampshire Public Radio, a photographer from Associated Press, and news teams from local television stations. And though they kept their air of total chill, this obviously impressed these teenagers greatly; not only were they finally on a high-school team, they were being interviewed just like the pros!

I ended up by the boat of one of the two Catholic high schools taking part, Bishop Guertin. One of their English teachers, Dan G., had come to cheer them on. He led the fishing club at school, but it had always been pretty informal ("Pond slop fishermen," he called his team affectionately), and the boys were pumped to be participating in a big-time tournament.

Dan worked with the New Hampshire Interscholastic Association, and was a good source of information. For all my bias against bass fishing tournaments, I had never actually attended one before or bothered to learn the rules.

Dan filled me in. The organization behind high-school bassing in Illinois and Kentucky, the Student Anglers Federation, had demanded that, in return for sanctioning the New Hampshire tournament, all participants had to join their organization. The NHIAA said nuts to that—no other high-school sport demanded similar—so the Federation relented, asking only that they be mentioned in publicity handouts.

As for the rules. Everyone had to wear life jackets at all times. Captains, the adults, could drive the boat and offer advice, but they couldn't touch a line or help with the actual fishing; students, if they didn't own any, could use the captain's equipment. While fishing, boats had to stay at least 150 feet away from other boats. Four fish could be kept in aerated live wells, and these could be culled (smaller ones released) when bigger ones were caught. Any injured or bleeding bass had to be kept and killed—and there was a quarter-pound penalty deduction in your aggregate score for a dead fish. Any thunder overhead, any lightning, and everyone had to get off the water. The boats would go out in two "flights," so as not to bunch, and teams were due back at 2:30 for the weigh-in.

I asked Dan what the reaction had been among teachers and administrators when they learned the students would be missing a day of school to go bass fishing.

"Some thought it was the dumbest thing they ever heard of. Others said it was the greatest thing. 'I wish they had that when I was in high school,' was a common reaction. I use fishing literature in my class, so I'm in the greatest camp."

"Who's your money on?" I asked, pointing to the boats.

"You have to like the locals, which would be Moultonborough High. They know the lake. I hear Laconia High has a woman bass pro as their captain, so they'll be right up there. A largemouth will win it, and that probably means a four-and-a-half pound fish. The good news is that—"

He stopped in mid-sentence, stared past me toward the boat launch. "Wow, will you look at that!"

The last high-school team had arrived, trailering not a sexy high-tech boat, but a lobster boat, the real deal, with the upswept bow and broad work platform of a craft made for blue water. This was Ports-mouth High, from New Hampshire's eleven-mile fringe of coastline, sporting a big flag with their school colors, becoming—the minute they launched—the fans' sentimental favorite.

"Yeah," the salty looking captain said, when all the reporters flocked over. "The rules don't say anything about what kind of boat, and this was the best we could find. I don't think she's ever been in freshwater before." He squinted at the lake with its tricky channels. "I can find my way around the Atlantic, but I'm not sure I'll be able to find my way back here."

Great stuff—but now the bass-meister, the beefy, jumpsuited guy with the bullhorn, was ordering the first flight out, and things got busy very fast. The boats had to keep headway speed for the first few hundred yards, and could only throttle up when they hit the open lake, so their progression down the channel was slow and stately, reminding me of gondolas on the Grand Canal or barges on the Thames. Bass moms and bass dads waved to their kids like they were going to sea for good—"Good luck!" they called and snapped pictures. At the leading edge of the procession, just when the boats were about to disappear over the horizon, came great roaring noises as the captains hit the gas, sending up angry rooster tails of vertical spray.

The first flight left, and then the second flight, and then it became preternaturally quiet, so we adults left at the dock felt abandoned and purposeless—the teams weren't due in for another six hours. It was like going to attend a high-school football game, getting all caught up in the pre-game excitement, and then watching as the boys ran off to play out of sight and hearing, so we wouldn't even know the score until they returned.

Time to hop the press boat. This was a pontoon boat operated by New Hampshire Fish and Game; they had sent fifteen wardens to help with the event, making it an ideal day to break the game laws elsewhere. A cheerful woman named Karina operated it; she helped me on with my life jacket, then, with a cargo of photographers for ballast, steered us toward the creamy froth left by the second flights' wakes.

And it was an interesting voyage right from the start. One of the boats, the Alvirne High School team, had decided to fish right there in the first bay near the boat launch. Not for them the crazy speeding up and down the lake—they had gotten into bass right away. Just past them we came upon the State Marine Patrol boat, which had already ticketed five antsy teams that had started speeding up while still in the no-wake zone, and then, for good measure, issued a ticket to the spectators' pontoon boat for having its registration displayed improperly.

The Fish and Game officers seemed worried we might get busted ourselves, but with a suspicious squint at our bow number, the water cop waved us on.

It was a while before we encountered any more teams. Winnipesaukee, before it spreads open, has many hidden inlets and coves, and we couldn't duck into all of them; then, too, if you have a bass boat with dual 200 horsepower outboards on the back, you're going to use them to *zoom*. With no teams to interview just yet, the public radio man swung his microphone toward me.

"What do you think of bass fishing tournaments?"

That was an easy one.

"I think they're bullshit," I said—the microphone jerked back.

Had others on the boat heard me? These were Fish and Game officials; bass tournaments helped pay their salaries (there are an astonishing 450 "sanctioned" bass tournaments a year just in our small state alone). I tried changing subjects.

"Look at those beautiful loons!"

An innocent enough remark—or was it? Loons and bass tournaments are currently a hot issue in New Hampshire. The bird, fighting back from its decline, has become the symbol of our lakes region, its image appearing on inn signs, decals, and sweatshirts; the New Hampshire Loon Center, devoted to preserving the birds and their habitat, was headquartered fifty yards from the boat landing from which we had left.

The problem was lead. Loons can swallow lead sinkers, mistaking them for pebbles they use as grit, or can eat a fish with a leaded lure in its lip; it's estimated that this causes almost fifty percent of adult loon mortality in the state. Flyfishers have largely switched over to nontoxic split shot made of tin or steel, but bass tourney anglers were showing up at hearings in Concord and fighting any restrictions, not just on sinkers, but on lead weights built into their lures. Jigs cost about $3.00 apiece if they are lead weighted; $8.00 apiece if they're nontoxic, and with bassassers packing 100 jigs in their tackle box, this could add up to real money—and some claim that national fishing tournaments would shun New Hampshire if tighter restrictions were imposed, hurting area businesses.

(A letter to the editor in the local newspaper summed up this point of view. "Someday, when the so-called do-gooders make fishing so expensive that no one will participate anymore, they will have to pay for the management of fish and wildlife themselves—the way sportsmen do now. Good luck with that!")

Gabe Gries, Warmwater Project Leader for New Hampshire Fish and Game, explained all this to me, and then suggested the solution had to come on a national level, since the big sporting-goods dealers weren't interested in making jigs just for New Hampshire. Okay, understood— but with loons stretching their lovely necks right there off the bow, ducking and diving in their gracefully iconic way, it didn't do much to sweeten my attitude toward bass tournaments.

I cheered up again when we started encountering the teams. Portsmouth was first—the boys in the lobster boat. "All we're catching is pickerel," the captain said ruefully. "You guys have any shiners we can buy?"

Laconia High already had their limit, and were searching for a big one out on a reef, hoping they could cull their smaller bass and keep a potential winner. They were captained by Terry Tilley, who, I was told breathlessly, had gone to the national circuit as a pro. Rose Therrien, the team member in the bow, yelled "Fish on!" and all the photographers got excited, but the bass broke off before they could get their pictures.

There was a lot of "structure" along this stretch of shoreline, so we began encountering more teams.

Franklin High School: "No fish yet!" Bishop Brady: "Just small-mouth so far, no largemouth!" Gilford High School: "Do white perch count?" Winnacunnet: "Nailing 'em on Wacky Worms!"

Most of the kids cast toward shore with the mechanical chopping motion of workers on an assembly line, but some—the ones who watched bass tournaments on TV—did it with more panache. They tossed it underhanded or pitched it sideways, "jerking" or "flipping," and one cocky blond, seeing the cameras approach, stepped up onto the bow, twisted sideways, and, like an Ultimate Frisbee player, cast one behind his back. Maybe he was the one who college scouts would be interested in; I had learned not only that universities like North Carolina State and Auburn were offering scholarships in bass fishing, but that a surprisingly high number of these kids knew that and wanted in.

We went from team to team, boat to boat. It was pleasant out on the lake, now that the chill had lifted. Winnipesaukee's shoreline is a blend of weathered summer homes that go back generations, and trophy houses that vie with each other in ugliness and ostentation. Above these shine the mountains, and springtime bands of early foliage were striping up the slopes.

And it was wonderfully quiet now that the teams had gotten to their fishing spots and the outboards were silent. In my day (in the course of the morning, I was tempted to use that phrase several times), you would have paddled the boat from spot to spot, but now it was trolling motors that did the work, controlled by foot-pedal remotes. They make a humming sound when they're on—a throaty purring that's soft and surprisingly soothing, like the motor is singing the lake to sleep.

The press boat visited four or five more teams—"How's the fishing?" we took turns shouting—and then we steamed back to the boat launch to see if anyone else wanted to go out. Weigh-in wasn't until 2:30, so I hopped in my car and drove to Center Harbor for lunch. We needed some marigolds for our garden, a new paddle for the canoe, so I hunted up both in the resort town busily readying itself for the season.

When I got back, it was almost 2:00. There were more spectators than in the morning—parents had left work early to watch their kids come in (they sat in sling chairs like at a soccer game), and the evening news show had sent out reporters to film the weigh-in. A lot of teams had already come back to the bay, where they were trying for a last-minute winner; if in the morning they had looked like Venetian gondolas, they now looked like LSTs waiting the order to charge Omaha Beach.

The sponsors' tent had been set up near the weigh-in scales, and here the notorious tourney commercialism was unapologetically displayed. Banners advertised: *Redneck Remedy* for sunburn; *Sta-bil* ethanol treatment for engines; *Numa Sports Optics* endorsed by Scott Martin, "Champion Bass Angler and host of the *Scott Martin Challenge*"; *Power-Pole* shallow water anchors; Toyota Trucks; Lowrance, Skeeter, Triton, Yamaha; *Dobyns Reds* (whatever they are) endorsed by Gary Dobyns, "West Coast All-Time Money Winner"; and *New Hampshire Junior Bass Masters,* sponsored by Li'l Hustler Tackle Co.

And it wasn't just the commercialism that cast an odor. The bass boats were idling offshore, and the stink of gasoline was overwhelming, flattened into a low cloud by the returning drizzle; if you stuck your finger in the air, you could have twirled carbon around it like a noxious licorice. (Later that afternoon, driving home, I heard on the radio that scientists had measured carbon dioxide levels in the atmosphere higher than 400 parts per million, a threshold not crossed in three million years.)

It was time for the weigh-in. The man with the bullhorn from the morning, the bass-meister guy, shouted out instructions to the teams about how this would be accomplished. Each team had a number, and when it was called they were to hurry their bass in the special mesh weigh-in bags over to the scales, where they would be weighed individually and then as a four-fish aggregate. Instructions were very precise on this—and it was impressive, watching these teenagers devote so much care and attention to insuring the fish went unharmed.

Gary Gries stood right by the scales making sure this was done properly. He told me later that, despite all the care, there was still some mortality.

"Two percent," he said, meaning two out of a hundred bass weighed would die as a result of the handling. This was considered to be a remarkably low number; down South, where warmer water stresses bass more, mortality after a tournament could reach thirty percent, a major fish kill.

Kearsage High went first. Their four-fish aggregate weighed 7.97 pounds, which flashed on the electronic scoreboard. It wasn't immediately clear to fans when we should applaud—when the weight lit up the screen, or not until the announcer, a popular New Hampshire DJ, announced the results?

Hopkinton came in with a 8.91 pound aggregate, to take the early lead. Moultonborough Number 1, the local team, took over with 9.9 pounds, but their Number 2 boat topped that with 11.86 pounds, good enough to take second place on the day. The winners turned out to be from Exeter High down on the coast, using a good 4.00 pound largemouth to push their aggregate to 12.43 pounds, making them the first state tournament winners in New Hampshire high-school sports history. Pinkerton Number 1, the team with Elizabeth Preble, finished a highly creditable fifth; Portsmouth, the team in the lobster boat, finished fifty-first.

Overall, 201 bass had been caught and released on the day, split evenly between largemouth and smallmouth. The biggest fish, in a species upset, turned out to be a 4.17 pound smallmouth caught by Sanborn High. Applause, photos, slaps on the back—and then the teams took their bass back to the live wells, motored at least 300 feet from the dock, and delivered them back to the water, not much worse for wear after playing high-school sports.

I talked to some of the organizers as the teams trailered out. Clearly, the tourney had exceeded everyone's expectations. They had been willing to go ahead with only five high schools participating, but instead they had nearly fifty; they were hoping two or three reporters might show up, and instead they had a dozen; they weren't at all sure any bass would be caught, the water being so cold, but the kids had caught and released hundreds; the weigh-in had gone a lot smoother than at most tournaments; and it was obvious, watching the teams as they left, that everyone was going home happy.

There would be tweaking needed to get the fall season up and running. More portable toilets would have to be available, and not just the one; smaller regional tourneys would allow them to fish smaller lakes; they would have to find more adult volunteers.

I got up the nerve to mention to Gary Gries that not all bass fishermen thought tournaments were a great idea, pointing to the commercialism, the carbon footprint, the competitive hoopla; I was tempted to quote Jim Harrison's line about how "fishing tournaments are like playing tennis with live balls." This wasn't just the NHIAA State High School Bass Fishing Tournament after all, but the NHIAA *Crestliner* State High School Bass Fishing Tournament. I'd been to my share of state soccer championships over the years, and while there might be a banner from a local car dealership, and home-team parents might be selling cupcakes, there was nothing like the in-your-face blandishments I saw here.

Then, too, if they are to have more kids participating, avoiding tryouts and cuts, they will need more bass boats, which means turning to B.A.S.S. members for volunteers. And while the volunteer part is commendable, the B.A.S.S. part means wedding themselves to a vast commercial enterprise whose goal is to hook kids early, not just on fishing, but on fishing *their* way.

The organizers knew these were concerns, but thought they were trumped by the kids' enthusiasm, the desirability of introducing them to an outdoor sport and so giving their generation a stake in conservation. And maybe they're right. But I came away as conflicted as I went in, glad to see the boys and girls out there on the water, convinced, as never before, that the whole tournament conception sucks.

Cynics would say that the bass is never more American than when it's bringing in the bucks, acting as poker chips in high-stakes tourneys, or as a kind of swimming ATM machine. And maybe the way to fish for them *is* to outfit yourself in 1970s-era jumpsuits, plaster ads and logos all over your chest, put on aviator glasses, power up your dual 200 horsepower Mercs, turn the electronics on, throttle down on your independence and nonconformity, and then go and pull them out as fast as you can reel.

Or maybe not. My hope would be that some of these young people, having been introduced to the sport through tournaments, might quickly tire of the razzamatazz and bullshit, decide to venture out on their own some evening, maybe in a canoe, alone or with a friend, maybe with a can of worms, maybe with a fly rod. Once they discover the quiet part of the sport, they will become true bass fishers, enjoying the intensely interesting competition that comes between man and fish, one on one, taking place in secret far from the madding crowd. They might find plenty of fun in tournaments, lots of good ol' boy laughs, but if they want to find joy, solace, and mystery then going out alone is the way to find it—and when the bass boats zoom by out on the open lake, they can tell their buddy how they used to do that, too, back in the foolish, callow days before, as anglers, they finally grew up.

Five

Every Forgotten Pond is forgotten for good reason. America is full of them. Off the main roads, away from tourist country, too small or shallow for summer homes, hardly visited, precious in the way lost and neglected things often are. In an age of blatancy, bombast, and hype, they're refuges of understatement—and not just for man. Largemouth bass love forgotten ponds. They take a long hard look at what their image has become in the larger world, see their cousins in more fashionable lakes being cranked in by jumpsuited men in muscle boats, held up for the TV cameras, transmuted into dollars, and they decide that living rough and forgotten is no bad thing.

This particular Forgotten straddles the border between one of Vermont's prettiest, most affluent towns and one of its poorest and shabbiest. Toward the end of the nineteenth century, this was the center of one of the largest copper mining operations in the country, with a thousand miners, Irish and Cornish, digging away at veins that ran deep into the hills. It was even the site of a labor battle, the "Ely War" of 1883, when disgruntled miners marched on the owner's house chanting "Bread or blood!" and were met by the bayonets of the National Guard.

There's not much left of this now except mine shafts known only to local history buffs (a buff fell down one last year and died), and a Superfund site that seems just as forgotten and neglected as the tailings it was meant to clean up. Almost everything in Vermont turns beautiful if you wait long enough—but there's a legacy of hardness here, even danger, and if you fish Forgotten at night, you don't want to fish alone.

75

Just last week, state police, called to a house near the pond, Tased an epileptic who had reached out for help, killing him instantly—so it's not just the tough guys you have to worry about here, but the trigger-happy descendants of those mining-company goons.

The dirt road leading up to the pond starts out in 1959 at the bottom and ends up in 1859 by the top. Aging hippies living in do-it-yourself houses Hobbits would be happy in; the trailers of misfits who don't want to be bothered by the world and have large handwritten signs announcing this in no uncertain terms; a last surviving hill farm, there where the forest gives way to an expansive green meadow. An empty brick mansion at the crest of the road once served as an inn—and haunted-looking inns, wildflowers growing high up the old bricks, are a sign that you have indeed entered forgotten country, where things are probably quieter now than they were in 1790.

Forgotten Pond lies within a bowl of open meadows, and seems, with the trees leaning back from the shoreline, even higher and loftier than it really is, giving the sense that cupped hands are lifting it toward the sun as an offering. It's surprisingly lush for a pond this far north, surrounded by the kind of tropical looking undergrowth you'd associate with the Deep South (well, deep South Connecticut, anyway). Weed beds, lily pads, sunken logs, mangrove-like roots marching out from the shallows. It's not quite Okefenokee, but for Vermont it's pretty close.

It's a pond that seems split between left and right, and I don't mean just geographically. On the west side is a small relaxed summer camp that's had various incarnations over the years, but started out as Camp Thoreau, a place for old New York lefties to send their kids. On the east side is a rough, improvised boat launch that's become the favorite place for the descendants of those tough Cornish miners to party and fish. In the middle, floating in a canoe at night, you can hear the boom boxes playing country on one side, children singing campfire songs on the other. Wait for the party to get going at the launch, wait for the counselors to put their charges to bed and come down to the shore to relax, and you can catch the straw-sweet smell of marijuana coming from both sides, coalescing over the center of the pond in a friendly, lefty-righty sort of cloud.

(The counselors think the rednecks are swimming nude and having wild orgies on their end of the pond; the rednecks think the counselors are swimming nude and having wild orgies on their end of the pond ... but speaking as someone who paddles from one side to the other in the course of a fishing night, I've never encountered evidence of either.)

If the rest of the world has pretty much forgotten Forgotten, then I'd forgotten about it, too. I first visited it twenty-seven years ago, on a memorable/not-so-memorable occasion, and, while I'd canoed it a few times since, this was the first time I'd come back with the deliberate intention of fishing.

In late April of 1986, Celeste was eight months pregnant with our first child. We were excited, happy, and, like most first-time parents, a little bit overwrought. While I don't remember the specifics, I probably said something like, "You know, once the baby arrives we'll never have time to do anything together, so why don't we go fishing today one last time? Someone recommended this pond over in Vermont."

Celeste was game, though at this point in her pregnancy she was carrying some serious added weight.

"Will I need a license?"

Money was tight those years. "Nah," I said confidently. "It's the boonies, a warden would never go up there."

The same friend who recommended it must have given us directions—this was years before GPSs—and, after loading the car with fishing gear and our picnic, I drove the twelve miles to the pond, getting more excited the rougher and lonelier the road became. Forgotten forms an almost perfect circle, with a narrow, canal-like extension on the eastern (right wing) side. On the far end of this extension is the grassy boat launch.

We pulled in and parked near the water. I was in no hurry to get out, which puzzled Celeste greatly.

"Aren't we fishing?"

"Uh, not quite yet."

"Why aren't we getting out?"

"See that man throwing rocks at the water?"

She squinted out the window.

"The one in uniform? He looks friendly enough."

"Game warden."

What he was throwing rocks at were the trout that a state hatchery truck had just dumped into the pond. They were clustered in the channel, hundreds of ten-inch rainbows, and he was trying to scare them out to the main pond where they wouldn't be so vulnerable.

Celeste, license-less, mad at me for assuring her she was safe, remained in the car until the warden drove off. So. There was a certain mood, even before we got into the canoe.

"I'm *not* fishing," she said, with great emphasis.

"Fine. I'll fish, you help paddle. We have the picnic? Life preservers? You okay up there? Balanced?"

She nodded, though balance for a woman at eight months pregnant is not what it is for most of us. I lay my brand-new Orvis fly rod across the thwarts, checked again to make sure Celeste was comfortable, and then, shoving the bow off, hopped into my seat in the stern.

Afloat at last—but not for long. Ten feet out from the boat launch, as the huge pod of trout parted to allow us passage, some unexpected disturbance in our equilibrium, perhaps from the baby's kicking (I like to tell my daughter), rolled the canoe over and deposited us in the pond.

"Stand up!" I immediately shouted. The water there was twelve inches deep.

Celeste was confused, frightened, struggling. In one of those flashes of clarity you sometimes get in these situations, I realized I had two choices: immediately spring to the aid of my pregnant wife, or immediately go after my brand-new fly rod, which was floating away toward the open pond.

I made the decision any man in that situation would make. I will not tell you what that decision was.

Celeste, when we climbed dripping onto shore, was not amused.

"First you nearly get me arrested, then you nearly drown me. You can fish by yourself. I'm going home."

She drove away, leaving me with sopping wet clothes, a canoe full of water, and a new fly rod looking even shinier and more lustrous after its brief swim. I stripped down to my undershorts, righted the canoe, got in, paddled out away from the stockies, and started casting, hoping the sun would dry my clothes out before anyone arrived—and that Celeste, once she calmed down, would drive back and fetch me.

When I started fishing, the pond was deserted except for 2,000 disoriented trout and *moi*. Ten minutes later, dozens of battered old pickups careened into the parking lot as if at the end of a desperate road race, people jumping out with spinning rods, buckets, and bait cans, running to the water to cast, a good many of them halfway drunk, though it was still early in the morning. This was the classic case of people following the stock truck, or spotting it driving by the house and hurrying in pursuit. Bush telegraph kicked in after that—people called their buddies who called their buddies who went knocking on doors calling out the troops. Forty fisherfolk, men and women, boys and girls, cast from shore, and more were arriving all the time. No wonder the game warden had tried scaring the trout out deeper.

I was snobbier about my fishing in those days—I refused to be part of such a mob. I started paddling back to the launch, and then remembered that not only was I wearing just boxer shorts, but that they were still wet and transparent. Even worse, I carried a fly rod, which meant, to the people on shore, I was likely an effete son-of-an-exhibitionist-bitch from Massachusetts. Returning to the boat launch was *not* an option—I had to fish until Celeste came back, like it or not.

People were catching trout now. People were hooking trout and snagging trout and killing trout, and I didn't know whether to be disgusted or amused. One man, the drunkest, leaned on his belly and reached as far out into the pond as he could, concentrated, then plunged his hand down and brought it out clutched around a trout's wriggly middle. His pal crawled out on the bank to join him, and did the same—and then almost everyone was trying it, not bothering with rods anymore, scooping out the fish with their hands like gluttons at an all-you-can-eat buffet that had run out of forks.

Once you have a morning like that on a pond, there's really not much more you can ever ask of it.

What finally brought me back was something that fisher friend mentioned when he first steered me to Forgotten twenty-seven years ago. "It's a bizarre kind of place all right," he admitted. "But in late June there's a Hex hatch you don't want to miss."

Hexagenia, the "Great lead-winged drakes," are the largest species of mayfly in America; they're the size of moths, not mosquitoes, and they only hatch in ponds with muddy, silty bottoms, which means that in Vermont they're very rare. Fishing a Hex hatch is something flyfishers dream about; usually, we're squinting in our fly boxes to tweezer out size 22 midges, which are nearly microscopic, but with Hexs we can take out those huge meaty size 10s that have sat on the substitute bench for years waiting their chance.

Flyfishers have long memories when it comes to this kind of thing. Some minor, otherwise idle neuron in my brain had liked the sound of that sentence, taken it in, condensed it, filed it for future reference. *Forgotten. Hexagenia. Late June.*

Rainbows are crazy for Hexs, but, remembering the mob from my first visit, I wasn't much interested in Forgotten's trout. Luckily, bass rise to Hexs, too (I caught my largest smallmouth ever on a Hex imitation), and so bass is what brought me back again—largemouth bass, this being one of the few ponds we have locally where they flourish.

When I picked up my pal Ray Chapin at his house just across the state line, explaining to him what we might encounter up there, I emphasized the trout more than I did the bass. Ray was typical (he's changed now) of a certain type of flyfisher, in that he was impressed all to hell when he had a bass on the end of his line, enjoyed the experience immensely, but, when he wasn't actually attached to one, let his thoughts drift back to trout. So—the closer we got to Forgotten, the more it sounded like a sales pitch I was delivering, but I wanted to make sure I had him along, not just for his usual companionship, but as backup.

"You see some pretty strange customers up there," I said, when there was no longer any chance we could turn around. "Some pretty tough *hombres*."

Approaching the boat launch, the underbrush seemed thicker than it usually did, the air heavier and more humid—and then I realized the thickness came from a percussive wall of sound. Country music, booming from twin speakers set on the open gate of a pickup. Oh shit, I thought, but the moment we turned in, a man jumped up from the bank, hurried over to his stereo, turned the sound down to a polite, considerate level.

He was the tough guy all right. Nail thin, wire hard, late twenties or early thirties, wearing a greasy hood with the sleeves cut off, with a saturnine kind of expression and a saturnine cast to his skin. He had so many tattoos that it was the rare islands of pink skin that looked needled into him, not the black and blue patches that seemed his normal coloring. Not much in the way of teeth were left. His forehead looked like it had been ball hammered, then burned, then hammered again.

He looked, in other words, like someone who had seen hard time in life and served hard time in prison—and I don't think this was just my hasty profiling either.

"And there he is," I said to Ray, as if pointing to one of the pond's famous denizens.

Ray squinted. "A pussycat."

"Yeah? We'll see."

He gave us a friendly wave, made a sweeping gesture to show us where to park, and then went back to the bank where his pole rested on a forked branch stuck in the mud, squatting on his heels in the hillman's classic posture.

"Any luck?" Ray asked when we got out.

He shook his head. "Not much. But she's in here all right. Just saw a school swim by heading out toward the middle there."

"Bass?" I asked.

"Muskie."

Forgotten is an odd and surprising pond that I'd believe almost anything of, but it contains no muskellunge. Still, if that's what he saw, I wasn't going to argue with him, and why I wasn't going to argue with him became apparent when he got up from squatting to make a cast. Strapped high on his right hip was a black holster topped by the silver butt of a very serious looking automatic.

Glock. I know nothing about guns, but remembering the various mass shootings and assassinations that's the word that occurred to me. *This guy is packing a Glock.*

Vermont has an open gun law, which means, theoretically, you can carry a pistol in public any way you want, but I'd never seen anyone take the law up on this until now. It clearly was a statement, but of what? I'm as tough as I look? Don't tread on me? Pay me that thousand you owe me from last time? Don't fuck with the Second Amendment?

Or was it just prudence on his part, self-defense? The state cops were Tasing people right down the road, killing them, and he wasn't going to take no Tasing from no staties.

"Good luck!" he called to us, when we got the canoe launched. His voice was high and girlish—he could have been one of the summer campers over on the liberal side of the pond. Ray was right—a pussycat—but he seemed to be waiting for friends, and they might not be as welcoming.

He waited until we had cleared the channel, and then turned up the music to the excruciating level it had been when we got there. It's not the first time I've bass fished to a soundtrack. Willie Nelson or Patsy Cline would have gone down just fine, but our friend was playing the bad stuff, country rock drenched in self-pity, and it wasn't until the weed beds were thick enough to absorb the worst of it that the sound became bearable.

"What do you get when you play country music backward?"

Ray twisted around in the bow seat to stare at me—I never tell jokes.

"What?"

"Get your wife back, get your dog back, get your truck back."

We started casting. Immediately, we were into a double—a large-mouth for me, a largemouth for Ray. Six-inch largemouths, but that was fine. The weed bed was full of them, cubby little fellas that seemed overjoyed at the sudden appearance of our poppers, rushing each other to grab one first. Baby assassins, cute as they are. My kids once had a freshwater aquarium filled with tiny sunfish and minnows into which I added a six-inch bass. Two days later, only one fish was left—and I don't have to tell you what species that was.

In the world of bass fishing, there's a perpetual—and quite heated—argument over which fights harder, largemouth or smallmouth. The old bass writers love to go on and on about this, contrasting the smallmouth's powerful counterpunching with the largemouth's exuberant strike, but then usually conclude that if caught in the same kind of water their fighting abilities are equal.

Fair enough, and the only thing I can add to the discussion is that baby smallmouth fight harder than baby largemouth. Baby smallmouth are a real handful on a fly rod, leaping and tugging and acting like Dennis the Menace on a day he's forgotten to take his Ritalin. Baby largemouth are late bloomers, hellions in the making, but not quite there yet—they seem to be learning how to fight, while smallmouth are born knowing.

But I'm pussyfooting here, being politically correct. Truth is, the adult smallmouth fights much harder than the adult largemouth, no matter what water they're found in.

We caught them on every other cast as we drifted clockwise around the pond. In between we caught bluegills, gorgeous plump ones, so dark and firm it looked like they had shoulders—and bluegills with shoulders are impressive fish. They fought harder than the baby bass, performing their favorite spinning sideways trick. Lifting one from the water was like scooping beauty up in our hands.

One of my favorite Winslow Homer watercolors dates from 1889. It's of a North Country lake, with a broad splash of white merging into layered strokes of watery green. In it, or hovering just above it (Homer plays tricks with the perspective), is a bluegill with a red fly in its mouth. Homer has captured it perfectly—the orange underside, the dark "blue" patch on the gills, the roundness, the feisty personality that would make it attack such a huge fly. In the background in a canoe is the mustachioed flyfisher who is attached to it. He looks bemused. Not particularly happy, but not particularly unhappy either. Bemused.

The title of the painting is an inside joke: *A Disappointing Catch*. Obviously, this fisher was after trout, not sunfish, and is disappointed at catching a bluegill. Or is he? This, after all, is a fish beautiful enough to star in a Winslow Homer watercolor; the expression on the fisherman's face, when you look back at it, is all grudging respect. There is nothing disappointing about bluegills.

Homer did another, more famous watercolor starring the fish. *Mink Brook* (1891) shows a bluegill beneath a lily flower staring eye to eye at a frog sitting on the lily pad, a secret moment done with a skill and sensitivity that takes your breath away . . . but then everything in Homer takes my breath away.

Have you ever seen his bass paintings? (I asked Ray, after telling him about the bluegill ones.) Homer is known for his watercolors of trout fishers in the Adirondacks or Quebec, but toward the end of his life he began spending winters in Florida fishing for largemouth in the St. Johns and Homosassa rivers. The watercolors he came back with are the greatest representation of bass we have or ever will have—luminous, tropical, exuberant, lush . . . but I'm not very good at describing art. Let me quote here from someone who is, writer Patricia Junker.

> The strike of a great largemouth bass could be an intensely visceral experience, as Homer shows us, the fish appearing brutal and balletic as it leaps to its death. The physical and emotional impact owes much to the dramatic notes of blood red color—the fish's gills—that punctuate these near monochromatic compositions in deep tropical green tones . . . By virtue of his fluid calligraphic brushwork and dramatic color patterns, Homer managed to create in his wrenching studies of thrashing, contorting, death-defying black bass, a pair of paintings that are, ironically, among his most beautiful and elegant works. And with them he distilled from his Florida angling experience a singularly powerful expression of the

joy and miracle of life, a proud sense of death, and the wonder and mystery of nature.

Homer has at least one North Country bass in his output, too. *Bass* (1900) was painted before his Florida trips, and shows a smallmouth horizontally suspended—Homer's favorite trick—over an Adirondack Mountain lake. It doesn't look quite at home there, perhaps because that kind of North Woods background is so closely associated with Homer's trout . . . but then the bass, in their eastward migration from the Great Lakes, would not have been present in the Adirondacks for very long at this stage, and Homer captures their exotic, somewhat alien beauty perfectly.

We followed Forgotten's shoreline, dipping in at the coves, drifting out around the points, laughing over the cubby bass, the gorgeous bluegills, maybe not confronting the joy of life as intensely as Homer did, but not oblivious to it, either.

An incident now occurred that the great artist would have found amusing. We had just passed the camp on the pond's western shore. The campers hadn't arrived for summer yet, but the counselors were there, piling wood scraps on the beach for a bonfire. From the way they were dressed (one had a T-shirt with a clenched fist), it was clear that, even though it wasn't called Camp Thoreau anymore, it still fell on the left-wing side of the summer-camp experience. We caught some bass in front of their swim dock and one of the prettiest counselors gave us a wave.

That's not the funny incident. The funny incident happened a little past this. As mentioned, Forgotten's shoreline includes a network of mangrove-like roots that coil out over the pond's surface as if the trees are tiptoeing out for a swim. I had just made a remark about how this was like snook fishing in the Everglades, when a bass—by far the biggest yet—came up and assaulted my Sneaky Pete not more than ten inches from shore. I hooked him, felt the fullness of his weight, then suddenly didn't anymore—or rather, I did feel it, but in a strange, yo-yoing kind of way.

It took us a while to understand what was going on. The bass, after grabbing my popper, had immediately jumped, looping the line over one of the overhanging alder branches, from which he now hung like a heavy Christmas ornament. When I pulled on my fly line, he went vertically up out of the water, sagging the branch; when I relaxed the tension, he sank vertically back into the pond. Up, down. Up, down. We laughed, and then paddled over to disentangle him.

The sun had disappeared behind those high meadows now, but in late June that still meant a good way to go before dark. We paddled out into the center of the pond, sat there with our rods across our laps waiting for the shadows to join edges and thicken.

"So," Ray said, with a decided note of skepticism. "Where are those Hexs you promised me?"

I pointed past his elbow. "Right there."

I was pleased at their timing—even more pleased that a twenty-year old rumor turned out to be true. For there on the surface a short cast away appeared a shape that managed to be erect, dignified, feathery, vulnerable, and angel-like all at once—less a bug than an apparition. *Hexagenia* are the mayfly equivalent of luna moths, spontaneously generated (it seems) from June's swelling fullness of life, and verging on exaggeration.

This one's life was brutal and short, for as we watched, a fish came up and with a swirl that mixed the indigo of the sky with the ebony of the water sucked it down.

"Trout," I said. Ray smiled.

The hatch started slowly, and we traced it less by seeing bugs than we did by watching the rises that meant yet another one was eaten. I had Hex imitations in my box, and we held the hooks up to the sky to get enough contrast to thread them on. It didn't take long to connect. Ray caught his trout—a long skinny rainbow. For them, feeding on *Hexagenia* was on the order of a felon's last meal, since the pond would soon warm up to levels that would kill most trout. I caught a bass—and that made me smile. You don't get many chances to catch largemouth on dry flies, and this one jumped higher than Ray's trout.

The darker it got, the more bugs we saw, so things were getting exciting—and not just on the water. Back at the boat launch the music turned rowdier, more metallic, and we could tell from the laughs and the glassy clanking sounds that a party was starting up. I wondered about our friend with the pistol and what he might be doing. Smoking with his pals? Drinking with his pals? Brooding with his pals? His wearing a gun on his hip was one thing in daylight, but something entirely different at night. Forgotten was *not* our turf, and this was a pond where the locals took such notions seriously.

Almost nothing would make us abandon a Hex hatch in progress, but we were street smart enough—pond smart enough—to realize the rowdiness would only get worse as the night went on and the empties piled higher. Best to go back now, get the canoe on the car, get out.

And yet . . .

"Oh, my God!" Ray whispered, pointing to a black, down-swirling vortex where another Hex had just been gulped. "A monster!"

I saw it, was just turning the canoe so he would have a good shot at it, when we heard glass shattering against something hard like a rock or a forehead. That decided it. We started paddling as fast and quietly as we could, staying to the far side of the channel so perhaps, just perhaps, we could slip into the boat launch unobserved by anyone on shore.

Lanterns must have been mounted on the roofs of the trucks, because the light rays were higher than the shapes moving beneath them—the tough guys looked like they were dancing at a disco, with exaggerated, strobe-like jerkings. It wasn't a dance though; it was hard to know what it was, unless it be a ritualized punch-up, people trading shots in the stomach, shots on the arm. We kept a wary eye on this as we snuck our way along the bank, but something else soon caught our attention.

Apart from the main group, standing at the shallow end of the boat launch where twenty-seven years ago I had capsized my wife, stood a solitary figure facing the water. He seemed to be hurling rocks or bottles stiff-armed into the water, but there were no splashes, or at least not big splashes, and it took me a few unbelieving seconds before I realized what he was doing.

Fly casting. The man with the pistol on his hip, the worm fisher, the walking tattoo parlor, the hard case, stood knee deep in the pond working a fly rod back and forth in his left hand, urging his line out into the darkness, and if he had been waving a polo mallet I would not have been more surprised.

He was a beginner, he didn't have the timing down, but he was doing better than most beginners—he wasn't the kind of man who would let a tool get the better of him for long. It was so black out now that his shape seemed blue in comparison, so we could see him quite clearly, his hand sweeping upward, his arm extending, his shoulders rolling into the uncoiling white wisp that was his line. There was something formal about that motion, something that seemed almost posed, so he could have been a dignified gentleman flyfisher from the 1890s, lifted from a Homer watercolor, with the mystery and promise of that June night draped across his form.

Our canoe hit the ramp with more noise than we intended. It was hard to say whether the partiers near the trucks were his friends or not; a woman called to him, but he ignored her and kept casting. He shifted his position just enough that he came into the yellow slats cast by the lanterns, so a little more of him became visible. We were on our way around him, hoping to slip away without anyone seeing us, when I noticed something that made the words jump out of my mouth on their own.

"I haven't seen one of those in years!"

Attached to the fly rod's grip was the thick, muffin-shaped silhouette of an automatic fly reel, the kind that had been popular back in the 1960s, mounted horizontally, with a lever you could press to spring back your slack line. I struggled to come up with the name.

"That's a Martin, right?"

"Damned straight. Got it in a trade off this fella. She's not half bad."

It was the start of a good conversation . . . we were going over to take a closer look . . . when he suddenly grunted and hauled back on his rod. A bass was attached, one of those cubby cute ones, and, pressing the lever, he shot it out of the water so it landed at our feet.

"My first fish on a fly rod," he said matter-of-factly.

"Good for you!" Ray and I said simultaneously.

We were happy for him, pleased to have our hasty preconceptions overturned—but not surprised when, instead of returning the bass to the water, he threw it in his bucket atop the other dead fish.

"You have to put the small ones back," we could have explained, but bringing up the Vermont fishing laws just then didn't seem like a good idea. I remembered the old gangsters from the 1930s, Pretty Boy Floyd and John Dillinger, and the slang term for their pistols: *rods*. This guy had both kinds of rods, one for fishing and one for shooting, and though all three of us were in the same fly-fishing fraternity now, how fraternal can you risk being with a man packing a Glock?

Six

Bass fishers often have a Memory Lake in their past, the place where they first fell in love with the fish, the place forever associated with the mystery, romance, and torment of being fourteen. My Memory, in Western Connecticut hard by the New York border, was said to be the largest lake in the state, and, with its two skinny arms extending northwards from a potbellied middle, gave the impression of a giant swimmer windmilling, a little wearily, through the hills.

The local newspaper liked to claim it was one of the five loveliest lakes in the world, but I've seen plenty of lakes in my travels, and Memory, sad to say, would not even crack the prettiest fifty. Still, it was pastoral enough, at least in those years, featuring a high wooded ridge separating the two arms, and modest summer homes stained brown to blend into the trees. The surrounding towns were still surprisingly rural, with farms that, having survived everything three centuries had thrown at them, would not survive much longer—creeping suburbanization would soon do them in. But my years there gave me a taste for country, for quiet places away from the world's mainstream; my parents, buying a summer cottage there the summer I was twelve, blessed me more than they could have realized.

As for the bass, the lake was said to be full of them, though it took me years to prove this was so. Every writer on fishing likes to wax poetical about the first trout he caught, the first bass she landed, but though I've spent the last few weeks racking my memory, I can't recall my first largemouth, though catching it must have been momentous. It probably came when I was spinning for bluegills with a plastic water-filled bubble ahead of a dangling wet fly—a deadly technique I'd read about in *Outdoor Life*, which, unlike most deadly techniques, actually worked. I've never caught such fat bluegills since—orange-black saucers bigger than my hand, peeing on me when I landed them, puckering those beautifully firm small lips to make it easier to get the hook out, still so feisty after I released them that they often swam around the rowboat and attacked the fly again.

The bass, my first one, must have walloped my black gnat or McGinty even harder than the bluegills, fought longer, dove deeper, maybe even jumped, before, miracle upon miracle, I brought it into the net. Momentous, undoubtedly, but maybe *too* momentous? Try as I might, I can't focus back fifty years to the actual moment, it's evaporated into the place defining moments go when they're done defining. The bass did its work—captured me hook, line, and sinker—and then swam back into the dark recesses of time where it resides still.

That's probably why bass fishing hit me so hard—I fell in love with the romance of it, the concept, the notion, before there was a reality to mess it up. Boys that age need romance, and needed it even more back in an era when there were fewer options/distractions than there are today. The romance of fishing, the romance of hunting, the romance of stock cars or skiing or competitive chess. It hardly mattered what you fell for, as long as it seemed even more alluring than it ever in fact could be in fact. Fishing gave me the chance to wildly, extravagantly, wholeheartedly exaggerate—and fourteen is probably the only time in life when wild exaggerations are possible without you seeming like a fool.

Only one romance could have competed with fishing during those years, but I was shy of girls, could hardly speak in their company, and was years away yet from girlfriends or dates. Our cottage was part of something called Candlewood Trails, an association of summer-home owners who shared a clubhouse and beach. An intense social life sprung up around these, at least for teenagers. A lot of families were from New York, and these city kids, not having been told the 1950s were over, still favored a tough, slick-backed look ("The Bronx Weasel," is what my grandfather called my sister's boyfriend), though they got along okay with the suburban kids, the ones wearing polo shirts and madras shorts. Me, I stayed away from both groups—shyness had more to do with my fishing trips than I cared to admit—and went around wearing khaki work pants my mother found for me in the "Husky" section of W. T. Grant's, and my father's old Eisenhower jacket.

In 1962, you fell in love with fishing pretty much by following a well-defined path, particularly if you were an avid reader as I was. You bought the big three fishing magazines every month, *Field & Stream, Outdoor Life, Sports Afield,* read them cover to cover, tried learning as much as you could, incorporating the latest hot tactics into your local fishing, never mind that these were methods designed for Florida or Montana.

My own favorite was *Sports Afield* and their fishing editor Jason Lucas. A. J. McClane wrote for *Field & Stream*, and I liked him, too, but he seemed to favor trout over bass, while Lucas was a bass man all the way. I saw an ad for a new edition of his book, *Lucas on Bass Fishing,* autographed by the author, and begged for it for Christmas. My mother sent away the order form, and so the book was under the tree that year—but Lucas had misunderstood, and when I tore it from the wrapping and opened the cover, it was autographed to my mother, not me.

(I still have it on my shelf, and I looked through it last night. It's honest how-to stuff. Lucas comes across as a no-nonsense, let's-get-them-in-the-boat kind of guy, and the only touch of genius is the pipe he always made sure was in his mouth whenever he was photographed; no fisherman ever looked wiser smoking a pipe than Jason Lucas.)

Reading tales of chivalry completely turned Don Quixote's head; reading "Bass Love the Fourth of July!" or "Go Deep Young Man, Go Deep!" or "Licorice for Largemouths!" or "Think Big for Smallies!" completely turned mine. I thought about bass fishing constantly, tried learning everything there was to know about it, practiced casting bobbers into laundry baskets on the lawn, tied my line to our cocker spaniel's collar to test my reels' drag, and became a sucker for every type of lure, gadget, or bait any huckster was peddling.

There was the Vivif, a plastic minnow with a tail so seductive that the bait shops would keep it in a special aerated tank where it could wiggle through the bubbles. Spoonplugs, which were said to work best if you trolled them at full speed. (When I tried this, they all snapped off.) Rapalas, the Finnish minnows, which I first read about in the *Life* article that made them famous. The Arbogast lures—the Hula Popper, Jitterbug, and Hawaiian Wiggler—or the Heddon plugs, like the River Runt Spook. And of course Dardevles, the red and white ones, which cast from here to China and were death on pickerel, particularly if you slapped pork rind on the hooks.

You read Jason Lucas, A. J. McClane, Tom McNally, or Erwin Bauer, bought every lure you could afford and shoplifted those you couldn't, got a huge tackle box to hold them all, stuck three rods under one arm, a net, stringer, and lunch box under the other, went out in your rowboat or fished from the bank—and caught not a goddamn thing. In 1962, that's how you fell in love with bass fishing. Foreplay was everything; the climax of catching a bass hardly mattered.

I probably hooked, fought, and landed a grand total of eleven bass in the three summers I was first obsessed by them. That is, three or four bass a summer. Looking back, it's hard to know why I did so poorly. I slept late if I could, like all teenage boys, so most of my fishing was in the hottest time of day when the bass were taking their siestas. I wasn't good with mechanical things, so I was always snapping off lures or getting the reel gummed up. My father enjoyed fishing, but his poor eyesight kept him from being serious. I had no older brother to show me the ropes, no avuncular old-timer smoking a pipe, like Jason Lucas, taking me under his wing. "Cast over there, young fella. Easy now, easy. THERE! Drive that hook home! A lunker, good for you! Give 'em the butt!" . . . Nope. I learned on my own, and progress was slow.

The old-timers I knew weren't much interested in fishing. Mornings when I woke up early and went down to the dock to cast out past the sleeping boats, Mr. Kelsey would be out walking his English setter, Lord Jim. He looked like a craggy old-timer, dressed in checkered red and black wool even in summer, but he was a hunter, not a fisherman, and a cranky one at that. I remember him standing near my shoulder while I cast, complaining about the state of the world—Russians, Democrats, beatniks, he was mad at them all—but he always remembered to ask me how the fishing was, which counted for quite a lot.

Bill of Bill's Bait Shop down on the state road was another old-timer—he was beefy and florid-looking, in a good-ol'-boy Connecticut kind of way. It puzzled me that he didn't seem to like fishing, him running a bait-and-tackle shop—and not just any bait-and-tackle shop, but as quintessential a bait-and-tackle shop as you can imagine.

Shack-sized, air-conditioned to keep the minnow tanks cold, trolling lures dangling down from the ceiling, worms snug in their bedding, rods in a carousel by the window so passing fishermen would see them and drool—all this, plus an indescribably delicious smell the component parts of which I never managed to identify, but was even better than a bakery's. Stacked by the cash register were those white cardboard bait boxes that always made me think of Chinese takeout—but no, my memory is playing tricks on me here, because Bill didn't use a cash register, but a metal tackle box with damp-looking ones and fives.

It became one of the favorite places in my small world—and yet Bill himself, when you asked him how the fishing was, didn't have much to say.

"Decent," he'd grunt. Morning, noon, evening, summer, autumn, spring. "Decent," and that was that.

Looking back, I think he must have suffered from some chronic illness, or his wife did, or his kid. In tenth grade, when my English teacher mentioned "choleric" as a possible SAT word, I immediately thought of Bill.

Still, there was a time when I daydreamed about buying the shop from him, running it as my business, and I still can't convince myself that wasn't a good idea. When I revisited the town after thirty-five years away, I tried hard to find the shop, or at least its location, but every trace of it was gone, sunk, like so much of our generation's childhood, beneath a mall.

So. No old-timers to learn from. If I was going to get advice on fishing, it would have to be from the bass boys in the outdoor magazines—Jason and A. J., Tom and Erwin. And the articles I began reading with increasing attention revolved around fishing at night. Clearly, trying for bass in broad daylight on a hot summer lake was not going to work, so I needed to change my *modus operandi*—and since waking up early didn't appeal to me, night fishing was the default strategy I was forced to adopt. Fishing at night, I decided, *must* be good, and the reason it must be good is that, while I was fifteen now and tall for my age, darkness—and what might be abroad in it—still scared the living crap out of me.

Because you're a coward, I told myself, but in retrospect I'm more forgiving. Evolutionary psychology rages powerfully through a young person's spirit, particularly when you're engaged in something so fundamentally primitive as fishing. I wasn't scared of drowning or lake monsters or being kidnapped when I went out at the lake at night; I was afraid of cave bears, saber-tooths, mastodons, or enemies from a rival clan, and no rationalizing, no pep talks, could prevail against what was, on a primal level, mere prudence.

One of our neighbors liked fishing, and he invited me out, saying (and this was a great revelation to me, that a grown-up would be willing to admit it), "I get a little scared fishing by myself at night." Mr. Cavendish wasn't the old-timer I was looking for, but a smooth, polished man in his thirties, with a beautiful young wife. He worked on Madison Avenue in advertising (a "Mad man"—he claimed to have invented the famous candy slogan, "Melts in your mouth, not in your hands") and, like Jason Lucas, smoked a pipe when he fished.

We went out in his aluminum runabout, and, once it got dark out, actually managed to catch a bass or two, which was as much a surprise to him as it was to me. They slammed our Jitterbugs on the edge of the weed beds, jumped high enough to make us yell, then powered their way through the lily pads where we had to chase after them.

I don't think we went out more than two or three times together or caught more than five or six fish, but these were important experiences, since I badly needed some bass reality to go along with my bass dreams. But I was still a beginner, and made dumb mistakes.

I read that the best way to land a bass was to grab its lower lip with your thumb, paralyzing it, allowing you to lift it into the boat with no fuss. And it *is* the best way—if you remember one thing. After you grab the bass lip and squeeze, before it goes still, it will always give one last head shake. Fine—but I didn't know that then. Reeling in a fish on a Heddon Crazy Crawler, I reached down into the beam of Mr. Cavendish's flashlight, readied my thumb over the thrashing, weed-festooned bass, saw its mouth gape open, reached, and grabbed. My thumb found its lip all right, but I got one of the treble hooks in the webbing of skin just to the side of it—*my* skin. I yelled from the pain, dropped the bass—the bass that was still attached to the Crazy Crawler that was still attached to my hand. I shook it desperately, flinging the bass off into the darkness, but my hand hurt for days, and, when I remember it, throbs even now. When it came to bass fishing, I still had lots to learn.

But now that I was beginning to actually catch a bass or two, I felt the need to improve my infrastructure. In those days, the spinning rods everyone wanted were Garcias, a Swedish company that also made the classic Mitchell 300 spinning reels. They had a clever marketing scheme, whereby their least expensive rods were blue, their medium-priced rods yellow, their expensive rods brown. I longed for the deep brown patina, but had to settle for the sunny yellow—and it's still the rod, of all the dozens I've owned since, that I remember most fondly.

It was well made, with beautiful cork on the grip, sliding bands of wedding ring gold, silky wraps of contrasting black and yellow thread, and agate guides, which I'd read were the best kind to have. I must have cast a million times with that rod, and caught, in total, probably not more than a hundred fish, counting bluegills and crappie. But I loved the way it flexed in casting—I didn't need the bonus tug of a fish, or at least not more than occasionally.

(It's on the desk beside me as I write, and it looks like it's been through the fishing wars. The cork on the grip, dried now and cracked, looks like it's been dusted with road salt. The ferrules are tarnished and blackened. The wraps are either in the process of unraveling or held tight by electrical tape. The agate is chipped on the guides and the tiptop one is missing entirely. The patina, once so smooth, is sticky with grit and more mustard than yellow . . . but it survived long enough to catch my wife's first bass, my daughter's, and if God forbid this house should ever catch fire, some instinct will make me rush to save it first.)

I bought another rod, an Abu Garcia bait caster with a bright red Ambassadeur reel (very important in its allure, that it wasn't spelled Ambassa*dor),* though this put a real dent in my savings, since I was still losing Hula Poppers in the weeds just as fast as I tied them on. Looking back, I remember an insatiable cupidity when it came to tackle—I wanted *everything* I saw in the advertisements, yet nothing ever satisfied me for long. I think what was happening was that I was searching for, stumbling toward, a fishing method that would absorb all my energy, attention, and lust . . . that I was thrashing my way, rod by rod, reel by reel, lure by lure, toward the wondrous simplicity of fly-fishing. I wasn't quite there yet, but I was reading about it in my fishing magazines, and now and then, when no one could see me, whipped my Garcia spinning rod back and forth like I was fly casting after all.

If I can't remember the first bass I caught because the occasion was too momentous to take in, then something of that awe continued blinding me through my grand three-year total of eleven. I remember the Crazy Crawler bass glaring up at me in the lemon beam of Mr. Cavendish's flashlight, but the only other fish that stands out vividly from the Memory Lake years is one I didn't really catch.

My sister was waterskiing, I was driving the boat, when I noticed something floating in the water that looked to be a ski that had come off someone's foot. After depositing my sister back at the dock, I sped back to fetch it—and saw it wasn't a water ski at all, but a largemouth bass three times larger than any I'd ever caught. It was floating on the surface and obviously in some distress, though I couldn't immediately identify what its problem was. I raced back to get my sister, and with her at the wheel I reached down and scooped it up with my net.

Anyone who's caught a bass will always be amazed at the willingness of even small bass to attack lures and/or prey much bigger than they are themselves. It's plucky of them, even reckless, but fatal? They seem to know just how much is enough, their mouths are well calibrated and judicious—or yet maybe not. The bass I pulled from the lake had attacked a fat bluegill which was now wedged broadside in its throat, unable to be swallowed, unable to be disgorged. The bass—which probably weighed seven pounds—couldn't move its gills or swim or submerge, and was well on its way to dying.

"Quick!" I yelled to Christina, who screamed when she saw its size. "Back to shore!"

She gunned the motor and two minutes later I had leaped over the side to begin trying to save the bass's life. I reached in the gaping mouth, groped, got enough of my hand around the bluegill to yank it out. Freed, it immediately swam off, none the worse for having been in Jonah's mouth.

That left Jonah to worry about. My quick Heimlich maneuver hadn't helped, and when I released it with an encouraging shove toward deeper water, its great body rolled majestically over on its side like the hull of a great ship, a *sinking* ship, the *Lusitania* or the *Andrea Doria*.

Its mouth didn't want to close—it was as if it had been hyperextended past the breaking point—and when I pressed the lips together, they opened again, as if gasping for breath. Girls sunbathing on the beach came over to watch, but I didn't pay them any heed, my shyness evaporating in my desperation to save the bass's life. I'd read that swimming a fish back and forth through the water could help revive it, forcing water through its gills, so that's what I did, stooping over until my back hurt, my thumb and forefinger on the bass's rope-like lip, my other hand supporting its huge sumo bell, steering it gently one way, then gently the other, trying, every few minutes, another encouraging shove.

I remember the feel of strength and power that the great fish gave off, even in its death throes—for it was obvious now that it was past the point of ever being revived. Still, I kept walking it through the water, leading it past the beach to a weed bed mucky enough no one would follow us. I was alone with it there—still the largest bass I've ever had my hands around.

I can see it now, that bass. There was something Cadillac about its shape, something luxuriously 1960ish. Its gold flesh was so vivid it seemed lit from inside (though the wattage was dimming), and the bars that crossed it were as black and masculine as the stripes down a drill sergeant's sleeve. The tail was the tail of a bomber, a B-17's. The eye, the one closest to me, was too red and desperate to look at. The gills were strong as a weightlifter's pectorals, and flexed in and out as the fish fought for breath. *Lunker,* I said to myself. I had always wanted to catch a lunker—and now I had, but not really, so it wasn't turning out anywhere near as happy as I thought.

Dead, it became a trophy—sort of. On the way up to our cottage I passed Mr. Kelsey walking Lord Jim.

"You caught that?" he asked in wonder.

"Uh, yeah," I mumbled. My forehead buzzed, but not in pride.

Next stop was Mr. Cavendish's house, but he wasn't in, and his wife, when I held the fish toward her, wrinkled her pretty nose up in disgust. I wanted to take it down to Bill's Bait after that, get a photo taken to hang on his wall, but my mother had more pity for the dead bass than I had, and I was sent to the garden to bury it under her tomato plants.

Looking back, I realize I was extraordinarily fortunate to have that—enough unencumbered time to fall in love with something so passionately. Boys that age would have been sent to work in the fields or the mills forty years earlier; boys not much older to fight in wars. When I wasn't fishing, I was reading my head off, devouring every novel the local library would let me check out (I always got funny looks when it was Dostoyevsky), beginning my apprenticeship when it comes to how to use words, though of course I never thought of it that way, not when all I was aware of were the stories the words told.

If I could lean back in time and give my younger version some advice, it would be this: Don't let your love for the quiet, lonely places you fish and the quiet, secret places you find in books lead you so far in solitary directions that you can't find your way back. Don't give up your teenage responsibility to be a little wild and a little crazy. Fishing is great, it saves you from being too bookish—but be careful of the cost. Nice, your trying to save the bass like that. But you need to try a little harder to save your teens.

I remember, in that connection, walking back to our cottage on the hill after fishing late at night. I was going out alone now—I didn't need Mr. Cavendish providing security. I'd fish until nine or ten, catch a largemouth if I was lucky, bring the boat back to the dock, button it up under its canvas, and then gather my equipment and start walking. It was a mile to the house—not far. But under one arm were three rods and a landing net, under the other a tackle box that probably weighted twenty pounds, and, strapped around my forehead, a flashlight so heavy it made my head tilt over, so I walked stooped like an old man.

Once upon a less sedentary time, everyone had one particular walk they remembered from their childhood—the walk, out of many dozens, that became *the* walk, so when you remembered those years, it seemed, for better or worse, that you were making it again and again. For my mother, raised on a farm, it was walking to school through the cold of an upstate winter, ashamed at the clothes she wore, afraid the other kids would mock her. For my dad, it was walking along crowded Brooklyn streets bringing lunch to his father at the firehouse.

For me, it seems I was always walking along a country road late on an August night, passing summer houses where parties were just winding down, people laughing in the lantern light as they said their good-byes, or couples whispering to each other and giggling from screened-in porches against which moths beat their wings . . . me walking past them, wishing I was part of it and yet glad I wasn't, never quite able to reconcile those two desires, and so burdened with a lot more than just the weight of my tackle box or the tangled clumsiness of those rods.

One night, when I finally made it to our porch, I found my mother and visiting Uncle Wesley standing there looking alarmed.

"Is that you, Walter?" my mother called.

They had heard me climb the steps to the porch, put my tackle box down (it made a distinctive rattle), and press the latch of the screen door. They had heard me do this *twenty minutes before I actually got there.* They waited for me to come in, but I *didn't* come in—and this is why, twenty minutes after they heard the sounds, they stood on the porch peering anxiously into the darkness.

A ghost, we decided, half kidding, half not. And, looking back, I think maybe it *was* a ghost, my own ghost, who had grown tired of all my worrying, my shyness, my anxiety, and struck out on his own.

And that reminds me of another incident, one I'd forgotten about until now.

It had been an exceptionally miserable fishing night. Casting toward the forested shore, I'd managed to lose a Hula Popper, a Jitterbug, and a Crazy Crawler, a perfect trifecta of ineptitude. Turning to cast toward open water, I sent my River Runt Spook sailing toward the stars— literally toward them, since I'd forgotten to tie a knot. The motor, when I tried moving down the shoreline, coughed, sputtered, and quit, so I was forced to paddle. The mosquitoes were bad. I caught, as ever, no bass.

(Extraordinary, that I didn't give it all up—that I'm not remembering this as an ex-fisherman.)

I somehow managed to get the boat back to the dock, covered it, started on my long walk home through the dark. It was quieter than usual—it must have been toward summer's end—and as I started up the small hill that led to our cottage, I began remembering the ghost that had scared my mother just a few weeks before.

The longer I walked, the darker the darkness became, until it seemed whatever shade comes after black. The longer I walked, the more human the trees seemed—and I don't mean friendly human either. They loomed over me, their hulking shapes in a perfect position to snatch and grab if I came too close. I began whistling to keep my courage up, and no sooner had I started than I heard a throaty humming noise right behind me, as if someone had decided to join in. But no, not a humming—a low rolling *thumpa-thumpa-thumpa* on the gravel that rolled closer, stopped, and then resumed, this time a little closer. I realized the sound had been there for a while now—that a car was slowly following me up the otherwise deserted road.

I stepped to the side to let it go past, but it only slowed down. I started walking again, this time faster, but it kept up with me, its headlights lifting from my ankles to cover my back. I thought about running into the bushes, but there was a cliff there, a thirty-foot drop to the lake—thought next about climbing a tree, but I was never very good at this, and even the lowest branches started well above my head.

Caught!—I almost shot my hands up in surrender—but this time, when I stepped to the side of the road, hoping only that my end would be swift and merciful, the car pulled over and the window rolled down.

Driving was one of my sister's friends, from the happy swarm of teenagers down at the clubhouse who always seemed to be having so much fun. And it seems important, remembering, that her name was Nancy. In those days, girls only had seven names (boys had six). The Susies were mischievous and the Lauras were flirty and the Pattys were daddy's girls and the Marcias were brainy and the Carols were cheerleaders and the Karens were all-arounders and the Nancys, without exception, were plain old-fashioned nice.

She was Nancy nice, Nancy Furillo. She drove, so she was probably two years older than me. She had actually talked to me once or twice, been very gentle with my embarrassment. Driving from her house down to the clubhouse, she must have spotted me walking in her headlights . . . Christina's brother, the shy kid who liked fishing . . . slowed down, thought about it for a moment, and then decided to do something very kind.

The dashboard light was Martian green, but she looked a lot nicer than any Martian.

"Hello, Walt," she said. Then, after letting that sink in, "We're having a bonfire down by the lake. Why don't you come?"

Did I say something in response? I must have—some tortured, mumbled variation on the word no.

She was close enough now that I could smell her perfume, see the pageboy of her soft brown hair.

"Yes," she said, taking that in. "But why don't you just come?"

I felt the weight of my huskiness, the braces on my teeth, my acne, my embarrassingly red, red hair. I mumbled another no. She only smiled.

"Just for a little while. I'll drive you. Please come."

Three times she asked me, three times I said no. It wasn't just Nancy asking either; it was the whole teenage experience, the world of parties, dates, dancing, necking, going steady and breaking up, drinking and smoking and taking chances, learning about life, embracing life. The world of friends. The word of sociability. The world of normalcy.

It was asking me to join, that world. It was asking me politely three times—but it wouldn't ask again.

Seven

The New Hampshire record for smallmouth bass is safe for another year. A lucky angler named Francis Cord pulled one out of Goose Pond in 1970 weighing a few ounces short of eight pounds, and no one has caught a bigger one since. Goose Pond sits right over the hill from us, I can be there in twenty-five minutes, and, with the potential of a fish that size, it's a mystery why I don't fish it more often.

It's an attractive body of water, once you get out in the middle and look north toward the bare summit of Cardigan and the other steep hills. Its feeder stream, Marshall Brook, drains some of the wildest, most forgotten land in the state, and the pond itself, if you stare down into the clear depths, boasts some of the biggest boulders in New Hampshire, which is really saying something. Trophy rocks—glacial erratics big as McMansions, under which a future state record is probably even now putting on size.

The shoreline is heavily developed—modest summer homes, but lots of them. The bassassers love it here, so I wait for a rainy evening before making my one trip of the season, hoping the weather will keep the boat traffic down. It doesn't. After the tenth or eleven wakeboarder cuts across my bow, I vow not to come back again.

Of the three ten-inch bass I caught last night, one looked like it might have potential. It was fatter than the others, fought harder, had a cocky glint in its eye that looked promising. A new state record, I decided—but not for another six or seven years.

It was raining hard by the time I left. I keep my bass bugs in a simple plastic box, and I'd opened it so many times that all the bugs and poppers got soaked. When I got home, not wanting their hooks to rust, I dumped them out across the picnic table—a table that sits right below my office window, so I'm staring down at it now. The morning sun is beginning to dry them, so, unlike the soggy mass they were last night, they're starting to regain their color, shape, and fluffiness. I've done the same thing with trout flies over the years, and when I look out at them they appear as realistic as you might expect—like a huge swarm of insects has decided to descend. Looking down at the heaped mass of bass bugs, I see something very different.

Halloween candy—that's my first impression. It looks like a kid has taken her bag of treats and dumped them out across the table, bite-size pieces wrapped in foil that glitters in the sun. But no—not just Halloween candy, but the trick-or-treaters themselves, shrunk and miniaturized, costumed in boas, capes, plumes, and tinsel, sleeping it off after a hard night's trick-or-treating.

A second after that image clicked, it was replaced by even gaudier ones. I saw the bugs as marchers in a Mardi Gras parade, drag queens or gaily feathered exhibitionists, kicking up their legs as they paraded across the picnic table's center, delighting in their extravagance and flamboyance. There are strippers among them—Sally Rand and Gypsy Rose Lee—and old-time burlesque comics with seltzer bottles, noisemakers, and cigars. A parade—and then it wasn't just New Orleans anymore, but Hollywood, Looney Tunes, a picnic table full of Elmer Fudds. The Muppets are there as well, the frog-like and the furry—"Hey Kermit!" I feel like shouting—and then my eyes, my imagination, really get going, so, seeing the sleeked-back bugs, the jazzy, mustached and whiskered poppers, the *way way way* over-the-top, I can't help thinking of Flash Gordon and pinball and W. C. Fields, carnival barkers and carnival freaks, the Sunday comics, Bozo the Clown, Las Vegas showgirls, barroom broads with shivs hidden under their skirts . . . and then, seeing the cupcake-shaped heads, seeing the frosting, I think of edible things that are bad for you, root-beer floats and soft-served sundaes, Twinkies, hot wings, pizza bites, Tootsie Rolls, and cheese-covered fries.

I thought, in other words, of everything in the American experience that has laughed at that experience, refused to take itself seriously, cocked a snout at respectability, rejected the sober for the bold, the colorful, the ridiculous.

That's what I saw, looking down at those bass bugs drying in the sun. Reading too much into them? Of course I am. But I have a hunch that this is what a non-fisher having not the slightest idea of what those bugs were designed for would think—that their first overwhelming impression would be that these objects, whatever their purpose was, viewed merely as objects, were hilariously *funny*.

Their names add to the fun. Boogle Bug, Cain Raiser, Poppercackle, Gutless Frog, Mississippi Mudflat, Grim Reaper, Endangered Frog, Sheep Walker, Dahlberg Diver, Charlie's Airhead, Pole Dancer, Gartside's Gurgler, Mouse-to-Mouth, Bar Nun, Dixie Devil, Bad Boy, Gerbubble, Little Fatty, Placebo Bug, Bling Bug, Sneaky Pete. Find two words that have an ironic cadence, toss in some alliteration, and, *voilà*, you've named a bass bug.

Funny stuff—and yet, once you stop smiling, there is a serious enough punch line when it comes to bass bugs. For all their extravagance, *because* of their extravagance, bass find them absolutely irresistible.

Bass bugs, bass poppers—floating, meaty-looking flies made of cork, balsa, deer hair, or foam—have not gotten the attention they deserve, not just as effective fish catchers, but as a unique and exclusively American folk art, one that, like making duck decoys and cedar-strip canoes, takes a craft that could be soberly utilitarian and turns it into something more attractive than it has to be and considerably more interesting. Trout flies get all the good ink, and America still boasts the best, most innovative tiers in the world, but to my mind bass bugs say more about the American spirit than all your Royal Wulffs and blue-winged olives combined. The English taught us how to tie trout flies, but bass bugs we taught ourselves, so it's a bit like the difference between imported classical music and homegrown Dixieland jazz.

That bass respond so freely, so enthusiastically, to this folk art is one of the reasons I love bass; who would think, under all that aggression, there beats the heart of an aficionado! Realistically tied bugs, ones that could pass as living insects, are usually of little interest to bass, while extravagant ones that look like nothing they've ever seen before capture their attention. While it would be going too far to say that they strike these bugs out of a bassy sense of humor, it's well-established that it's these bugs' difference, uniqueness, and flamboyance that tickles some adventurous spot in their omnivorousness—and difference, uniqueness, and flamboyance make for a lot of laughs. Even if they hit the bugs out of prudish outrage that anything so outlandish could ruffle up their lake, the point remains—it's their difference from naturals that is key. Not always, of course. But often.

Joe Brooks, writing about bass bugs in the 1940s, vividly makes this point.

> I've always wanted to make a bug that was different. Drastically dif-
> ferent! I've thought up what it will be. This bug when on the water
> will look like any other cork-bodied popper. But—as you give it a
> pop—an American flag will spring out of the cork body and wave
> merrily in the breeze.

That's the bass-bugging spirit for you—and I'm sure a bass would immediately come up to salute . . . But here, the sun has dried off the bugs on the picnic table, they've regained their perkiness, and it's time to examine them up close.

I've pulled two out from the swarm. The first is called the Fire Tiger and it's tied by Walt Cary, a much respected old-timer from Virginia who's been crafting bugs for more than fifty years. "Watch Walt create his masterworks," one writer puts it, "and you'll be mesmerized; most devotees don't mind waiting as they watch his weathered hands craft what are arguably the world's best popping bugs."

The Fire Tiger, from the eye at the front to its trailing rubber legs, is half the length of my pinkie The meaty "head" is cork—it looks like it might have been pulled from a small wine bottle—and it's finished with six coats of paint, so it shines with a vibrant gloss. A slash of orange crosses the underside of the head where the fish can see it, then, circling up the sides, the color blends into a chartreuse color deepening to a marbleized green on the very top; red eyes with black pupils sit on either side of the head—a flat-cut "burping" head, without the concave slant or cup you see in poppers designed to raise a ruckus. From black spots toward the middle of the head green rubber legs emerge and flop languidly sideways; at the back of the head, chicken hackle of a grizzly yellow color is wrapped around the upper part of the hook creating a bushy fringe, while hackle of a grizzly red color is flared back in two matching tails intermixed with more rubber legs of red and green. The hook extends under these tails, and then curls back toward the body with a good, deep gap; the barb is positioned directly below the rear of the head.

Hard to describe—and yet when you have one in your hand the overall effect is of great simplicity matched with considerable art. Clearly, Walt Cary's bugs are much more beautiful than they have to be (the bass will probably never see the beautifully marbled pattern atop the Fire Tiger's head), and, while Cary likes telling people "I'm not a pretty tier; I'm more interested in function than I am form," you could mount his creations in shadow boxes on the wall or exhibit them in a gallery of folk art and no one would think them out of place.

Here's another bug, the Rollie Pollie Skunk by Neal Pultz, who's made a name for himself as one of the best fly tiers of a younger generation. As befits its name, it's skunk-like, at least in color. Round black head, big yellow eyes, white rubber legs—and then a pert, skunk-like tail, with a mix of black and white marabou feathers. It's adorable—no other adjective fits—in the way small toys can be, so, if a child saw this on a table, you'd have to be careful it didn't end up in her mouth. It makes you think of all those little troll figures popular back in the '90s, with long silky tresses. Or earrings—these would look good on the right kind of woman, a stylish brunette with a lively sense of humor.

Like Walt Cary's bugs, the Rollie Pollie is prettier than it has to be. Most bugs are—and if you have doubts about that, take a look at their eyes. They're usually placed high enough on a bug that a bass would never see them before striking; most resemble no eyes ever seen in nature. On the bugs spread before me are eyes that are coy and doe-like, eyes as big and baleful as a giant squid's, eyes that bulge out of their sockets like the bug has been electroshocked, eyes that are beady, startled, aghast, eyes that are bloodshot, eyes that are walleyed, eyes that look teary and eyes that squint, eyes mounted like headlights, eyes that rattle in their glassy sockets, eyes that are silver, yellow, orange, and blue. Obviously, there's a lot more going on with bug eyes then, well, meets the eye.

The older bugs tied of deer hair often don't have eyes at all, and that makes them look blind, Lear-like, repellant—and it tips you off on how important eyes are in a bug, not in making the bass rise to them, but making a bass fisher decide to buy them in the first place. Is it because we want to look our bugs straight in the eye, decide if they have what it takes? Well, yes, sort of. We want the vicarious sense that, via those eyes, we'll be scoping out the water we cast to, or staring down into those gaping mouths as they hit.

That's where the art, the "extraneous" beauty comes in; for a bass bug to catch a bass on the lake, it must first catch a bass fisherman in the store. Nothing wrong with this, of course; as Joe Brooks put it, bass bugs "must have a tremendous appeal for *both* fish and man." The writer Ray Bergman echoes this, not so much on artistic grounds as on pragmatic ones. "You are more likely to have good luck on a bug you like the looks of than on one which doesn't appeal to you. Faith is an important item in any bug."

Flyfishers coming to bass after trout will often bring along their assumption that in order to catch fish you must match the hatch. These are the ones buying the detailed, very realistic bass bugs you can find in the catalogs, ones that faithfully replicate a moth, dragonfly, or mouse. Master fly tier Joe Messinger's Frog has been famous for decades (and I see his son is still selling them at $9.50 a pop), with its frog-kicking legs, but it probably looks a lot more froggy to us than it does to a bass. Some of these realistic ones, mice especially, work very well, but you get the impression it's despite their realism, not because of it. Given a choice in my bugs between nature and art, the sober or the gaudy, I'll choose the arty extravagant ones most every time. "Freaks," Bergman calls these—bugs that bass take, not because they look like familiar food items they're likely to find on the water's surface, but because they don't.

Another important point to keep in mind about bass bugs is the catch-22 that's in effect. At times, bass will hit *any* bug that's thrown to them, it could be a pencil wrapped in pipe cleaners, while at other times they will hit *nothing* that's cast over them, it could be the most perfect bass bug ever invented. It's the gray area in between where a bug has to earn its reputation, not just taking the easy ones (any bug can do that), and not taking the impossible ones (which are indeed impossible), but the skeptical-but-not-completely-so ones, the bassy middle class, who, when it comes to rising to a bizarre-looking concoction of cork, chicken feathers, and rubber, are occasionally willing to be seduced.

The origins of many traditional arts and crafts are often lost in the mists of time, but with bass bugs, though there's quibbling over the details, history pretty much agrees on the broad outlines.

The Seminoles are given credit for inventing bass bugging, or at least a rough and ready version called "bobbing." This was first described by the naturalist William Bartram, one of those writers who, like Audubon or Meriwether Lewis, we read to marvel at their descriptions of American when it was still a paradise. Writing in 1791, he describes how the Seminoles of Florida fished for enormous largemouth bass using ten-foot-long poles that swung "bobs" over the surface, lures tied of "the white hair of a deer's tail, shreds of a red garter, and some parti-colored feathers, all of which form a tuft or tassel nearly as large as one's fist, which entirely covers and conceals the hook."

Shreds of red garter? Parti-colored feathers? Sounds like bass bugs had a sense of humor right from the start.

This method of fishing spread north in the nineteenth century. In North Carolina, the bob evolved into something close to modern deer-hair bugs, being constructed of deer-skin squares cut into stringy strips and soaked to make them pliable, and then wound around a hook. Fishermen soon learned that a piece of cork floated as well as deer hair, and worked even better if you stuck some chicken feathers in it. This was called "spat" fishing or "jiggling," and often these bugs would be fished on only six inches of line, the fisherman dapping the corks over likely looking pockets from hiding places on shore.

The big debate among historians is whether or not Dr. James Henshall, the father of American bass fishing, did or did not invent the modern deer-hair bug as we know it. He wrote about bobbing, and he traveled enough in the south that he probably knew about the spat, but in his published writings about fly-fishing for bass, it's gaudy wet flies like the Montreal or Queen of the Waters he talks about using, not anything resembling a deer-hair or cork bug. The famous Henshall bug was named in his honor, it seems, rather than being his own invention.

The truth is the bass bug was "invented" roughly simultaneously by various tiers working independently of each other, building on the old bob tradition or adapting trout flies to better take bass. Emerson Hough and Fred Peet of Chicago learned to make bugs out of spun deer hair in 1912, and William Jamison, another Chicagoan, was selling his Coaxers commercially by 1910, while Tennessean Ernest Peckinpaugh began selling bugs made out of cork at about the same time.

If anyone can be credited with singlehandedly inventing bass poppers, it's probably "Peck," who began tinkering with them in 1901 or 1902. He liked to bass fish well into the evening using bucktail streamers, and discovered that the bass would take them when they skittered across the surface; looking for a way to keep them floating when they were wet, he added cork to the hook—and, with that simple addition, the popper was born. By 1913, he was selling his Night Bugs to bass fishermen stopping in Chattanooga on their way to Florida, and then in catalogs to anglers across the country.

Chicago—not usually thought of as a bassin' hotspot—continued to play an important role in bass bugs' evolution. An outdoor writer from that city, Will Dilg, popularized Peckinpaugh's patterns and added some of his own. With this kind of publicity, Peck was able to go into business full-time, and by 1940 the E. H. Peckinpaugh catalog listed sixty different bass bugs with hundreds of color combinations; the company employed nearly a hundred workers, who turned out more than 300,000 bugs a year.

Other pioneers from this era deserve mention. Tom Loving of Baltimore invented the famous Gerbubble, Orley Tuttle chipped in with his deer-hair Devil Bug, Joe Messinger's Frog appeared in the 1930s, and Cal McCarthy's flat-winged Cal-mac Moth made a big reputation for itself at around the same time. By the 1940s, most writers on bass fishing included chapters on bass bugging; what's interesting is that they all talk about it being something that was developed within living memory, in their youth. They stress that it isn't just a wonderfully effective method for catching bass, but one that's an enormous amount of fun, Bergman flat-out stating "even the thrill of trout dry fly fishing can scarcely surpass the rise of a large bass to a popper or bug." By the time World War II ended, bass bugging and bass bugs were entering a short-lived golden age.

It's fun to go back to bass books of that era and look at the colored plates. At first glance, the bugs pictured there are similar to today's, and you can even recognize a few perennials like Messinger's ubiquitous Frog. There's a different style of naming in effect, with the tier's name given prominence; a bug isn't just called the Mystery Bug, but Knight's Mystery Bug; it's not just the Spouter, but Harvey Harnden's Spouter. Understandable—these were men trying to make a living—but the names don't have the sassy, ironic flavor they took on later.

It was an art in the process of evolution. There are winged monstrosities that must have been impossible to cast, and others that look like they've been electroshocked, with rigid whiskers sticking out from their heads. But there's a leaner style beginning to emerge—many bugs looked streamlined, sleek, futuristic, like the designer has watched a lot of Flash Gordon. Some are plain silly looking, with exaggerated cupped lips—they remind you of Rube Goldberg or the early Walt Disney. Many are bullet and/or torpedo shaped, as befits bugs designed during a world war. Some are "fly rod" versions of famous casting plugs like the Flatfish, and I'm just old enough I can remember buying these as a young man.

Color? Yellow predominates—Joe Brooks writing in 1947: "Yellow is the best color"—ranging from soft margarine shades through lemon to gold; there are also more whites than you would see today. A lot is going on with scale patterns, cross-hatching and striping. A few are masterpieces of decoration; John Scott's Amphisbaena, with its black freckles, looks like a work of abstract impressionism. (And if you, like me, don't know what amphisbaena means, I've just looked it up: "a serpent in classic mythology having a head at each end and capable of moving in either direction.")

Over the years I've scored a few old-time bugs at tag sales and flea markets, and I'm looking down at four of them now, three made of deer hair and one made of cork. The cork is that Flash Gordon/streamlined style—the head is tapered front to back, and white wisps of hackle are glued to the sides so they stream back toward the hook, increasing the minnow-like sleekness. The hair bugs are bulkier than they are today, meatier; to my eye, the hook gap is too shallow, so actually hooking a bass on one would probably be tough. One of these I've never had a name for, but, sure enough, there it is on one of the color plates: the Weaver Frog, with a striped deer-hair head and outspreading deer-hair legs. A sixty-five-year-old bug—and it makes me wonder if there are any bug lovers out there smart and dedicated enough to be collecting these while they still can be found.

So that was the state of things circa 1949—lots of bass bugs on the market, lots of fly fishermen bugging for bass—but then spinning reels came along and nearly wrecked the whole tradition. Instead of having to learn to fly cast, struggling with those heavy rods needed to overcome a bug's wind resistance, the casual angler could take a spinning outfit and, with a short learning curve, cast a Jitterbug or Dardevle thirty yards.

While diehards like Roy Yates (whose Deacon with its distinctive comet shape is still a killer) continued to experiment with new designs, bass bugging was being dismissed in the pages of *Sports Afield* as "an extremely crude form of fly fishing, if fly fishing it can be called." Even a writer sympathetic to fly fishing could lament that the bass bugs had shown "almost no design development in the last fifty to one hundred years."

The renaissance in bugging came in the 1970s, spurred on, on the one hand, by the introduction of light and powerful graphite fly rods; and, on the other, by new and innovative bugs tied and popularized by an Ozark fisherman, writer, and artist named Dave Whitlock.

Whitlock, calling his methods "the new realism," worked under two influences: the example of trout fly tying, with its emphasis on precise imitation of the living insect; and the spinning lure revolution, with its crankbaits, stickbaits, and plastic worms. He tied deer-hair bugs that combined the two influences . . . the Near Nuff Hair Frog, the Hare Water Pup, the Damdragonsel Moth . . . and while some old-timers sniffed as his bugs "dressed with unnecessary appendages and decorations," a new generation of bass buggers eagerly took them up, with tiers like Larry Dahlberg, Art Scheck, Bob Clouser, and Jack Garside taking the old tradition and running with it in fruitful new directions.

It's telling that even a sober realist like Whitlock makes bass bugs that look like Muppets. What's more, he seems to know this—that a sense of humor is something any good bug should have incorporated into its design.

"Each time I tried my new flies or fished them, I had a new sensation of playing the role of a master puppeteer. I made my puppets fly, flutter, twitch, pop, shake, dive, wiggle and swim . . . My new flies were tied with special materials, shaped to accent the animation."

Whitlock built his reputation making deer-hair bugs, while tiers like Walt Cary and Harry Murray specialize in making their poppers out of cork. This brings us to bass bugging's great schism (every folk art deserves a good schism): which material makes for better bugs—deer hair or cork?

There are many good arguments on both sides. Deer-hair bugs are older, going back to the Seminoles, but cork has nothing to apologize for, with a pedigree of at least two centuries. Whitlock and the hair boys insist that bass will hold on to deer hair longer than they will cork ("Bass are extremely sensitive to food texture, preferring a firm meaty object to one that is very hard"), while the cork fans will argue that their material casts better, floats better, and is equally as durable.

The biggest difference, having all kinds of implications, comes in how they are tied. Deer-hair bugs are tied like trout flies, one at a time, with the emphasis on "tying." Shanks of hollow deer hair are either spun around the hook shaft one small bunch at a time so they flare outward at right angles, or stacked, where hair lies flatter, allowing for easier mixing of colors. After either technique comes hedge trimming with barber scissors to get the desired shape.

Making cork poppers is much more time consuming, which can discourage amateurs. Bodies have to be cut and shaped out of cork (or balsa, tupelo, or foam); fastening them to the hook is tiresome; hackle and legs have to be attached just so, and up to six coats of paint have to be applied before it's all finished. Most tiers, if they want to turn out more than one a day, have to adopt assembly-line tactics, carving out bodies one day, attaching hooks the next, etc.

A schism—but most bass buggers come down somewhere in the middle, so our fly boxes contain a good assortment of both hair and cork. Yes, bass will hold on to a deer-hair bug a tad longer than they will cork; yes, cork floats much better, and doesn't cost quite as much as deer hair. And if tradition is important to you, the two materials come out even. Bass bugs, no matter what they are crafted of, are prime examples of the American genius at improvisation ("Deerhair tiers, are, inevitably, inventors," William G. Tapply wrote, "liberated from the need to imitate something, they can't help fooling around"), combined with the American genius for mass production ("Making bugs out of cork," Harvey Harnden says, "is a construction job")—or at least *were* prime examples, back in the days before everything changed.

Is the art of the bass bug alive and well in the twenty-first century or, like so many other traditional arts and crafts, is it becoming a nostalgic relic from the past? I decided to talk to some men and women professionally involved in the business, to see if I couldn't get a handle on how things stand.

Don Davis lives in Chesterfield, Missouri, near some excellent bass ponds and the Big Mo. Growing up in Mississippi, he learned bass bugging from his father; later, moving north a couple of states, he was disappointed not to find any convenient source for the bugs and poppers he fished as a boy. In 2006, he started his own web-based distributorship, Breambugs, which gathers bass bugs and bluegill flies from the best tiers across the country. A good idea—but would it work? Very shrewdly, he took out an ad in *Confederate Veteran* magazine, not just for any bug, but for the famous Dixie Devil. Those old Confederate reprobates went for that name like a largemouth after a frog—and simple as that he was in the bass bug business.

"So," I asked, after we swapped a fish story or two, "what's new in the bass bug world?"

Don's a cheerful man, but he sees things plain.

"Dying off," he said sadly. "Moving offshore and losing its quality."

A depressingly familiar story. Labor costs are driving this quintessentially American art to Nicaragua and China. Lots of popular bugs are being "handmade" offshore, like Betts and like Boogle, while renowned American tiers like Tony Arcado, unable to compete, were closing up shop.

We chewed that over for a while (I wondered what Chinese bug tiers make of their work, never having seen a bass, having only the faintest notion of what the work of their hands is used for), and then, since neither of us had a solution, got to talking about that part of the tradition that still lives.

"We sell bugs to all fifty states in the union," Don explained, "though the Southeast is our biggest market. Walt Cary's Belly Frog is one of our best sellers, and it's very similar to a pattern Peck Peckinpaugh tied years and years ago. Chartreuse is our best-selling color by eight to one over white and black. We have an expression down here, 'If it ain't chartreuse, it ain't no use.'"

Don suggested I call Neal Pultz out in Fresno, California, to get the perspective of a skilled, imaginative tier making a living off his bugs. His Little Fatty is one of Breambugs's favorite—a feather-light balsa popper with a beautifully "distressed" look, thanks to a splattering of black dots, a bouquet of legs, hackle, and marabou, and six celluloid enamel coats.

Neal is fifty-something. When he was younger he worked at an assortment of jobs—truck driver, meat packer, short-order chef—earning just enough to go off on fishing expeditions up and down the length of California. He taught himself how to tie trout flies, and that helped bring in some cash; there was a time when he was singlehandedly tying nine hundred dozen elk-hair caddis a year.

"I started tying bass bugs for gas money," he told me. "I'd drive up to fish the Klamath and stop in at tackle shops along the way to see if they'd sell my bugs."

The shops liked what they saw, and orders started coming in. At a fly-fishing show, he met the great Dave Whitlock, who told him that if he was going to be successful he needed to find a niche where he wouldn't have much competition—and making some of the country's most beautiful bass bugs, when Neal thought about it, seemed just the ticket. He took some of his creations to another fly show, spread them out before fishing writer Lefty Kreh, and Lefty liked what he saw—a tremendous boost to Neal's confidence.

He works at it full-time now, with two or three helpers. Breambugs alone orders 7,000 bugs a year from him, and he's hard-pressed to keep up with demand. He buys 1,500 board feet of balsa wood at a time, the hardest grade he can find, taken from the heart of the balsa tree; he shapes these on a lathe, and has his shop so organized that he can paint upward of 2,000 bugs a day.

It's the steps in between—the tying on of hackle; the insertion of rubber legs—that are terrifically time-consuming. He did the best he could with this for years, but then was forced into a decision he is still ambivalent about: he shipped that stage of production down to Nicaragua.

"An agent called me, asked if I would try their tiers. 'Okay,' I said. 'I'll ship you five hundred bodies, and if I like what they tie, we're in business.'"

He sent down a box, not expecting much, but when they came back, "Four hundred and seventy-five out of the were tied better than I could do myself," he said.

He's definitely an American bug man, and, with companies like Umpqua being mostly Chinese now, he takes great pride in that—but the fact is that an essential part of his operation is now offshore.

"It's the only way I can survive," he explained honestly. "And I want to go on with this as long as I'm having fun doing something I love."

At least one company still makes bass bugs start-to-finish in the U.S. The Gaines Company had its start in 1947 in the same north Pennsylvania town where it still operates. Russell Garlick, the original owner, sold it to Tom and Lael Eggler in 1971, and Lael continues to operate it today, in what is almost certainly the last operational popping-bug factory left in the United States.

Lael answers the phone when you call Gaines, and it's a delight to talk to her—though she's protectively closemouthed when it comes to company details.

"So, Lael, how many employees do you have?"

"We don't give out that information," she says, as sweetly as possible.

"How many poppers do you sell a year?"

"We don't give out that information," she says, even more sweetly.

"Do you have any plans to outsource to China?"

That prompts some passion all right. "We are an American company and WE ARE ALWAYS GOING TO STAY AMERICAN!"

Gaines makes the Sneaky Pete, invented by Russell Garlick in 1950 and a best seller ever since. I have one on the desk beside me—if I rummaged through the house, I could probably scavenge up several dozen—and it's a beautiful piece of work. It's a slider bug, meaning one with a pointy, almost vulpine nose that doesn't make much commotion on the water. The eyes, to my eye, are feline and very feminine; the legs are made of a particularly tantalizing rubber; the mix of hackle and marabous on the back gives it a seductive wiggle in the water even when it's fished absolutely still. Most of mine are chartreuse, and Lael, like Don David, confirmed that it's indeed the most popular color. Whether it's because the bass just like the fact that nothing in nature is truly chartreuse, or because it gives terrific visibility to the fisherman, it's hard to say, though it seems significant that the chartreuse we're talking about is exactly the same color as the safety vests worn by highway workers and emergency personnel all across America.

When it comes to the criteria for a perfect bass bug, the Sneaky Pete ranks high. It's wonderfully aerodynamic, a pleasure to cast. It's hookability is outstanding—a bass that rises to a Sneaky is a bass that's hooked. It makes a light touchdown on the water, displacing just enough water molecules to tickle a bass's literal line, its "hearing," and make it curious. The only place it gets low marks is in durability, particularly if you like to bounce it off rocks, but a drop of epoxy on the head will help with concussions.

The name is also part of its appeal; its name plants it squarely in that offbeat, alternative American tradition I spoke of earlier, and it only takes a quick search in the dictionary to confirm this.

Sneaky Pete is American slang for 1) a hustler's cue in a pool hall, one that looks shabby and crooked but is actually the best one in the joint; 2) a cheap bottle of fortified wine popular on skid row; 3) making love to your partner while they're asleep, as in "Last night I gave her the old Sneaky Pete."

No wonder it catches bass!

When my kids were little, I'd come back from a fishing trip and they would ask me what I caught. "Three bass," I'd say, or, "Six big ones," and then they'd ask an even more important question: "What did you catch them on, Daddy?"

"Sneaky Pete," I'd say, and they always collapsed in giggles, running off to tell their mom, "Daddy caught one on Sneaky! Daddy caught one on Sneaky!"

Indeed Daddy did. Many times. Hundreds of times. Thousands of times. When the bass were stubborn, I'd hit them with that hustler's cue, tempt them with fortified wine, poke . . . But no, I don't think I'll go much further with my analogies than that. It's a wonderful bass bug. May it always stay American!

But that's the rub. We're used to seeing things that seem quintessentially American move to China, Vietnam, or Brazil, so even our trout flies are now more likely to be tied in Kenya or Thailand than they are in Montana or the Catskills of New York. And yet bass bugs moving offshore seems like the final, saddest indignity. You would think that they were too small a business to be subject to macroeconomic trends, too secret, too humble—but no. The gnashing, wailing sound you hear is Will Dilg, Tom Loving, E. H. Peckinpaugh, and Harvey Harnden spinning in their graves.

The future is not without hope. Neal Pultz enjoys showing young people how to tie bugs and they're wonderfully enthusiastic. Amateur tiers, working at their vises at home, are keeping the art alive on their own, never mind what the big boys are doing. Making bass bugs, like quilting or fine woodworking, seems to be going back to its roots as a folk craft, not an international business. So good luck to you all—and always remember that a good bass bug has panache!

For that's what I love about them. When I fish trout flies I'm working *with* nature, feeling reassured that if it can be understood and replicated the trout will do their part. Bass bugs teach us the opposite lesson—that working aslant nature can bring great results. I can understand why a rainbow rises to my gray midge on a river thick with them—I'm pleased when one hits, but not terribly surprised. When a bass rises to my Boogle Bug, never having in its life seen anything like it, I'm greatly surprised—as surprised probably as the bass is. Realism works in fishing, but so does the outlandish, and bass bugs prove it.

I wish I had the dexterity and patience to tie some myself. I'm not good at that kind of thing—but what I'd enjoy doing is naming them.

Yesterday at lunch, looking down at the old plates in Ray Bergman's book, I started trying to come up with bass bug names on my own, ones that are suitably twenty-first century. Once I started it was like a fit I couldn't stop . . . every spare piece of paper in the kitchen was soon covered in ink . . . and after due reflection I've selected out my favorites. Any tier out there is welcome to appropriate any that catches his or her eye, and all I ask in return is for you to send me your bug when it's perfected. None of my names are as classy as Scott's Amphisbaena, but at least they're pronounceable.

Crispy Critter. Dominatrix. Panic Attack. Pop-u-lure. Empty Nester. Harry Popper. Wings of Fire. Louisville Chugger. Merchant's

Copy. Fill-a-buster. Snack Attack. Bass-a-holic. Direct Deposit. Pop Pie. Don't-Bee-Shy. Girl on Top. Bass Vader. Bee Bopper. Mouse Pad. Bass Lash. Kiss of Death. Piece-a-Cake. Bassie Lassie. Momma Poppa. Pop Quiz. Dinky Pinky. Gig-a-Byte. Forgeddaboutit. Zulty Zoe. Poppa Bear. Surface Beauty. Snug-a-Bug. Mopsikon Flopsikon. Seal the Deal. Slip Slider. Wing and a Prayer. Pop Tart. Boston Pops. Pop and Prejudice.

Eight

If the trout is the fish of the famous tributaries—the Madisons to the Missouris, the San Juans to the Colorados, the Batten Kills to the Hudsons—then the bass is the fish of the great American rivers themselves, the Tennessees, the Potomacs, the Susquehannas, and the Mississippis. Bass are mainstream fish, in every sense of the term. They flourish in the midst of us, so instead of getting on a plane, flying across a continent to play with them, you can amble down to the river on your lunch break, cast your lure out, very possibly catch a lunker.

Great rivers are the seams of American life, the binding sutures, so it's no wonder the great American fish is right at home there. Yes, bass love quiet, forgotten places just like trout, but they can prosper and thrive in the hurly-burly of the larger world. Bigness suits them, breadth, bustle—they aren't just specialists in pristine. Trout sometimes stumble into these main stem rivers, but they don't last long; bass seem to want to be there, and are often friendlier, more gregarious, easier to approach than they are on lakes and ponds.

My own great river, the one I know best, is the Connecticut, New England's longest, flowing four hundred miles from Canada to Long Island Sound. Bass can be found throughout most if its four-state course, but the stretch I fish, splitting Vermont and New Hampshire, extends from the Cornish-Windsor covered bridge to the village of Orford thirty miles upstream. Wilder Dam, built in 1950, splits this reach into two very distinct halves: a fast-flowing tailwater downstream; a slower, lake-like reach upstream. The bass love both stretches. They're bigger, stronger, warier downstream; smaller, feistier, more abundant upstream.

I live along this upper section ... if I walk to the end of my driveway, stand in exactly the right place, I can make out the flat sheen of its water in a gap between a barn and a small knoll ... and so within these thirty miles there is a shorter mile-and-a-half stretch, my home water within my home river, that I will fish forty times in the course of a season.

It's a beautiful river—it's astonishing how beautiful the Connecticut can be. It runs through pastoral hills and forested eskers, with only the occasional oxbow to wrinkle things up. It likes to stay just out of sight from the roads, and when you're actually on the river in a canoe or kayak, the high banks make it surprisingly secret and tunnel-like—a self-contained corridor where you can spend a summer morning without seeing another human being. Serving as the border between New Hampshire and Vermont, it acts like one of those in-between kind of places that doesn't really belong to anyone. It's a river of vine-covered banks, slanting white pine, spreading silver maple; it's a river of sudden drop-offs, gravel bars, tangled weed beds. It's a river of fizzy white water and marshy backwaters; it's a river than can be oddly tidal for a stretch so far from the sea, thanks to the releases of the dam. A river of modern transfer stations and nineteenth century midden heaps; impromptu riverside shooting ranges, nuclear power plant discharges, shopping malls—and, in a characteristic Connecticut River touch, the stretches behind the malls are among the loveliest, most forgotten of all.

A river's personality can be a hard thing to pin down, but, if pressed, I would compare the Connecticut to a seventy-five-year-old man, who, after surviving a raucous youth of wild and violent misbehavior; a middle age of work, loss, and tragedy; has now at long last entered upon a serene and accepting old age, with a hard-won gravitas, a gently ironic sense of humor, that makes spending some time in his company well worth your while.

The wild youth? Go back far enough and this was border country, no man's land, bitterly fought over by the first English settlers and the

French and Indians raiding down from Canada. State-sponsored terrorism we would call this now—"asymmetrical warfare." The French war parties had it all their own way at first, descending the Connecticut to take unawares Deerfield or Northfield, or, farther north, the lonely outpost called Fort Number Four. By 1759, the English adopted terror tactics of their own, sending Major Robert Rogers and his Rangers on a raid north of the border that resulted in the butchery, at St. Francis, of mostly women and children—and then a famously desperate retreat down the Connecticut back to Number Four.

The violence eased off by the nineteenth century (but never entirely—murderers, even now, find the river is a convenient place to dump corpses), but the wildness continued, with the storied Connecticut River log drive, the longest log drive in world history, bringing millions of board feet of timber down from the headwaters to the voracious mills of Massachusetts. Rivermen were a rough and tough bunch, and, talk to the oldest old-timers up here, they can still tell you stories of famous punch-ups and riverside brawls.

The tragedies came with a series of destructive floods, starting in the 1920s, and continuing through the early 1950s, after which a series of dams helped control the worst ravages. If anything, this resulted in a false sense of security; during Hurricane Irene in 2011, a lot of people learned to their sorrow how destructive and greedy the Connecticut and its tributaries can still be.

By the 1960s, and the passage of the Clean Waters Act, the Connecticut began settling into its serene second youth. By the time I began fishing it in the early 1980s, it was on its way to becoming a rare environmental success story, with a new generation of fishers and boaters rediscovering a treasure that the previous generation, pinching their fingers over their noses, had resolutely ignored.

Like many great American rivers, it has always served as a corridor for a lot more than water. The railroad was constructed along the Vermont bank before the Civil War—at the turn of the century, there was better passenger service than there is today. The telegraph followed the tracks, and even now you can see the surviving poles leaning to the side with their wire descending right down into the water, as if ghosts of telegraphers past are tapping out Morse to the walleye and pike. Interstate 91 went in on the ridge above the river back in the seventies, cutting farms in half. I take it they were a pretty wild bunch themselves, the construction gangs who built it. They always needed reinforcements, so some of the original hippies left their communes and went to work, teaching the rednecks how to smoke grass while the rednecks taught them how to chug Blue Ribbons and Buds.

So, a wild and colorful past. It's hard to read that now . . . the river has no wrinkles, no obvious facial scars . . . and, afloat on its prettier reaches, casting toward where the branches of maples stroke the water with their shade, you'll think it was all created yesterday—that you're the first person in the world to ever discover it, the first one to figure out it's loaded, absolutely loaded to the brim, with smallmouth bass.

It's continental-class in that respect, the Connecticut—continental-class meaning it's worth hopping a jet anywhere in North America to come fish it. We have trout fishing in this valley that ranges from poor to middlin'-good, but if I were guiding flyfishers, it's to the Connecticut I would bring them, with full confidence they would catch an experience worth remembering. The fifteen miles below Wilder Dam is usually good for at least one trophy twenty-inch smallmouth on a morning's float, while the upstream stretch can provide big numbers, with thirty-fish afternoons a real possibility.

The fish aren't everywhere, which is why you'd be well-advised to find a crusty old-timer like me to guide you. Within the thirty miles there are long featureless banks where you won't catch squat, and even some of the classic bass spots, like weed beds and lily pads, are not as good as they are on other waters. If I send someone out, I tell them "Fish the rocks," which is usually all the guidance they need. The cliffs, the spots where the gravel banks suddenly become sheer, can be good places to try, as are the deadfalls, the fallen white pine that stud the shoreline. And the backwaters, the marshy widenings where tributaries come in. Give them a shot, too, for they can hold largemouth that don't like the current out in the mainstream.

As for the pronounced tidal quality the river has here, it comes from the releases of the Wilder hydroelectric dam. These can range from 900 cubic feet per second during low-water periods to 20,000 cfs when they're generating at full capacity—and 150,000 cfs during storm "events" like Hurricane Irene. Downstream of the dam, the water level rise and fall is dramatic, even dangerous, on the order of the Bay of Fundy, so you shouldn't venture out without paying close attention to the "flow forecast" reported on the Internet. Above the dam, the effect is gentler, more on the order of the tides you see on Cape Cod, though still powerful enough to put a noticeable flow in the current—a downstream one when the dam is generating, an upstream one when the gates close. The bass are sensitive to these changing water levels, particularly above the dam, where they seem to feed heavier on a falling "tide"—a release of 4,000 cfs—than they do on a stagnant or rising one.

It brings them goodies, the increased flow. Brings bass moths, mayflies, spinners, spiders, beetles, caddis, mice. They like sipping these from the surface as they float past, and, if the supply that day is a little skimpy, they can root in the rocks for fat crayfish that must taste to them like lobster. There can't be many bass rivers in the country where the fish stay so tight to the banks, even in summer, which is one of the reasons the fly rod is so effective. That said, in more than thirty years I've never seen anyone fly-fishing the upper stretch but me. Not just a few flyfishers . . . *none*.

You seen spin casters and bait fishers casting from the bank, at least in June, though they quickly disappear after that. Bass guys in bass boats—you see them, too, or at least their wakes, as they zoom past, perpetually on their way toward somewhere better. They don't catch much, the macho boys—they're victims of their fantasies and their technology. Having spent Saturday morning watching TV shows about catching largemouth on Florida lakes, they think the bass must be in the weeds, forgetting that these are smart river smallmouth who much prefer rocks; having invested so much in their bass boats, they can't risk them in the shallow, unpredictable water below the dam, and so cut themselves off from some of the biggest bass in the Northeast.

I give them a wave when they rocket past, their wakes bullying my canoe. I give them a wave with my middle finger, but I feel sorry for them, too.

Because the river warms up slower than the lakes, I don't start fishing it until the second week in June. By then, the fishing on stillwater has begun to slow a bit, whereas the Connecticut is just entering prime time. Because of the drastic rise and fall of the water level, the bass spawn deep in the river, deeper than the eye can discern; if they did this any shallower, their nests would be exposed at low "tide," and you wouldn't be reading this chapter.

Our river fish are darker, leaner, scruffier than our lake fish—their cheeks are often grizzled up with lice. They'll jump sooner than lake fish; since you catch them so shallow, with hardly any water beneath them, they have no choice but to take to the air. The current probably adds thirty percent to their pulling power, and dealing with it acts like isometrics, building up their muscles. And, since lakes (geologically speaking) have long since arrived and rivers are still going, there's a certain here-today-gone-tomorrow aspect to their personalities. They enjoy moving around, and, when you catch them, they look like transients yanked off the highway, not burghers snatched from their homes.

But all this is overview. Time now to get out on the water, try to show you what a morning on the river is like. And you're lucky in your choice of days. It's the middle of June, warm but not yet hot, with a southerly forecast for later, but perfect calm right now. This is the pattern we've had for a week, which is very good news; Connecticut River bass hate change, love regularity, so they should be receptive. I've called the information recording for Wilder, and the forecast is for a release of 2,000 cfs until noon, which is just enough to get some flow going, switch the conveyor belt to *on*.

The launch is six miles downstream of my house, and it's not officially a boat launch at all, but just a gravel pull-off. I slide the canoe off the car top, load it on its little cart, toss in my rods, flies, and paddle, and then, before pulling the rig to the water, take an appraising squint at how things stand.

The bank is high enough that I can see almost a mile of river. Directly below me the river's surface is ribbed with reflected white contrails of jets passing out of hearing overhead; out toward the middle the gray looks slippery, like a child's playground slide; over by Vermont, the water is pebbled in impressionistic dots, some gold, some emerald. A 500-yard-long island divides the river into two and partially hides the Vermont shore—a long, tapered, river-shaped island, which is a smart shape for an island to be, rather than presenting its blunt side to the current and being constantly at war.

The river is moving in its lazy 2,000 cfs way. Below me, I can see the tops of weeds streaming leftward as if a comb is tugging at each pliant strand. Further out, twigs and bits of flotsam drift endwise with the current, not broadside like they would if the current was still. The surface, clean and steel-colored from the distance, is much cloudier up close. A good cloud—the cloudiness of life. Spinners from a night-time hatch, their gossamer wings waterlogged in the surface film; moths that became confused by the full moon and plunged toward its watery reflection; midges the same size and color as the pollen strands they float among; various bugs I have no name for, forming a thin, anchovy-colored paste. From a bass's point of view, the entire river looks edible.

Upstream, I can see a pronounced kink where the river jogs to the west, and then, where it straightens again, the steep, birch-lined bank with the railroad—and just beyond, a ridge swelling into two sugarloaf hills. I can see a farm, or at least its broad, marshy hayfield flattening down to the water. Willows occupy a corner of this field, and, even though it's windless, seem to add the same kind of motion to the sky that the current does to the water.

With the sun still low behind me, New Hampshire looks hard, Vermont looks soft, and while this will even out as the morning progresses, I'll be doing most of my fishing on the Vermont side of the river.

I slide the canoe down, being careful not to slip on the treacherous, slick-as-ice clay that forms a shelf between the scrubby bank and the water proper. It's a new canoe, at least for me. Tired of lifting my heavy fifteen-footer on top of the car, I've switched to a lighter ten-footer, a one-man pack canoe a man was selling over on Lake Sunapee. Compared to the solid, dependable steed I'm used to, it's like riding an unpredictable colt, so I'll have to go easy before I learn all its tricks.

There's good water right here, but, saving that for later, I paddle across the forty yards of water to the island's eastern side. It's privately owned, forested with old pine, but back in the 1800s its soil was rich and open enough to farm. There's a photo in our town history of a farmhand who worked out there, John Latham—a "burly man, a bit of a renegade, known to be a hard worker," though, judging by his ferocious scowl, his massive head and arms, he wasn't just a bit of a renegade, but the genuine article. He was famous in town for having webbed feet; not having access to a boat, he would swim to the island with his scythe every morning, drape his clothes on a rock to dry, start in haying.

The bottom here is sandy, with a few skimpy patches of weed that are worth trying as a warmup for what lies ahead. It takes me two or three false casts to work out the sixty feet of line I'll be casting and re-casting all morning—and on the third cast, the first where my Boogle Bug actually drops to the surface, a bass rolls over it and takes hold. Not a big one—eleven inches, and noticeably paler than the usual Connecticut River fish—but an eleven-inch smallmouth fights hard in a river, particularly on a fiberglass fly rod as flexible as mine.

This is the best of all possible omens—finding a fish so fast, from second-string water. Right above this, at the upstream end of the island, comes much richer stuff. There are blowdowns here, chocolate-colored pine trunks lying athwart the river, and they're the obvious targets for my next few casts. And that's where bass number two takes it, at the downstream end of the biggest log, underneath which its been lurking. It's a better one, fifteen inches, and gives me a fight serious enough to tow the tiny canoe out to the middle of the river—a Nantucket sleigh ride, or damn near. First fish, and then first good fish, and I haven't been out ten minutes.

There's an extensive weed bed above the island, which, when the water level is high, you can just make out waving below the canoe—

green, silky, mysterious. My father, the last time we ever went fishing together, took a good bass here trolling a Rapala (with his bad eyesight, trolling is all he could manage), and, after a few empty casts, I end up trolling myself, resting the rod on the canoe seat and letting the fly drag behind the canoe as I head upstream. Trolling a Boogle Bug? Yep, it works, and I haven't paddled five yards before a fish makes . . . well, I was going to say, "makes my reel scream," but what it does (I'm using an old Pfleuger Medalist reel) is make it click, wobble, and squeak, which is still enough to startle me. By the time I put down the paddle and pick up the rod, there's nothing to tighten on, the bass is gone.

I get startled here a lot, now that I think of it. One morning, fishing in a fog thick and clingy as cotton, something struck the canoe hard on the side, almost tipping me. My first though was that, like the *Titanic,* I'd hit an iceberg—a low shape in the water swept heedlessly past—but it turned out to be the oar of a racing shell, a hit-and-run sculler from the Dartmouth boathouse ten miles downstream.

Another morning I was enjoying the quiet when I heard a sudden loud *whoosh* right behind me—again, I nearly capsized, this time from fright. It was a hot-air balloon on its way across the river; spotting me, the balloonist (Brian Bolland—we later became friends) dropped down to have some fun, waiting until he was inches from the river's surface before making his burner whoosh him upward.

"Catch anything?" he called from the gondola. My arms, which had automatically shot up in surrender, fell back to my sides.

No such surprises today—the only sound are cars over on Route 5 heading to work. A pleasant sound at this distance, buffered by the water; if makes me feel I'm playing hooky, which is a feeling we fishers enjoy. This stretch above the island can get quite shallow if they're releasing lots of water at the dam, and from time to time I see bass rising here just like trout. It surprises me the fish don't do it more often, with so many flies on the water, but bass are steak eaters, not grazers, and most of the time they wait for thicker cuts.

The submerged weed bed ends here, as the river curves westward toward Vermont. It does this in three successively larger indents—a secret cove, a slanting ledge, a scalloped bay . . . and there, the river has turned, and paddling upstream you're heading northwest instead of north.

The cove looks bassy as get-out, but I've never caught much here, and except for a token cast or two don't give it much attention. This is the self-reinforcing loop fishers fall into; not having caught anything in a spot, you don't really work it, and, since you don't really work it, you never catch anything. But as I said, it's beautiful, with a flat terrace atop steep banks, providing an expansive view of the river framed by massive white pine.

A perfect spot for a house, I always thought, while at the same time praying no one would ever build there. But then of course someone did—last autumn when I wasn't around to blow it up. In size alone, it's really quite modest, and displays on its roof all the latest in green technology. Whoever built it never seems to use it except on July Fourth and Labor Day, and yet arranged in a semicircle on the lawn are fourteen green Adirondack chairs—and I don't mean the $18 plastic ones made in China, but $400 wooden ones built in the Adirondacks. You do the math—and this is why, paddling by their bass-less cove, I always shake my head in dismay.

(This is far from the ugliest trophy house on the river. The ugliest trophy house is a few miles downstream. A man who owns a hotel chain, the kind that are found near malls, decided to make his summer house look like one of his hotels, which, $3 million later, it does—a cement blockhouse that would not have been out of place on the Maginot Line.)

Above this first bay, the river's hydrology becomes interesting. There's a steep granite ledge visible on shore that juts fifteen feet out into the river, becoming briefly its bottom. The current, sweeping down from the north, comes against this with its full weight, and then flows on, but—so hard and adamantine is the ledge—with a significant eastward deflection in its course. The bass love this kink—on the great conveyor belt of food, this is the most reliable place for them to wait. I will *always* catch a smallmouth here, at any time, under any circumstances—which is why I'm surprised, after six or seven casts, when I come up empty.

I give the Boogle Bug a time out, tie on a brown Wooly Bugger resembling a crayfish, cast it upstream of the ledge, and let it drift down with the current, keeping my rod tip low, not working the fly but staying in touch with it until it's time to lift for another cast. This is like nymph fishing for trout—and, as in trout fishing, the line suddenly tightens, I lift the rod, and I'm attached to a good fish without ever having to strike it.

He's got a scar, this one—something attacked him and fairly recently, since the scales behind his jaw look like raw meat that has been splashed with iodine. The mark of the vampire—the mark of the pike. The bass are so at home in this river, so perfectly attuned to its environment, that it comes as something of a shock to realize that it's not total paradise for them—that dealing with catch-and-release flyfishers like me is far from their worst problem. Most of these dangers threaten them when they're small . . . when they get big, *they* do the bullying . . . but the scar is clear evidence that even adult bass have much to worry about.

I change to a Tapply bug before moving upstream, let it dangle behind the canoe while I search for my sunglasses, and another bass comes up from the ledge and clobbers it—which is another sign of a good fishing day, that you're catching smallmouth entirely by accident.

The shoreline scallops inward here to form the second cove. Wild iris grow in the shallows, pliant yellow ones and a few clumps of purple. A pair of orioles are building their nest in a tree on the bank, using moss left draped on the bushes after springtime high water. Kingfishers like it here, too—they're oddly clumsy in flight, rise and sink like wooden yo-yos. And mergansers. They keep their babies as close to the bank as possible, so, if any predators are about, one flank at least is protected.

I mentioned the hydrology. The same current that hits the ledge with full force creates a back eddy in this cove and flows for a surprising distance upstream. If I want some easy paddling, all I have to do is stay tight to shore—the eddy drifts me up while the rest of the river drifts down.

Nine o'clock now—the sun is out full strength. I take off my hat, tug down over my face my newest fashion accessory—a nylon, balacla-va-style Buff like the bonefish guides wear in the Bahamas. It's said to be breathable, so I pull it right down over my nose and mouth until I look like a bandito; I remind myself that under no circumstances should I ever wear this where anyone can see me, particularly a child.

Where the bank straightens comes another weed bed, a sloppy one that looks like wet brussels sprouts. A classic spot, at least for the largemouth fisher, but here on the Connecticut the smallmouth shun it. I give it a casual cast or two as I paddle past, aiming for the flat pancaked beginnings of lily pads that won't blossom until August. I catch a bass here once every three years—which means, having caught one last year, two years to go before another strike.

Prime water is just ahead. The railroad tracks follow the river up from White River Junction at varying distances from the bank, but here they're as close as they can possibly be, on a shelf blasted out of rock in the nineteenth century. This resulted in lots of boulders, blocks, and stones falling into the river, which means lots of hiding places for smallmouth; the next 150 yards comprise the best fishing spot in fifteen miles of river.

Railroads and bass go together, as we'll see in the next chapter—the fish spread across the continent by hopping freights—so there's something fitting about fishing in sight of trains. Two a day head north here (I never see any heading south), and yes, right on schedule here comes the Vermont Central freight, sixteen cars loaded with, from the look of it, nothing but graffiti. The engineer leans out the locomotive window and gives me a wave, and I wave back—and that exchange, simple and brief, seems quintessentially American.

Nothing sends out vibrations like a train, but the bass don't mind—if anything, they respond to it like I do, with nostalgic satisfaction. My next three casts bring me three nice bass, though the caboose isn't yet out of sight.

It can be a tricky play to fish the railroad stretch. If the river level is high, those rocks remain invisible, and all you see along shore are berries, leaves, and vines. The bottom drops abruptly, as it does along much of the river; two steps out from the bank and you're over your head. (Which helps explain the surprising number of people who drown each year in its waters.) The bass are either tight against the rocks, or five yards out where the scum line is, the frothy channel of bugs and midges that forms a smaller, juicier conveyor belt within the larger belt of the river. Sometimes after a windstorm the scum line becomes so thick with twigs and pine needles the bass won't poke their heads through it, and the release, the "tides," can also complicate things, moving fish in or out in ways that are hard to predict.

I find two more fish, the same size as the others—twelve inchers, and just starting to trade their sleekness for a belly. The breeze comes up from the south, gently, and while a soft wind from the south is no bad thing on the Connecticut, it makes navigating the canoe increasingly difficult. Along shore the current, the back eddy, is moving upstream with my bug; underneath me, the current is moving downstream thanks to the dam release; meanwhile, the breeze is blowing the canoe upstream. Three separate, contrary forces to deal with (and a fourth, when a bass tows me across stream), so I'm constantly putting down the fly rod and picking up the paddle in order to compensate.

(And while we're talking about wind . . . Read the bass boys, and they all have a theory about which wind is the best to fish on, which the worst. Even doggerel is invoked, as in "Wind from the east, fish bite least." I have no hard-and-fast rules about this, or at least only one: when the wind is from the northwest, STAY HOME.)

I'm catching bass every ninth or tenth cast now, in intervals of ten or twelve yards. Small fish, but while jumping they seem to shed more spray than they usually do, like dogs shaking off after a swim. Rock bass (faux smallmouth) are mixed in with these. They hit just as hard as bass, with a pronounced *puhtooie!* sound. Their first tug is hard, too, and then they immediately give up, and by the time I've heard my fourth or fifth *puhtooie!* I'm not even bothering trying to hook them.

Above the railroad tracks runs old Route 5 and above old Route 5 runs I-91, but the high bank keeps the river quiet, and whenever I hear what sounds like a truck it always turns out to be a motorboat—and, deep in my guilty soul, I always decide it must be the game warden come to check me, though I haven't seen one in twenty-five years. The river belongs to New Hampshire up to the low water line of Vermont, which was the price the latter paid to be admitted to the Union in 1791. (This could eventually work in the state's favor; if the Connecticut ever dries up in global warming, Vermont will own New Hampshire all the way to the seacoast.) In practice, the river acts as No Man's Water, and the wardens like to patrol places where their jurisdiction is less ambiguous.

The speedboat powers down the middle of the river, sees my canoe, and, remembering the proper ethics, slows so his wake won't threaten me. A gentleman of the old school, and I give him a grateful thumbs-up.

Powerboats have a long tradition on this river. Samuel Morey lived just upstream in Orford, and if you don't know who Samuel Morey is it's because Robert Fulton had better patent lawyers. In 1792, more than ten years before Fulton's *Clermont* ran on the Hudson, Morey navigated a primitive steam-powered dugout down the Connecticut here, managing a respectable five miles per hour; he chose a Sunday so his church-going neighbors wouldn't see him and laugh. He made a larger, more sophisticated boat, brought it to New York, but investors there decided to put their money behind Fulton. "Blast his belly!" Morey would say, whenever his rival's name was mentioned. "He stole my patent!"

There's a boulder here I always use as a target—it's shaped like Half Dome in Yosemite, with one side shaved sheer—and when my bug rebounds down into the water, a bass immediately grabs it, making me laugh. This marks the upstream end of the rock garden. The railroad tracks veer farther from the river as the banks become higher and sand-ier, with a pronounced curl on their tops like the crests of frozen waves. The birch give way to white pine, which isn't good news for the bank's stability; most of the pines lean outward over the river, and when they fall they take great scoops of earth with them.

Until now, I've had it pretty easy as regards casting and tactics, but now I need to work harder. Casting underneath pine limbs can be chal-lenging; your casting stroke has to be more horizontal, so you're false casting along the plane of the river, sliding your bug in sideways like a jet landing on a runway rather than dropping it down like a helicopter to its pad. I've become reasonably proficient at this over the years, but this still means I frequently blow it and get my fly tangled around a branch. I usually just point my rod at it and break off, not wanting to frighten the fish, and then come back later to try and salvage what I can; sometimes, if I'm clumsy, the pines will resemble Christmas trees hung with ornaments and tinsel.

I'll be writing later about the big-fish water below Wilder Dam, but up here tactics are different. Poppers, those concave-faced floaters that pop, don't work well on this part of the river, and neither do the mice imitations that downstream bass love. Local bass are turned off by any splash or commotion. They're lovers of quietude, connoisseurs of calm. They favor sliders like the Sneaky Pete or the Boogle Bug, with noses that sit low in the water and don't make any fuss.

I'm guessing this is because they see so many dead insects, food that sits still on the table and doesn't hop about; to mimic this, you have to fish your fly slowly and/or have it play dead. Cast close to shore, tighten up on your slack, lower your rod tip, and wait—and wait and wait and wait. These bass like to look their bugs over before they take—they can't be rushed. This is true on most bass rivers, but is doubly true on the Connecticut—where the lazier you fish, the better.

The last pine, the tallest, forms a canopy over the water—my favorite spot for a tea break. The bottom here is firm red sand, which feels good on bare feet. I pull the canoe well up on the strand so the "tide" doesn't make off with it, find a contemplative spot to pee, come back to the canoe for the thermos, stand there in the blue-green shade of my miniature private beach, looking things over while chewing on a blueberry muffin and sipping away at my mug.

You get in a zone while fishing where the wider picture can be lost. Sometimes I come away feeling I haven't seen anything beside the water under my fly, the fly itself, and the bass that come up for it—and yet I've seen these with extraordinary clarity and focus. This can carry over to the wider picture if and when I remember to look up, as the intense, concentrated beam I bring to fishing catches a flash of light, a play of water, a cloud. Heightened reality? Not quite that—but reality one or two clicks sharper than when I'm not fishing.

Take the bank right behind me, the one rippled in overlapping chevrons of sunlight that become more pronounced where they enter the water and refract. If I were fishing this stretch from a canoe, concentrating on my casts, it would just be background, literally *back*ground—a sandy, barely noticeable haze backing the vibrant halo of light that was my fly. Now, staring up close at it, I can see this section of bank is its own self-contained world, with enough variety and movement that you could stare at it for an hour and not be bored.

It's eroded, concave, rising a steep twenty feet above me and extending for no more than five or six yards before its width is absorbed by the softer mass of undergrowth on either side. The erosion has exposed the pine roots, which bulge like cords out from the sand, and then taper to beard-like gray whiskers as they approach the river. The breeze doesn't penetrate the pines, it's perfectly still here, and yet little runnels of sand slide down in miniature avalanches the width of my pinkie—reaching water, these spread apart into finger-shaped deltas. Reddish-green vines crisscross the center of the bank, hunting for objects vertical enough to wrap themselves around them and climb; some of these vines are so thick, so looping, a Tarzan could use them as a swing. Spiderwebs use twigs for anchors, then bulge outward, inhaling and exhaling in gossamer breaths. The concavity of the bank acts like an oven, trapping the heat, but this is softened by the shade cast by those pines.

A lot to look at and enjoy—but then, when I back away to peer up toward the crest, some barely noticeable disturbance or sixth sense makes me turn around and face the water. I've left my fly dangling out back of the canoe with my rod resting on the seat. The line has come tight now, as the current swings the fly into the back eddy near shore. A bass has seen it . . . he's clearly visible against the sandy bottom . . . and he's slowly adjusting his position until he's ten inches below it and ten inches behind; a Spitfire stalking a Messerschmitt would assume just this pose. He waits there . . . in total indifference, it seems at first . . . and then, the very second I grab for the rod, comes up in the water and takes the Sneaky with solid muscularity that instantly turns (I feel this in my wrist) into total surprise. He jumps in exclamation marks—straight up, straight down, with a splashy circle—and then, before the surprise wears off and he can really start punching, I have him over to the bank, unhooked and released, none the worse for this thirty-second lesson in life's unpredictability.

You don't often do this on the Connecticut, sight fish for bass—of all the fish I catch today, this will be the one I enjoy the most. Time for celebration. I pour myself a second cup of tea, break off another piece of muffin, and then wiggle my butt around until I've scooped out a comfortable platform in the bank.

The upstream view is one I never tire of, including as it does a sweeping expanse of river, low hills beginning their serrated rise toward Mount Moosilauke, and a beautiful reach of marshland, with pliant green bullrushes that make me remember Sunday school stories about Moses. Gorgeous stuff—and yet, in all the years I've lived here, I probably have fished it only four or five times. The reason is partly logistical . . . the canoe launch is a good distance downstream, and I've about reached my limit when it comes to upstream paddling . . . and partly pragmatic: I've never caught a bass in that upstream section, not a one, and see no reason to do anything but admire it from afar.

This brings up a puzzling theoretical I think about often. Would I visit the Connecticut if it didn't hold bass? Would I just come out and admire its beauty from the canoe, float leisurely down the current, paddle in to examine the banks, marshes, and coves, rod-less, content just to look?

Probably not. No—certainly not. I need the bass, the possibility of encountering them, to make the river's beauty come to life. I need the atavistic sharpening of focus that fishing brings; I need the connection to the fish, the literal connection, to tug me into the experience rather than just drifting over its surface. Fishing for bass, guessing where they might be, deciding how to tempt them, pulling back against their power, allows me to enter; without this, I feel horribly passive, locked out of the experience with no way in.

This is a difficult concept to explain to non-fishing friends. I'll be hiking along an upland brook with them, ask if it contains any trout, and, being told that it doesn't, will immediately lose interest in even looking at it; whereas, if they answer yes, my eyes immediately go binocular, even if I'm not carrying a rod—every rock, crevice, and trill becomes coated in significance. I probably love water more than I do fish, but I only love water that has fish in it—and I don't know how to say that less paradoxically.

The bass, an immigrant, has over the course of two centuries become the Connecticut River's quintessential creature, and if you learn where they live and how to catch them, you will be well on your way to making the river yours. And that's the last question I'm going to ponder before I shove off and resume fishing: how long *do* you have to fish a river before it becomes an essential part of you?

I've been exploring this stretch for thirty years now, have fished it countless times, caught more than a thousand smallmouth. Not once have I been bored. Between the satisfaction of renewing contact with a place so wonderfully familiar, and the delight of encountering new, never-seen-before variations, I come away feeling reassured and renewed. The world spins as it always spins—we're always glad to hear that. The world can still surprise and astonish us—at my age, we're glad to hear that, too.

For many years, I always returned the same way I came, staying tight to the Vermont bank, working any rocks I may have missed on my way upriver, catching holdout fish that avoided me the first time. Five years ago, on a whim, I paddled instead straight across to New Hampshire, explored that shore—and so that's the way I go home now, down the eastern side of the river.

A totally different waterscape. Cooperman Brook empties into a large cove so shallow and weedy it could be in Lousiana. A cluster of islands, none very large, creates maze-like passageways where kayakers often get lost, and call out asking the way back to the river. The flatness extends to the first downstream hayfield; unlike most of these flat areas, this one doesn't meet the river at an abrupt bank, but gradually flattens into a shallow fringe of marsh.

You get a saltwater feel, fishing this side. The release of the dam is exaggerated by the islands, the tidal effect is more pronounced, and the bass seem to move in and out of the delta based on what the flow is doing; you're thinking bonefish flats one moment, tidal rips the next. The bass are smart, wary, and scarce—but maybe I'm wrong on the "scarce" part, because last August I fished here during a flying ant hatch, and bass rose everywhere.

The best spot is where the outermost island curves toward the eastern bank, creating a weedy channel. I never use weedless hooks, but I probably should here, since every third cast brings in spinach. The other thing I should do is put on a wire leader, because pike will come up and slash off your popper, mugging you of five dollars and ninety-five cents.

Sometimes I manage to land one—sometimes as in right now. I stand up in the canoe to increase my casting range, flip my bug past the outer band of weeds into the clean water near shore, and the moment it lands there's the famous *explosion!* that fishing writers like to refer to when they describe the strike of a pike. Usually when this happens I lift my rod into nothingness . . . the pike's teeth have already gained purchase on the leader and snapped it . . . but this time my fly finds a corner of the pike's mouth where he can't get leverage, and for the next five minutes I have my hands full trying to bring it in.

It's strange about pike. Some will fight hard, some will fight medium, some won't fight at all. This one is bigger than what I usually catch, a good thirty inches, but its fight is schizoid—all fury one moment, all passivity the next. In the middle of things, out of curiosity, I let the line go slack. Immediately, the pike stops struggling . . . he hovers motionless in the water, a boxer on his stool between rounds, the bug dangling like a mouthguard from his lip . . . and then, when I resume pressure, he's all fight again, zipping this way and that, but somehow eluding the weeds that would surely mean his safety.

I handle him carefully—the vulpine, bayonet sharpness of his jaw would frighten you even if you didn't get a glimpse of those stiletto teeth. The fact that pike are slimy adds to the difficult of releasing them; they're beautifully slimy, silver-and-white slimy, naturally slimy, bursting-with-health slimy, but slimy all the same.

The pike comes as a bonus, a gratuity, on an already good day. I pick up the pace, casting every ten yards instead of trying to fish every inch. The wildlife viewing is better along this shore, with so many hiding places. Deer on the island are a common sight, sloppy beaver lodges (never so round and neat on a river as they are on ponds) get mixed in with the blowdowns, and this is the most likely place on the river to find otters.

I see three of them now out in the middle, bobbing like the humps of an undulating river monster, a local version of Scotland's Nessie or Lake Champlain's Champ. They get a wave, since they're fishing just like me.

I've been out three hours, worked fairly hard, and yet there are still plenty of spots to try on the way home. One is ten feet from where I launched the canoe this morning, ten feet from where I'll be shoving it back up on shore. An old stump sits on the bottom in a salad-like bed of weeds, and is clearly visible even when the flow is high. It's probably a leftover from the log-drive days, and, facing upstream, the current has hollowed it out over the years, so it resembles a topless, bottomless barrel lying on its side.

Bass like to sit just upstream of its rim. Why is hard to figure out, since it doesn't really shelter them from anything; maybe they find it comforting, the way tropical fish find ornaments comforting on the bottom of an aquarium. When I bring a friend out fishing, I always let them have first crack at the bass here, since my guiding reputation is immediately enhanced if they manage to catch it. "Like shooting fish in a barrel!" I'll say, and we get a good laugh.

It's my turn today. I paddle just upstream of the stump, so the current will sweep my Sneaky over the sweet spot before the bass sees me. And since it's all about reassurance today, of going out to a place you love and finding it more lovable than ever, the bass immediately cooperates, splashing in a way that seems far more sudden and explosive than the pike's strike, even though I'm expecting it.

A good fish—and it gains in stature, in size, in desirability, but immediately breaks off. "Shit!" I yell, meaning good shit, priceless shit, the regret that *should* end a fishing day. This isn't New Zealand after all. This isn't even Montana. It's my home water, I don't have to fly here or spend big bucks. I can come tomorrow morning if I cancel that dentist's appointment, or tomorrow afternoon if I can't.

There's one last ritual I follow, before dragging the canoe back to the car. I stand on the bank and point out toward where I've been fishing, ticking bass caught off on my fingers—which today means all ten of them on the first pass, and eight more fingers on the second. We catch-and-release boys like bringing *something* home; for some, it's pictures; for me, it's a number—and so I'll be holding eighteen in the creel of my memory until I get home and write it down on the calendar.

And since I'm describing an ideal day, one where against all odds the world acts like we'd like it to act, there's one last image to bring home. A shadow crosses my shoulder and its coolness makes me glance up, just in time to see an osprey slanting down from a high pine toward the island, as if riding a zip line put there for that purpose. Osprey can whistle, but they can't carry much of a tune; if they could, this one would be singing *"America the Beautiful" or "This Land Is Your Land,"* so perfectly does it animate all that's classic in this riverscape. I watch as long as I can, until its brown blends into the trees, and the morning goes with it, as the river, my river, rolls on.

Nine

The bass I catch near home are wild fish, not native ones. The distinction is important and often overlooked. Whether a fish is wild, meaning spawned in a river or lake, not a hatchery, and/or native, meaning present in a body of water when Europeans first arrived on the scene, is something trout fishers talk about obsessively, but that bass fishers pretty much take for granted. Most of us realize there is really no such thing as a hatchery bass, so perforce the fish we catch are all wild, but we go on to assume that the bass has been here forever, so they must naturally be native, as well. At least here in New England—and in places like Oregon, Nevada, Montana, and Hawaii—we couldn't be more wrong.

There are old-timers up here whose grandfathers, fishing local waters, never caught a smallmouth or largemouth, probably barely knew the fishes existed. Bass only appeared in this state one hundred fifty years ago, and how they got here, *why* they got here, makes for an interesting story. A very American story. For if you compare the black bass's conquest of the continent and the white man's conquest of the continent, the similarities are striking.

A population is established in a confined corner of the continent, and then, sensing a opportunity, a vacuum, it begins to spread outward, gaining tenuous footholds beyond its original range, displacing the natives, reproducing prolifically, adapting to new conditions and challenges, encouraged in some places, fought against in others, becoming more and more aggressive, exterminating competitors when it has to, fulfilling an unstoppable version of Manifest Destiny, until at last, in our own day, its domination is complete.

The analogy is perfect—up to a point. For while white men came to America from Europe, spreading westward from a thin coastal fringe, bass were here all along; when they spread across the continent, it was in four compass directions from their ancient home in the central heartland. So—if we're comparing degrees of American heritage, throwing priority and precedence into the equation—the bass has us beat. We were good at pioneering, but the bass proved even better.

The heartland I'm talking about, for smallmouth, were the waters of the lower Great Lakes and their tributaries, down to the watershed of the Ohio. It touched western New York in the east, the Ozarks in the south, and Iowa in the west—with the line of one hundred degrees longitude acting as a kind of bar on one side, and the Allegheny highlands blocking them on the other. The largemouth's original range overlapped this on the south, and continued down to the Gulf of Mexico.

Bass, in other words, held the continent's midsection, and they would probably have been content to remain there forever—but then, about the time the Civil War finished, something major happened, something that took the bass from being America's greatest homebody—the Midwesterners who liked things just fine where they were; the Southerners content to sit in a rocker on the porch—to becoming America's greatest migrant, the compulsive hitchhiker, the hobo, the rolling stone.

What happened to bass? The white man happened. Pails happened. Milk cans happened. Canals happened. Railroads happened. Roads.

Let's start with canals, since it was their rapid construction, starting in the 1780s, that gave black bass their first great chance to roam. The completion of the 360-mile-long Erie Canal in 1825 allowed the Great Lakes bass to spread eastward through the barrier uplands of New York—but the Erie was only the most famous of the 18,000 canals constructed across the country, adding more than 3,000 miles of inland waterways to the network that was originally here. On their own, without any additional help from man, bass began spreading up these to rivers and lakes they never had access to before. Bass, while not long-range migrants like salmon or shad, will still cover serious distances if given the chance; fishery biologists in Wisconsin using acoustic transmitters have tracked individual bass traveling as far as forty-five miles to seek out a place to spend the winter, and they can be carried even farther in springtime floods.

By the 1850s, bass had accomplished something vitally import-ant when it came to evolutionary politics: convinced man they were a highly desirable species, worthy of being transplanted to waters where they had never been found. This was first accomplished by their taste, their edibility—"As a food fish," one writer of the day put it, "there are few, if any, more palatable, its flesh being firm, white and flaky, and when cooked, nutty, tender and juicy"—and then by Civil War days, by their fighting ability on the end of a line. Everyone wanted bass now, for food and/or sport, and with the extensive canal system already in place, with railroads about to enter their golden age, the infrastructure to transport them across the continent was readily at hand.

This was mostly low-tech at first—nothing fancy was needed to transport bass. It's not a fish that lends itself to hatchery reproduction, since, unlike trout, the fingerlings are hatched with a very small yolk sac, and, to seek nourishment, they must start hunting almost immediately after birth. The good news is that you can dump young fish into a river or lake and they will almost always thrive there—many famous bass waters were originally stocked by a mere handful of fish and have never needed stocking since.

Here's where the milk cans came in. Doctor Henshall, writing in 1881, described for his readers the appropriate containers to use for transplanting:

> For small bass, the largest size wash-tubs are well adapted; if barrels are used, they need not be perfectly new, but they should not retain any vestiges of their former contents, as vinegar, oil or whisky. Metal tanks, constructed of galvanized iron, though more expen-sive, are to be preferred.

Fill a whisky barrel with bass, load it on a canal boat or train, have a horse and wagon ready for the last stretch, and you could easily stock almost any body of water you wanted to stock. And sportsmen, now that the salmon runs were extinguished in the East by overfishing and dams—and the native brook trout were taking a hit from pollution—had no compunctions, environmental or other, in bringing bass in to fill the vacuum.

You can go back to the sporting pages of the day and read the history of these stockings. In 1853, for example, a General W. W. Shriver of Wheeling, West Virginia, welcomed the completion of the Baltimore & Ohio Railroad to his city, since he immediately saw the possibility of taking smallmouth from west of the Alleghenies and stocking them east of the mountains. He enlisted the aid of Alan G. Stabler, a conductor on the railroad and an avid bass fisher. (In the history of the bass's diaspora, railroad conductors played a prominent role.)

The men took thirty smallmouth from a creek in Wheeling, the general personally accompanying them on the ride to Cumberland, Maryland, "carrying my fish in a large bucket, perforated, which I made to fit in the opening in the water tank attached to the locomotive, which was supplied with fresh water at the water stations along the route."

Reaching Cumberland, the bass were dumped into a canal basin, which gave them access to the Potomac River. This meant two hundred miles of river to colonize—and, in the Shenandoah, a tributary that suited them even better. All this . . . the untold numbers of bass caught in the years since, the million of hours of angling pleasure . . . from a single initial stocking of thirty fish!

And so it went. Bass were introduced in Massachusetts in 1850, with a tank of twenty smallmouth imported from Saratoga Lake in New York. Maine got is first smallmouth in 1869, the same year bass were introduced into Pennsylvania's Susquehanna and Delaware. There were catastrophes along the way—barrels spilled, water became too warm, hobos would help themselves to a free dinner—but, when you read about it, what's striking is how *easy* it all was, thanks to the bass's hardiness and adaptability. The white man fought hard and suffered much as he expanded across the continent; all the bass had to do was wave a seductive fin at the conductor and hop aboard a freight.

Henshall is a good source of stocking stories, both successful and otherwise. He explains how the South Fork Fishing and Hunting Club of Pennsylvania took 650 bass from Sandusky, Ohio, and transported them to their lake ninety miles east of Pittsburgh in 1881, using fifteen oak casks to which ice was added, and oxygen via a special pump. The stocking went well—in a few years, club members were enjoying fabulous fishing—but they should have been paying more attention to the state of their lake's dam. It gave way under heavy rainstorms in 1889, unleashing twenty million gallons of bass water all at once, killing 2,209 people downstream in the Great Johnstown Flood.

If you have a cache of old *Forest and Streams* in the attic, or are willing to pore through old musty fisheries reports, you can get a rough idea of how the process worked. More formal studies, ones that examine in great detail how bass came to waters that had never known them before, are much rarer—and so it gives me much pleasure to report that one of the best of these histories concerns the state that is mine.

It's called *The Bassing of New Hampshire* and it's written by a friend of mine named Jack Noon, who lives across the hills from me in Sutton. About thirty years ago, while researching local history and genealogy, he became interested in the history of the great salmon runs that once upon a vanished time graced the Connecticut River along the western part of the state—so interested that he began extensive research at the state archives in Concord. The deeper he delved into the history of the state's fisheries, the more he was struck by how, into the great vacuum left by the salmon run's extinction (and the decline of such local treasures as the Lake Sunapee golden trout), smallmouth bass opportunistically rushed. This, he realized, was *the* big story when it came to New Hampshire fishing, and he was soon devoting a considerable amount of time discovering just exactly how bass conquered the state.

Jack's book begins by describing the vacuum, and it makes for sad reading. In Colonial days, the Connecticut River teemed with salmon and shad, but overfishing (not only for local tables, but to supply dried and pickled fish to feed slaves on sugar plantations in the West Indies), and the early construction of dams (one was built across the Connecticut as early as 1794), severely depleted the runs of anadromous fish.

The completion of a high dam at Turner's Falls in Massachusetts in 1797 completely sealed off the upper river; by 1800 the spectacular spawning runs of salmon were already a thing of the past (though forlorn efforts to restore the run were only abandoned in 2011). Various fisheries commissions established by the state of New Hampshire lamented the sorry state of things, and called for something dramatic to be done about it. The commissioners had heard good things about smallmouth bass, though they had probably never actually seen one. Could importing the feisty Midwesterner be the fisheries' salvation?

Private citizens were already well ahead of the government. I mentioned earlier that Massachusetts had gotten its first bass in 1850, as detailed in a report by the U.S. Commission of Fish and Fisheries.

In 1850, twenty-seven bass were taken by Mr. Samuel Tisdale of East Wareham, Mass., from Saratoga Lake, New York, and put into Flax Lake near his home. In the years 1851 and 1852, others were brought to the number of 200 and reared in ponds in the vicinity. The matter was kept quiet, and fishing discouraged for five years, when the fish were found to have increased very rapidly. Some twenty-five ponds were stocked in the same county; afterwards, black bass from Mr. Tisdale's pond were supplied to a lake in New Hampshire in 1867.

Tisdale was a wealthy, well-connected man, numbering Daniel Webster among his fishing buddies. In 1849, he gave a commission to a friend named Preston H. Hodges who ran a hotel in New York. "In the proper season next year," Mr. Tisdale proposed, "if you will procure the bass at some convenient point and convey them to Wareham, I will pay all bills, except your time, which you must take from the fund of amusement consequent in the capture of that historic game fish, which, to me, is a stranger."

Hodges accepted, and the following June traveled west to Saratoga Lake near the fashionable resort, promptly caught twenty smallmouth, put them in tanks, and started by rail for Wareham.

> On his arrival at Springfield, Mass., the vitiated water was drawn from the banks and ice water was introduced in its steady, and, strange to relate, in a few moments every fish turned up dead. Mr. Hodges took the first train west for Saratoga, and again was successful, as he captured twenty more bass, and again shaped his course for Wareham, via rail to Albany, from thence by boat to New York where he changed the water. He then embarked on a Fall River steam to Fall River, from thence by rail to East Wareham, where he arrived with his nineteen bass, one having died on the trip. The fish were placed in Flax Pond, a small sheet of water near Mr. Tisdale's residence, at 10:45 o'clock on the 4th day of July, 1850.

Nice, that last touch—the All-American fish arriving in their new home on the most All-American of occasions. And how fitting—the bass starting its conquest of New England from within casting distance of Plymouth Rock. I've fished Flax Pond, waded around its edges, and caught some of the original fish's descendants.

It's not quite certain which was the New Hampshire water body that got those first Massachusetts imports, but Jack Noon thinks it was probably Rust Pond in the center of the state. This is our Lakes Region, and once the bass were established in Rust, it was simply a question of filling a few barrels with water, loading them on a horse and buggy, dumping some bass in, then carting them over a ridge or two until you could deposit them in a bigger lake like Winnipesaukee or Winnisquam.

Working independently over on the western side of the state, a fish culturist named Livingston Stone established a fish hatchery in Charlestown on the banks of the Connecticut River; he began advertising "Eggs in Season, Trout of all Ages" and, as something of an afterthought, "Also Black Bass." He apparently found his fish in Lake Champlain and transported them by rail back to his hatchery, and became accidentally responsible for putting the first bass into the Connecticut River when, in 1867, some of his fish escaped from the hatchery down a convenient feeder stream.

(Mr. Stone went on to play a significant role in the bass's continental expansion. Working as a U.S. Deputy Fish Commissioner, he established an "aquarium car" for railroad transport of live fish from coast to coast, and used it to bring the first black bass to California in 1847.)

Seeing what private efforts had achieved, the state decided to get in on the act, and began its own stocking program in 1868, although, as Jack explains, they had to proceed by trial and error.

> It would take several years for the fisheries commissioners to learn that the best way to establish bass in new waters is simply to stock live fish and protect them from fishing for a few years, and to avoid trying to work with bass eggs. The fish hatchery methods used with trout and salmon didn't work with bass. Trout and salmon eggs occur singly and are easily stripped from females by hand pressure, and fertilized artificially, with similarly stripped milt, on hatching trays. Bass eggs are linked in strings and are difficult to impossible to strip, artificially fertilize and incubate.

Dr. William Fletcher, a Concord dentist, was deputized by the state and sent to Lake Champlain to bring back enough bass to stock as many New Hampshire lakes as possible. At the same time, in one of the earliest fishing laws ever passed in the state, fishing for bass was prohibited for five years, meaning no one could legally take one until 1873.

The modest stocking program, the sensible five-year restriction, worked spectacularly—by the time fishermen were allowed to keep bass, there were reports coming in of numerous smallmouth in the four- and five-pound range. Some of these fish were put into a millpond on the Sugar River in Newport in 1870, and it didn't take them long to find their way down to the Connecticut, reinforcing the cadre that fled there from Livingston Stone's porous hatchery.

It's important to remember that the state's initial stocking effort was prompted by a desire to provide a new and abundant source of food to help make up for the salmon's and shad's disappearance, not by any sporting motives. The 1872 report of the fisheries commission made the point that "the sooner we get bass into all suitable waters in large numbers, the sooner we shall have an abundance of valuable food for all classes of people."

Admirable—but this is New Hampshire we're talking about, and even in those days it was a notoriously conservative and cranky state. Wasn't providing free bass perilously close to providing free welfare?

The commissioners had their answer ready:

Some have objected to the enterprise of stocking bass into New Hampshire on the ground that the more fish we have, the more we should encourage a set of lazy fellows to fish, who are too lazy to do anything but fish. Now, suppose we admit that to be a fact, it is an argument in favor of the enterprise, for we all know that these lazy fellows catch next to nothing now, whereas if bass were plentiful, they would catch fish for themselves and others to eat, and would thereby keep themselves from the poor farm. If the number of lazy who will not work but will fish is half as large as some would have us believe, would it not be wise for the state to create an industry by which this large body of its citizens might with certainty benefit themselves and the whole community?

And yet the motive for stocking bass soon changed, going from supplying food for layabouts, to providing cash for the eager beavers, the entrepreneurial, the wide-awake. Hotel owners, their local lakes now bereft of trout, found that sportsmen were just as willing to come north for the smallmouth fishing, and, even better, to bring along their families, taking advantage of the latest American social innovation, the two-week vacation.

More leisure time, more disposable income, a flourishing network of fishing publications eager to tell people where to spend the first and how to spend the second, a passenger railway system more efficient than anything we have today, enabling vacationers to leave the city in the morning and be fishing by late afternoon. All these formed the perfect cultural and economic conditions for bass fishing to take off. Bass, not for the last time in their history, were bringing in the bucks.

Picture an avid New York City angler planning his summer vacation with his family circa 1898. He could wire ahead for reservations at the Lakeside House on Lake Sunapee, lured by its advertising "one hundred and fifty feet of piazza, free from dust and dirt, rowboats free, everything new and nice, with A-1 tables and beds, prices $7.00 to $12.00 per week"; or, if that was too pricey, he could book a week at the Grandliden hotel on the lake, which claimed to have "the best bass fishing in New England."

Reservation booked, it was time to see to equipment. Our angler could go to E. Vom Hofe's shop on Fulton Street in lower Manhattan to purchase one of their highly regarded reels; or, if he lived uptown, drop in on the famous William Mills & Sons shop on Park Place, which, as well as being the "sole agents for H. L. Leonard Split Bamboo Rods," stocked Henshall rods for bass fishing, starting at $1.50. And a visit to the Goodyear Indian Rubber Glove M'fg Co. on Broadway might be in order, too, to purchase "a complete rubber outfit for fishing." And let's not forget something for those annoying mosquitoes and black flies. *Forest and Stream* carried an advertisement for "Jumbolene" made in Maine, with a picture of Jumbo the famous elephant squirting repellant from his trunk to scare away the flies pestering his back. Surely Mills must stock some? And, while we're there, let's outfit ourselves in a fishing suit made of "Olivauto Cloth," the fabric adopted by the new U. S. Forestry Service.

Lures? Best to purchase these ahead of time, in case they're hard to find up in the mountains. The Stanley Smelt sounds promising—"The most natural artificial bait, made of solid aluminum, invented by Fish Commissioner Henry O. Stanley." Hildebrandt spinners were said to work well, as were Crab Wigglers made by James Heddon Son's Co. of Dowagiac, Michigan—"the biggest teasers ever tossed to a bass." For seventy-five cents more, you can add in a Rush Tango Minnow, which glows at night, or, for the same price, Louis Rhea's dynamite new bass plug, the Waga-Waga—though, if you want this with a carved wooden propellor instead of the normal steel blades, you have to fork over twenty-five cents extra.

A lavish outlay, even before it's time to leave. But no matter—you only go on vacation once a year. You take the Boston & Maine coach to Claremont, transfer to a horse and buggy, and then, to reach the hotel proper (the wife's decided on the Lakeside House on account of its piazza), you hop the "staunch little *Lady Woodsum* steamer," which drops you right at the hotel's dock.

If you're lucky, the hotel supplies a beautiful Adirondack boat, like the kind advertised by Frederick D. Graves of Boston for $70. If not, you content yourself with a lowly rowboat, though maybe there's a newfangled Waterman Porto motor on the back, which allows you to "troll at any speed with any size or type of boat." And, if those expensive new lures don't coax up the bass, the bellhop has told you about a lad named Zane Pushee over in Sunapee Harbor who can dig you up all the worms you'd ever want and only charge you a nickel.

(I'm just old enough to remember participating in this vanished world myself. Lured by an advertisement and the recommendation of a friend, my parents drove our family up from Long Island to Lake Sunapee for our summer vacation in 1955, when I was seven. We stayed at Indian Cave Lodge, a rambling spread of a place right on the water. I remember fishermen coming to the dock with stringers full of fish, though I never learned what kind they were. I also remembering participating in a "scavenger hunt" and our team finding everything on the list but the last item, a "Gray Ghost," something none of us New Yorkers had ever heard of, but which frightened me just by its name.)

By the 1880s, New Hampshire could claim total victory for its smallmouth program—there was no longer any need to stock them, they were flourishing on their own, despite there being no catch limits whatsoever. In future years, smallmouth would occasionally be brought into new lakes as contract hit men, to deal with overpopulations of yellow perch, but the next time the state did any large-scale stocking would be in the 1950s with largemouth bass.

Even a dogged researcher like Jack Noon isn't sure how or when largemouth reached New Hampshire. They may have snuck in with the smallmouth . . . no one was going through aquarium cars checking identity papers . . . or they may have been privately stocked from largemouth waters in Massachusetts. There were largemouth haters . . . "In the New England states," a fisheries expert lamented, "the smallmouth bass has thrived while its brother has been neglected because of an absurd prejudice of considering the big-mouth bass to be an inferior fish" . . . but other fishery people recognized that largemouth were suitable for muddy, weed-choked ponds in the state. Soon enough there were fishermen who preferred them to smallmouth, to the point they began illegally stocking them on their own.

The bass program's success led the state to try introducing other species: landlocked salmon in 1867; walleye in 1876; Loch Leven brown trout, and rainbows from the West Coast, in 1888; Chinook salmon in 1904; cohos in 1909. The landlocks did reasonably well, the walleye somewhat better, the browns and rainbows, with frequent restockings, survived in their artificial way, and the Pacific salmon disappeared. None of them flourished like the bass did.

"By the end of the first half century," Noon concludes, "a bass could pass as a New Hampshire native as readily as any human whose third or fourth generation ancestors had been from away. Both fit in, and both had come to stay."

In looking at the history of the black bass's conquest of America, it's important to remember that they weren't welcomed everywhere with open arms. One man's desirable import is another man's invasive alien, and there was a kind of fishy xenophobia at work in the nineteenth century, an anti-immigrant prejudice that, with some justice, worried that the bass would gobble up what salmonids were left. This, after all, was well before the days of environmental impact studies. People, often amateurs, thought it would be a good idea to put bass in their lake, the means to do so were cheap and simple, and so they did it, end of story.

Even in New Hampshire there were second thoughts about whether the stocking program had been worth it. "It is impossible after bass have been once established ever to get rid of them," one fishery commissioner lamented in 1908.

> It is true we think that there are more fishermen come to New Hampshire to fish for black bass than any other variety of fresh water fish. But for all that we wish that lakes that are adapted to salmon and trout could have been reserved for them and the black bass confined to selected waters by themselves.

Too late for that. And the bass, when impugned, had no shortage of defenders, including the irrepressible Dr. Henshall, who pooh-poohed the bass's reputation at a killer.

> In reference to objections urged against the introduction of black bass into eastern waters, upon the theory that the presence of the "voracious" bass would mitigate against the increase of shad, trout or salmon. The objections are not founded on fact, for the black bass prefers a diet of crawfish, varying it with minnows, insects, larvae and frogs. While the bass will take a young shad or salmon if it comes his way when hungry, he will not make them special objects of pursuit . . . The man who alleges that the bass depopulates the streams of valuable food fishes, or asserts that he kills "for the love of it," has never looked into the mouth of the bass with his eyes open, for its teeth on both jaws are brush-like, incapable of wounding.

Henshall is being disingenuous here—with a mouth like an industrial crusher, the bass has no need of teeth. But to Henshall's credit, he urges that bass *not* be introduced into waters where trout flourish, but only to those where cold-water species have disappeared. And he correctly points out that the damage being done to trout and salmon came more from unregulated fishing with nets and spears, construction of dams, and industrial pollution, than it did from bass.

Welcome newcomer? Invasive intruder? The bass as hero or the bass as villain was a long-running debate, and it's still not over. Witness this recent article from a California newspaper.

A highly aggressive species of fish has been found in Lake Tahoe, and environmentalists are afraid the non-native invader will gobble up native fish and ruin decades of work to improve water quality. A smallmouth bass was recently spotted by a team of researchers, ripe with eggs, indicating that the fish are reproducing and have probably already spread around the mile-high lake.

"It really shocked us," said Sudeeep Chandrfa, a university limnologist working with the California Department of Fish and Game on a study of invasive species. "You can think of it this way: There is a new bully in the neighborhood."

Introduced species like bass have hurt water quality by excreting nutrients that cause algae blooms; they are ferocious predators that are likely to feed on Tahoe's native redside dace, suckers and chub; they could also hamper efforts by the U. S. Fish and Wildlife Service to reintroduce native Lahonta trout to the Sierra lake, which is the second-deepest in the world.

The article says nothing about how the bass got there, though the usual suspect in these cases is bass tournament fishers stocking on their own; it's a lot more fun chasing smallmouth around Lake Tahoe with your bass boat than it is chasing redside dace.

Even here in New England, just when you'd think it was a settled issue, the expansion of the bass's range still causes controversy. Lake Umbagog, straddling New Hampshire's northeastern border with Maine, was for many years the region's last stronghold of salmon and wild brook trout. Bass began showing up in Umbagog in the late 1980s, stocked by bass lovers gone rogue. The wheel had turned full circle by then; bass were the desirable fish now, thanks to tournaments and the

Saturday morning fishing shows, and trout were looked upon by some as elitist and effete.

But Umbagog is not just any body of water—it's part of the Rangeley chain of lakes, and its feeder stream, Rapid River, has long been one of the most famous salmon and trout waters in the country. Bass, once they were established in Umbagog, found nothing to stop them if they swam up the Rapid, much to the dismay of flyfishers casting for trout.

(I was one of them. Bowing to no one in my admiration for smallmouth, I was still bitterly disappointed to find one on the end of my line when I had driven many hours to fish for landlocks and brookies. But it's worth pointing out that when I gave up fishing the Rapid fifteen years ago, it was the hordes of fishermen and kayakers that drove me away, not the bass.)

Maine's fisheries department has had some success beating back the bass from the Rapid by using Middle Dam to lower water levels during spawning season in the spring. Biologist Dave Boucher reports, "We may be seeing some stabilization in bass numbers," but stabilization is a long way from eradication (picture Samoset telling his tribe, "We've seen some stabilization in Pilgrim numbers"), so it looks like the bass has added the Rangeleys to his long list of conquests.

Further north in Maine's northeast corner, it's not the smallmouth that's the enemy—the smallmouth is the fish the region is famous for now, the one that brings in sportsmen's bucks—but the largemouth, which is seen as the intrusive evil brother. Again, individuals acting on their own decided to stock largemouth in the St. Croix flowage, and so the state has declared war.

(Who *are* these people, I sometimes wonder. Do they wear camouflage? What kind of music are they listening to, what are their politics, what are they drinking? "Largemouth stocker!" you feel like screaming at them—but it's not an epithet that rolls easily off the tongue.)

"Washington County is one of the nation's premiere smallmouth fishing destinations," Fisheries Commissioner Chandler E. Woodcock declares, "and this single introduction of largemouth could jeopardize the fishery in more than 18,000 acres." Then, speaking directly to

Maine's anglers, he flat out says it: "If you catch a species that you believe is not known to inhabit the waterbody, kill it."

Kill! Form war parties! Drive the white man back across the Mississippi! The drama and melodrama of the bass's expanding range is far from over. The next big challenge will come—is coming right now—from how well they deal with climate change. Will increased water temperatures stop bass expansion dead in its tracks, or will it suit them perfectly? These are, after all, "warmwater" fish.

The answer seems to involve latitude. New York and Ontario have their fisheries experts studying the issue—and *Effects of Climate and Global warming on year-class strength and relative abundance of smallmouth bass in Eastern Lake Ontario* is the result. Its conclusion, reached after many closely reasoned pages, is that, for bass this far north, global warming may be no bad thing. "Climate warming could substantially increased the recruitment and abundance of smallmouth bass at this latitude, not only dramatically increasing smallmouth abundance, but increasing available habitat in inshore waters."

The study's authors add a caveat—if water temperature heats up by more than four degrees centigrade, all bets are off.

The Great Lakes represent the northern edge of the smallmouth's original range, the coolest edge, so there's some wiggle room if things heat up. Studies done in the Pacific Northwest also predict smallmouth expansion. But in lower latitudes, famous smallmouth rivers like the Susquehanna, Delaware, and Allegheny are already taking a serious hit, with record summer temperatures heating the water to above 90 degrees Fahrenheit, enough for major bass kills, and a dramatic falling off of the fishing, to the point many devoted smallmouth fishers are hanging up their rods.

As for largemouth, global warming seems to suit them just fine, or at least that's what the various bass magazines claim, with, it must be said, unseemly glee. Summers of unbearable heat? Virginia become Florida? New Hampshire become Virginia? "Bring it on!" you can hear them saying—and in the meantime, plans for climate-controlled, air-conditioned bass boats are surely well advanced.

And there's another irony to throw in the equation, one that works to the bass's advantage, bizarre as it sounds.

Increasingly high levels of mercury and/or cadmium in bass tissue . . . the residue of power plants and industrial burnings . . . have made them dangerous to eat. New Hampshire and many other states now recommend that pregnant and nursing women, and women who may one day become pregnant, eat not more than one eight-ounce serving a month (and none whatsoever from the Connecticut River); everyone else can safely eat just a little more. This toxicity keeps them out of the frying pan, so catch-and-release becomes, just not a sporting imperative, but a health one. And irony upon irony—that New England bass are being poisoned by airborne pollution blowing from their original home in the country's midsection.

Bass, if they make the mistake of taking your lure, can now do so in almost complete confidence it won't result in their being eaten.

At the start of this chapter, I wondered aloud how and why the bass I catch in the Connecticut River came to be there. It turns out the answer is complex, involving biology, environmentalism, the history of American transportation, changing cultural attitudes, journalism, chemistry, industrial poisons, bureaucratic activism and bureaucratic neglect, and a multilayered web of circumstances, some planned, some accidental. A lot of history for a twelve-inch bass to carry on its back—and yet it's part of the wonder when I catch one, this fish that, when it comes to conquering the continent, is even more American than us.

Ten

Raymondo and I drove up to Maine last week to fish the Penobby for smallies—and when we weren't casting bass bugs, we had fun slinging around nicknames, the kind our guide liked to use. "Hey Raymondo!" I'd yell, or "Penobby's looking fishy this morning!" or, "Those smallies sure can fight!" After a week of this we went back home, Raymondo restored to Ray, Penobby to Penobscot, smallies to smallmouth, harmed not the slightest by having been called something sillier. A great five days, and while I never take photos, I came back with a notebook full of impressions.

It was an occasion of sorts, this fishing trip of ours. In fifty years of chasing bass, I'd never left home to fish for them. I travel plenty for trout—Montana, British Columbia, Labrador, and, just last autumn, Slovenia. We daydream about trout and salmon in a way we don't about bass—our fantasies involve rising browns on the Rio Gallegos, not largemouth in Lily Pad Pond. And that's not to diminish bass in any way. Quite the opposite. We have to travel to trout because in most places we've chased them away, banished them into exile, made them exotic, to the point where the first step in fishing for them isn't grabbing your waders and filling the car with gas, but booking tickets for destinations half a world away.

Not so with bass. Because of their greater adaptability and tolerance, they're right out the door waiting to play. This cheapens them in some eyes—How can they be a great fish if they live right *here*?—but not mine. And then of course I'm lucky to live in great bass country, where I can encounter fifteen bass in a morning's fishing, with every expectation that one of them will be pushing twenty inches.

So there are few bass destinations to rival the Patagonias of the world, or even the West Yellowstones. Among the most famous of the few is the northeast corner of Maine, Down East Maine, where the smallmouth fishing is aggressively advertised and promoted, attracting bass fishers from more crowded parts of the country. (But not, oddly, all that many from the state itself. "Even today, some Maine residents scorn bass as a tourist fish," wrote Charles Waterman. "'Oh, bass are all right, I guess,' a resort owner told me. 'There's a man over in Portland who even eats the damned things!'")

Within Maine, the Penobscot River is the most storied stretch of water, with many claiming it's the best smallmouth river in North America. Why I waited so long to fish it is a real mystery, since I live only a half-day's drive away—but now I've done it, and found it's the water I should have been daydreaming about all along.

Even those who vacation in Maine, sticking to the lobster coast, don't realize how big the state truly is. The rest of New England works on a cozy scale, with a landscape cushioned by hills and softened by ponds, but Maine is almost as large as the other five states put together—and once you drive north of Augusta, the land takes on a Western sort of feel, with big sky, giant clouds, and a long way between exits. The speed limit on the interstate is seventy-five mph, and, with the landscape so low and vast, doing that down the inclines gives you the soaring sensation of flight.

Ray likes to drive, while I like to push the seat back, prop my feet up on the dashboard, and play tour guide. I pointed out the spiky lupine growing on the shoulder in clumps of purple; I pointed out the low bluish protuberances in the east, the Camden Hills; I talked about the Maine Woods' most famous visitor.

"So, Thoreau made three trips up here, but the one we're interested in was his 1857 visit, when he canoed down the Penobscot right past where our cabin reservation is."

Ray glanced over at me. "Then it's a good thing we fished Walden Pond last year. Remember those carp sunning on the surface?"

"The wilderness made a huge impression on him. The last words he uttered before he died were 'moose' and 'Indian.'"

Once we passed Bangor, we hoped to get glimpses of Katahdin, Maine's iconic mountain, but where it should have been in the northeast was one of the most towering, impressive thunderheads I'd ever seen; it was as if the wilderness had been chopped off at its base, whirled into blackness, tossed as a concept into the sky.

Ray handed me his camera and I did my best, continuing as I did so my little spiel.

"On one of those trips Thoreau shared a stagecoach with the greatest white hunter in the woods, a man called Hiram L. Leonard. Hiram L. Leonard? Leonard fly rods? He was a gunmaker in Bangor, but in 1871 he began making the split-bamboo rods that made him famous."

"Yeah? Think Henry bought one?"

"No, because by then he was dead."

That's the kind of conversation we had, because it's always the conversation we have when driving to rivers—factoids from Wetherell, quips from Chapin. And then he frequently notices things that he thinks as a writer I shouldn't miss.

"That rest area we stopped at back there?" he said. "Did you see the signs on the trash? 'Barrel picking prohibited.'"

"Times are tough up here. The Great Recession—only here it started twenty years ago when the paper mills began closing."

Ray nodded, grimly. "I'm just saying."

We saw signs for Old Town now and decided to get off the highway for lunch. Old Town is where Old Town canoes have been made for over a century, and since I own four Old Towns (one of which sat on the car roof), it made sense to make a brief pilgrimage to see where they came from—it was like someone who's eaten bread all his life pulling over in Kansas to see his first wheat field.

In Thoreau's day, Old Town was famous for being where the Penobscot Indian tribe lived, on an island, in the middle of the river—and they live there still, on Indian Island reached by a short bridge from Main Street.

It was to this island in 1857 that Thoreau went to find a guide for his trip up the Allagash.

We were ferried across to the Indian island in a batteau. The ferryman told me that the Indians were generally all gone to the seaboard and to Massachusetts, partly on account of the small-pox, of which they are very much afraid, having broken out in Old Town. The first man we saw on the island was an Indian named Joe Polis, who was dressing a deerskin in his yard. He was stoutly built, perhaps a little above the middle height, with a broad face, and, as others said, perfect Indian features and complexion. We asked him if he knew any good Indians who would like to go into the woods with us, to which he answered, out of that strange remoteness in which the Indian ever dwells to white man, "Me like to go myself; me want to get some moose." We thought ourselves lucky to secure the services of this man, who was known to be particularly steady and trustworthy.

Forty minutes north of Old Town are the Scotty Cabins on the river's west bank. Ray has one peculiarity—and only one—that has caused some friction between us over the years. On a fishing trip, he likes to go fishing the moment we arrive at our destination, never mind how long it took to get there. Thus, on a trip once to Yellowstone, we left New Hampshire at 4:00 a.m., drove three hours to Boston, flew four hours to Phoenix, changed planes, flew an hour more to Salt Lake City, rented a car, drove five hours to Raynolds Pass, and were wading into the Madison at 10:00 that night.

I try to be a good sport—if Ray wanted to go fishing, it was fine by me. It had been a rainy month, and the Penobscot was far too high to risk floating, so Jeff, the cabin's young, affable owner, suggested we try one of the nearby lakes.

"South Fork Lake," he said, pulling out his DeLorme Atlas to show the back roads that led to it. "Lots of big bass come out of South Fork."

We liked the sound of it—like the fact we could actually pronounce it. One of the characteristics of the Maine woods is how difficult the place names are to say correctly, and how, when you stumble over the syllables, you feel like a helpless outsider. Nesowadnehunk. Debsconeag. Passadeumnkeag. Wytopitlog. Sysladobis. Mattasmisomis. We'd see intriguing place names on the map, try to ask Jeff about them, get the first syllable right, approximate the second, then mumble out the rest in a fast clumsy blur that didn't hide our incompetence. Jeff was used to this—he was very gentle with his corrections.

The road to South Fork passed through what used to be called a hamlet—a scattering of houses so isolated and lonely they didn't look to be part of any town.

"Look at all the flags," Ray said, as we slowed down.

Every house had an American flag out in front, some stuck in planters, others draped over mailboxes—but that was just the start. Flags flew from the telephone poles, from road signs, from backhoes, from trees. The impression they gave, with the rain, the isolation, was the exact opposite of festive.

"What happens if you don't want one on your house?" I asked.

Ray frowned. "Love it or leave it."

The flags continued all the way to the boat launch, where a bunch of bass boys were trailering out after a tournament. In the old days, we would have gone right over and asked about the fishing, maybe gotten a few tips as to where the best place was to start; nowadays you don't do this, now when you're fly-fishing and the other guy is spinning.

We got some baleful looks, loading a canoe, not a bass boat, stringing up fly rods, not Ugly Sticks. The great cultural divide in America extends even to recreation, so hikers disdain ATVers, snowmobilers hate ski tourers, kayakers look askance at Jet-Skiers, who in turn try to drown them. There's Blue recreation and Red recreation, just are there are Blue states and Red ones. It's the American Divide. You know—the *Divide*.

Or was this my imagination? The bass boys studiously avoided looking at us, and, when they did, I felt more the outsider than ever.

"It's not your imagination," Ray said helpfully. "It's that thing you're wearing."

That thing was my Buff, the breathable nylon balaclava I wear over my face to ward off sunburn. Apparently they haven't caught on yet in backwoods Maine.

(Boat launches, normally the most sociable of places, were freaking me out lately. Earlier in the month, fishing the Connecticut from a launch well north of my usual haunts, I came across a shrine where the macadam entered the water—one of those faded floral arrangements you see on highways where someone has crashed. But it didn't commemorate a crash or a drowning. Last winter, a schoolteacher, a wonderful woman, was brutally murdered by a husband and wife, a thrill killing done on a whim, and the victim's friends had put this wreath and a photo where her body had been dumped into the river.)

South Fork is a big, sprawling lake, very much in the Maine style, which means lots of islands, lots of rocks, lots of places bass can hide. We mounted the electric motor to give our arms a break, and then followed the shoreline out toward where the lake broadened, being careful to work all the jetties and points. And we caught fish—bluegills mostly, but now and again a bass, including a largemouth, which in a land made for smallmouth came as a real surprise.

We fished until the wind turned the rain horizontal, and then let it push us back to the landing. Ray had got his first afternoon of fishing in, I had started filling my notebook with scribbles, and the elements were just bad enough we felt justified in retreating back to the cabins for our reward: tuna casserole, rhubarb pie, Glenlivet Scotch.

Perfect fishing cabins are all alike. Made of logs, or half logs, without a foundation but raised up on concrete blocks. Small and cozy, with three cots in a sleeping loft reached by a ladder, and a narrow downstairs bedroom with bunks. Piled at the foot of these bunks, scratchy wool blankets, charcoal colored or dark green. A simple kitchen, gas range, a dented assortment of pots and pans, mugs from different NFL teams and/or stolen from local diners, a sugar bowl with no more than three teaspoons of sugar left, a saltshaker that, with a few hard taps, dispenses salt.

A shower wedged into a corner of the bathroom—a real fishing cabin never has a bathtub—and a broken bar of soap left in the drain, since you will have forgotten to bring your own. An end table piled with local newspapers (for lighting fires, not reading), and plenty of fishing magazines, none of which should be fresher than three years old. A screened-in porch, with lots of pegs to hang rods or nets on. A gas-operated refrigerator circa 1963. A Formica table circa 1957. No signs or warnings posted on the walls—this isn't some cheap motel—only just the one: *Generator will be turned off at midnight*. Plenty of windows facing the river, so when you get up at night to pee, you can see moonlight flowing downstream with the current.

That's the easy part, getting a cabin to be all this. Where the real art comes in is having it be in exactly the right state of disrepair. A new cabin, a perfect cabin, would be boring in the extreme, giving you nothing to talk about. A real fishing cabin, a weathered cabin, a cabin with character, has a certain style of decrepitude that only adds to its charm.

The door to the porch must not close entirely, even if you bang the edge. Daylight must be visible out cracks in the cabin walls, at least in some areas. The paneling should be knotty-pine veneer. The refrigerator must keep things too cold, so the milk is always frozen on the morning, and the beer is almost—but not quite—frozen in the afternoon. The toilet should rock when you sit on it and/or run all night. The frying pan must be so cheap you can fold it in half; the spatula, plastic, should me melted and scraggly. The heater can't work, or at least not until you fetch the owner. While you're cooking breakfast you should feel the cabin move, as the hired man, working early, tries yet again to jack it back up to level. Mosquitoes are needed, the kind that are impossible to swat. And mice—the more aggressive the better. The lights mustn't work, or at least not all of them. Extra rolls of toilet paper should be kept well hidden.

You get all this, the coziness and quirks, you've got yourself a *real* fishing cabin, the kind you can really settle into. And even better does it get when the people who run the cabins, owners like Jeff and Mary of Scotty Cabins, are so friendly and helpful, so ready to do anything to ensure you a great time, that you want to hug them—and want to even more, when Mary bakes a big apple pie while you're out fishing and leaves it on that Formica table for your dinner.

I had only fished with a Maine guide, a "registered" Maine guide, once before. This was back in 1976 on Grand Lake Stream, when, a young man on vacation, I flew up from New York to fish for landlocked salmon. George came with all the accouterments—a battered felt hat with flies in the band; Old Crow in a flask ready to add to the coffee; Bean gumboots the same color and texture as his skin—and his face wore that droopy, somewhat sad expression of a man who had caught thousands of fish and shot hundreds of deer without having very much to show for it.

His boat was the traditional Grand Laker canoe, long and beamy, canvas and wood. "I like to fly-fish," I said timidly, when I met him at the dock. "Fine with me, sonny"—then he reached into his bait bucket, took out a smelt, impaled it on my streamer.

Charge for a full day's fishing, a great shore lunch, his well-honed witticisms ("You might as well try and shit in the top of that pine tree over there than get Tommy Liscomb to act reasonable")? Fifty dollars.

Styles in guides have changed from those days, and Charlie, when he met us at the Howland exit, was trailering a Hyde driftboat made in Idaho. But you can't just buy a boat, stencil up your truck, call yourself a guide in Maine—you have to be registered after passing stringent tests. And prices have gone up, too, but Ray and I felt it was worth it for one day. We could pump him for information we could then use ourselves, while enjoying a luxury we don't often get the chance to indulge in: Letting someone else take us fishing.

When you first meet your guide, there's a certain wariness to work through. The guide worries that his sports may be demanding, bossy, and clumsy with their casting; the sports worry that the guide may be demanding, bossy, and critical of their casting. It took about twenty seconds to get past all that with Charlie—we hit it off immediately.

He's in his fifties, a chemistry professor in college, someone who talks with the rhythm and pace of an urban hip-hopper. "Know what I'm saying?" is his favorite expression, and he uses it to keep the beat with the rest of his comments. A long neck leads upward to a friendly, open face, and atop that sits a Red Sox cap. As we drove north up the Interstate, he talked nonstop about his favorite subject: Maine; the Maine woods; Maine people; Maine fish; Maine's future.

"The real Maine starts north of Bangor," he told us. "How long it will last is anyone's guess—know what I'm saying? Canada wants a big east-west highway to link the Atlantic provinces with Montreal, and that will mean the end of things if it cuts through here. I won't be alive to see it, thank you very much God. And there's talk of a national park, which no one up here wants. I won't be alive to see that either—know what I'm saying?"

One of the most Maine things you can do is talk about the real Maine. The further north you go in the state, the further north people draw the line—liberal hippy-dippies south of it, rugged individualists north of it. Up in Fort Kent, hard on the Canadian border, people must talk about the "real" Maine starting just below town, giving reality a kilometer of breathing space before it becomes New Brunswick.

Charlie turned off at the Millinocket exit. Plan A, floating the Penobscot's main stem, was ruled out by record high water after a month of rain, so he was proceeding to Plan B: floating the Penobby's West Branch, not upstream for landlocks, but lower down for bass where the river widens and slows. This was known as Dolby Pond (at last—a name I could pronounce!), more commonly called The Flowage, which is a great Maine word meaning a dammed impoundment that spreads and scraggles its way over and around a drowned forest. He had called some guide friends, and they told him the water would be clear and fishable there, and, with the bass not having eaten for a week because of the flooding, we might have ourselves a very big day.

"Where's the turn?" he asked himself, slowing. "We take a left at the strip club—there it is! Great. You guys feel like going later, tell Daicy I sent you and you'll get a discount."

Ray and I glanced at each other—he was kidding, right? As fast as he could talk, his humor was still dry and laconic, in the approved Maine guide style.

Thoreau paddled through here on his 1846 West Branch trip, spending several days at McCauslin's "farm" on what was then the free-flowing river's south bank.

> McCauslin was a Kennebec man, of Scottish descent, who had been a waterman and had driven on the lakes and headwaters of the Penobscot five or six springs in succession, but was now settled here to raise supplies for the lumberers. He entertained us a day or two with true Scotch hospitality, and would accept no recompense for it. A man of dry wit and shrewdness, and a general intelligence which I had not looked for in the backwoods. In fact, the deeper you penetrate into the woods, the more intelligent do you find the inhabitants, for always the pioneer has been a man of the world . . . His clearing was bounded abruptly, on all sides but the river, by the naked stems of the forest, as if you were to cut only a few feet square in the middle of a thousand acres of mowing and set down a thimble.

Great Northern Paper dammed this part of the West Branch in 1903 so they could store pulp for their plant in East Millinocket—if we were going to find any traces of McCauslin's old farm, we would have to fish deep. And yet it was still beautiful—not wilderness water, but lonely, forgotten, and, like a lot of good bass water, hidden right out in plain sight. It's river-like upstream, lake-like down, and Charlie's plan was to get us as high on the river part as he could with his motor, and then drift down to where the water spread open to a view of Katahdin.

A bald eagle met us as we trailered in—it croaked like a seagull, and then whistled like a hawk. Ray, on his third cast, encountered a sixteen-inch smallmouth, while I was soon involved with one nearly as big. Clearly, Part A of Plan B was working to perfection—the bass were famished. We worked the shallows with our bugs, casting as close to the trees as possible. "Painting the shoreline," Charlie calls this, and it's an apt analogy, for there was something painterly in the way we cast and re-cast, stroking our bugs along the water's surface.

Flyfishers have a big advantage in this kind of fishing. Spin fishermen using surface lures have to retrieve all the way to the boat before they can cast again, eating up valuable time, wasting good amounts of river, while with our fly rods we could cast, let the bug drift a few feet, pick it up, deposit it right back again a short way downstream, so between us we covered nearly every inch of shoreline.

I get lots of practice back home casting under pine and silver maples, but here the banks were lined with cedar trees, arborvitae, with their denser weave of branches. The good news was that if my fly hit these branches their denseness acted like a wall, so instead of becoming tangled, the bug would plop down onto the water, often eliciting an immediate strike.

We usually fish from canoes, down low to the water, and it was a treat to be up high in the driftboat where we could watch the bass take. It let me see something I don't remember ever having witnessed before. A bass, a big one, spotted my fly drifting past in the current, but instead of clobbering it immediately, he swam just downstream so he was waiting when the bug arrived, then and only then taking it, timing his rise perfectly.

The water has a tannic tinge here, as befits a river that begins in the North Woods—our bronzebacks came steeped in tea. We encountered bluegills, too, which, after weighing the other options (chub, dace, pickerel, rock bass), we decided was the happiest default species to catch.

"What's a rock bass?" Charlie asked, genuinely puzzled—or was he putting us on?

We encountered bass all the way down the river part, found them off the rocky islets out in the lake, and then motored back upstream to find a place for lunch. Charlie had spotted a picnic table set in a meadow for the convenience of raft trips that come down later in the summer, and he didn't think anyone would mind if we helped ourselves. He spread out a lunch of smoked mussels, turkey and cheddar sandwiches, and Oreo cookies, which suited us just fine. While we ate, we talked about a lot of things, and not all of it was fishing.

One second Charlie was saying, "You really nailed those smallies, Raymondo," the next, "My wife, Annie, died last month."

I was staring up at the tree where the eagle sat watching us, as if he or she had a craving for our mussels, so my first reaction was a startled, clumsy "What?" Ray—whose strength comes from gentleness—immediately found the right note.

"Oh my god, Charlie! That's awful! What happened?"

We heard the story, which was every bit as sad as you'd expect. He talked about her illness, her last days, the memorial service to which hundreds had come. She didn't love fishing, but often went out with him and their kids, becoming the specialist in netting their fish. In all the years she did this, she always, *always,* got the fish on the first swipe, something she became famous for, so three different people mentioned it at her service.

We didn't need much more than this to see how much he loved her. Neither of us could imagine what it took for him to carry on—to pick up two strangers, for instance, and show them a good time fishing. Still, that was how he was coping, by carrying on as normal, and after a time, just the right amount of time, the subject went back to the job at hand.

"If you guys paint like you did this morning," he said, packing up the cooler, "those smallies don't stand a chance."

He called that right—we did even better in the afternoon, working the shoreline even more assiduously, catching increasingly bigger and darker bass. Charlie used the motor to take us as far upstream as he could before the current became too strong, and then we floated back down, plucking bass out from beneath the cedars like (so desperate were they to grab on) survivors from a boat that had overturned.

"Let's try the Cribs," he suggested, swinging the bow around. This is a series of side channels left from logging days that are only floatable when the river is high.

Charlie slotted the driftboat between an island and some rocks, and there we were—the Cribs. I've never fished in a prettier spot (this remained true for forty-eight hours, when I met its equal). Imagine a series of narrow channels, parallel to each other, often merging, but each distinct and individual, like variations on a riverine theme. They had a Southern feel, with weed beds along their edges and mangrove-like tangles of roots—but no, not Southern, *Western* . . . they made me think of Depuy and Armstrong and those other Montana spring creeks, laid out in rows so you could compare their virtues. With the water so transparent we could look down and see chains and spikes on the bottom left from logging days; with the channels so narrow, Raymondo could cast to one side, I could cast to the other, and for most of the journey we played fished simultaneously. And we didn't just float down all this, but waltzed down, elegantly, at just the right tempo.

But all this, beautiful as it was, hardly explains my extravagant reaction. I had never felt so good, not for a long time—and maybe it wasn't just the Cribs working on me, but Charlie's story, with its implicit reminder: *savor it all while you can.*

Where the Cribs ended came the landing. Time to trailer out, take our rods down, pee into the woods. We drove back to the Howland exit, had Charlie circle spots on our maps we could try tomorrow, said goodbye to him with real regret.

"Don't forget," he said. "If you guys come back to The Flowage, it's the first left past the strip club." Winking broadly now, in the registered Maine guide way, he said, "It's Daicy if you decide to go in."

When we woke up in the morning, the Penobscot, even with the sun out, still looked intimidating. Charlie said he never fished it unless it was flowing below 19,000 cfs, and according to Jeff it was racing by at almost 30,000.

"You'll be able to try it tomorrow," he said confidently. "The guides up here are too timid—the fishing can be great when the water's high."

What do you do when you can't go bass fishing? You go trout fishing. Baxter State Park wasn't far, and we decided that fishing for wild brookies in the shadow of Mt. Katahdin was a great default option.

There is something sentimental and nostalgic about trout fishing in the Maine woods. The big ones are gone, and the rituals of the sporting camp—the canoe ride in; the guide with his laconic wisdom; the brook trout for breakfast—have mostly disappeared with them. Muskie, pike, ATVers and GPSers, and, yes, bass, have chased and harried the trout to ever more remote places, including, as one of their last refuges, the 200,000 acres of Baxter Park.

Baxter Wilderness Park they call it—and those who manage it take the wilderness part very seriously. Only two rough dirt roads enter it, campgrounds are primitive, and there's hardly any signage—it's as close to a wilderness experience as you can get in the East. This keeps out the casual daytrippers and sightseers (even views of Katahdin, its centerpiece, are fairly difficult to obtain); in a recent year, it only had sixty thousand visitors, compared to the three million visiting Yellowstone.

Its brook trout are small, but every one is a native. We stopped and asked a ranger for advice, and he told us the streams were still too high to be safe.

"If I were you, I'd try Daicy Pond," he suggested. "Daicy's famous for her big ones."

(Daicy? Daicy? I thought to myself. Where had I heard that name?)

It's ten miles to the pond, but the road is so rough and twisty it took us forty minutes. When we passed a clearing, we'd get a view of fortress-like Katahdin to our right, and, with the sun out now after weeks of rain, it looked freshly scrubbed and polished. Ray was driving and I played tour guide.

"Thoreau climbed the mountain in 1846, or at least tried to. He got to the lower summit, not the real one. A big moment for him—he had an epiphany on top, or what some critics think was an existential meltdown. The weather was bad, and he had never been where nature was so savage and awful. It was a long way from Walden Pond."

> The mountain seems a vast aggregation of loose rocks, as if sometime it had rained rocks, and they lay as they fell on the mountain side, nowhere fairly at rest, but leaning on each other, all rocking-stones, with cavities between but scarcely any soil or smoother shelf. They were the raw materials of planets dropped from an unseen quarry, which the vast chemistry of nature would anon work up, or work down, into the smiling and verdant plains of earth. This was primeval, untamed and forever untamable Nature. There was felt the presence of a force not bound to be kind to man.

We found Daicy Pond, helped ourselves to one of the canoes that are yours for the asking, fished around the rocky perimeter, with nothing to show for it but a few sluggish strikes—those, and incredible views of Katahdin's snow-streaked gullies, and the equally impressive mountain to the west, the steep doubled tops of Double Top.

We ate our peanut butter and jellies at a table overlooking the pond, and then put our waders on and hiked down the Appalachian Trail along Nesowadnehunk Stream. There are two dramatic waterfalls here, Little Niagara and Big Niagara. (As is Baxter's style, hardly any signs point to these, and once you get there on foot there are no protective railings or cautions or anything to spoil the wilderness feel.) Both were raging, but we edged our way carefully along Little Niagara's bank and caught fish in a back eddy, right up against the granite base of the falls. Wild brookies, none longer than six inches, but feisty, beautiful, and full of life; it was as if the spray had been sliced into fish, and we laughed like kids when we extracted one from the foam.

We stopped in Millinocket on our way back, the famous old paper town. I hadn't been there in twenty-five years, and in place of the rough, brawny, vibrant place I remembered was a sedate, sleepy downtown, with a Main Street that at four o'clock on a bright June afternoon was entirely deserted. Great Northern had closed one of its huge mills, and the town's population had shrank by a third; rather than working a good paying job in the mill, Millinocketers were now waking up at 3:00 a.m. to make the long commute down to Bangor. (The mill's workforce had gone from 4,000 to 200.) The town smelled better now, with the stacks being cold—but that's the way unemployment often does smell: clean, cold, antiseptic.

The town was trying to pick up the slack by marketing itself as an outdoor destination, but this only helped a little. Whitewater rafters spend money at the convenience stores, and then keep on going; snowmobilers come in winter, but that's about it. The only establishment on Main Street that showed any activity was the Appalachian Trail Cafe, and that's where we ended up, perusing, as we waited for our coffee and squash donuts, the notes scribbled on the walls by Appalachian Trail "through hikers," who, having conquered Katahdin, come to town to celebrate.

I turned through some local papers left on our table. Millinocket and East Millinocket, though only a few miles apart, maintain their own high schools, with tiny graduating classes. The grads beamed in their pictures, but their future lay to the south, not in rural Maine. It was the same situation as in a thousand other aging U.S. mill towns. The boys and girls with guts and ambition join the army; the ones without those qualities, at least the boys, get menial jobs and save their money so they can buy the same assault rifles their friends use in the military.

Cynical? Hard not to be, reading the two lead articles. People were rejoicing because the one remaining paper mill had just gotten an order to make 3,000 tons of bright white stock for a major publisher trying to keep up with the demand for its soft-porn mega-bestseller. The other article talked about the Florida woman who had just won the lottery of $347 million; she was from East Millinocket originally, and the paper expressed the hope that she would remember her roots and do something worthwhile for the town.

(I read this with more than a little fellow feeling. Novelists, at least those who don't do porn or vampires, face the same problem paper towns face: too many texters, not enough readers.)

There was cheerier news on the paper's last page. Under the local court docket, with its listing of shoplifters and DUIs, there were a lot of fish-and-game violations—a *lot*. Was it because money was tight and people couldn't shell out for a license? Were people so desperate for food that a moose out of season was their only recourse? (Ray and I had fished in the Ozarks the previous winter, and seen rural poverty, but little as bad as you find in northeastern Maine.) Or was it the old cops-and-robbers game at work, sneaky wardens versus crafty poachers, those hereditary enemies going at it once again?

My fishing ethics were appalled, seeing how many had been busted for fishing illegally, but the rest of me had a different reaction. Compared to the brutal mercies of capitalism, fishing anarchy is no bad thing.

A long day. A good day. When we got back to the cabins, drooling in anticipation of finishing Mary's apple pie, we found our cabin door wide open, and there with his paws up on the Formica table, munching happily away on the crust, was Gus, the cabins' resident Labrador.

We fished the lower Piscataquis the next morning, the Penobscot's bass-filled tributary. It reminded us of the Connecticut back home; the same breadth, the same rural beauty, the same slippery clay banks oozing down to a lining of rock. We paddled upstream as far as the interstate bridge, then floated back down to the dam, picking up bass almost everywhere along the way. The houses on the bank got shabbier as we moved downstream, going from elaborate summer lodges to modest ranch houses to flimsy trailers.

The Piscataquis has what we were beginning to recognize as the characteristic Maine woods touch: remnants from logging days; in this case, rocky, island-like foundations once used to hold back logs, and now quickening the river into fast, pinball-like slots.

This was fun, but what we really wanted to do was float the Penobscot proper and see if it really is the best bass river in the country, as writers such as Lefty Kreh like to claim. When we checked back in with Jeff, he told us now was the time, with the cfs having dropped some and the river running clear. We would have our hands full, we'd have to wear life jackets at all times, but he had sent some spin fishermen out and they had done well.

This was good enough for us. We threw the canoe on the car roof, and Mary—whose forthrightness and feisty humor we were appreciating more each day—drove us to a clearing below a broken run known as Mohawk Rips.

Thoreau, who paddled down this stretch in 1857, explains where the name originally came from.

> We paddled and floated, looking into the mouths of rivers. When passing the Mohawk Rips, or, as the Indians called them, the "Mohog Lips," four or five miles below Lincoln, Joe Polis told us at length the story of a fight between his tribe and the Mohawks there, anciently—how the latter were overcome by stratagem, the Penobscots using concealed knives—but they could not for a long time kill the Mohawk chief, who was a very large and strong man, though he was attacked by several canoes at once, when swimming alone in the river.

We mounted the trolling motor on the canoe to help push us upstream against the current. We'd been in powerful rivers before, so we knew the drill . . . use the motor to get as high as we can, and then turn and drift back down . . . but the Penobscot's current was so strong it was only when we added paddle power that we managed to do anything better than hold our own.

In a routine started so long ago we've forgotten when, where, or why, I'm always in the stern of the canoe, Ray sits in front. Painting the shoreline had been easy from Charlie's driftboat, with him rowing, but now it was much trickier, as I had to play guide myself. With the canoe heading upstream so slow, and the bug drifting downstream so fast, the arc in the line made it difficult to connect when a bass came up. (The bug's eyes I could see very plainly; they looked aghast at the current's speed.) Playing one, with the current going one way, the canoe going the other, was no picnic either, but if I turned the motor off we'd hurtle downstream and lose too much river.

But that they were coming up at all was encouraging. After about fifty yards I landed my first one, a fourteen-incher the color of tempered brass, and Ray followed that up with three in a row—bang, bang, bang. It was immediately apparent that Jeff was right; with the river having been high for so long, the fish were famished—and we knew within fifteen minutes we were in for a very big day.

The Penobscot is the biggest river in Maine, and with the edges flooded, there was four-hundred yards of water between us and the opposite bank. In normal summers, it flows in lazy meanders, exposing sandbars and reefs, but with a record amount of rain needing transport to the sea, it was surging along with serious purpose, and even the rocky Mohawk Rips, when we finally got there, were only visible as finger-shaped swirls; it was as if the dead Mohawk chief, lying on the bottom, was reaching up a pleading hand.

Our bank, the west bank, was low enough that we paddled past flooded picnic tables in forested riverside parks, but the east bank looked steeper, with a cruller-shaped ridge and the only house visible for a mile on either side. Both banks are forested—cedar, pine, silver maple, the last growing in weird loops and overhangs that cast a marbleized shade.

It's not deep, the Penobscot—Jeff told us eight feet down was bottom—and, while I'm no hydrologist, this seemed to make the river flow even faster, like a hose pouring down a playground slide.

But slowly, carefully, we learned to cope with this power, be comfortable with it, turn it to our advantage. The bass helped—we were catching them everywhere. Raymondo had on the same popper he had used on the Dolby and the Piscataquis, and it was on its way to bass bug immortality, with more than one hundred bass to its credit and counting.

Me, I had my hands full maneuvering the canoe, but then we got as high on the river as we could manage, and everything after that was all downstream, so I could concentrate more on casting. On The Flowage, or on the Piscataquis, or even back home on the Connecticut, there are sterile stretches where you never get a bite. On the Penobscot, at least under these circumstances, every single inch seems to hold bass.

My arms ached from catching them is a cliché that makes my fingers ache from typing it, but, truth be told, our arms ached from catching them, and I started casting left-handed to give the other arm a rest. The bass weren't huge, but they weren't puny either—a fourteen-inch smallmouth, with the inertia of Maine's biggest river backing it up, is fourteen inches of solid pull. Oddly, they didn't jump much, which Ray thought might be due to the water being cold. After a break on shore, we began seeing rises close to the bank and thought for a moment they might be trout (or Atlantic salmon; the Penobby has the biggest run in the U.S.). But they were bass, rising to drowned Goddard caddis, and other bugs the high water had rinsed from the trees. I tied on a big Royal Wulff and cast downstream to them, and they took it differently than they did Ray's popper, with delicate, trout-like sips.

The current was so fast it threatened to get us back to the cabins sooner than we intended, so we ducked in between islands, exploring the channels where the current, mystified by all its options, momentarily eased.

"What's that sound?" Ray said, as we entered the first of these.

"Sound?"

"Big animal."

A moose plunged down the island's steep bank, bulled through the collar of driftwood, started swimming—a young moose, swimming like a beginner at summer camp, with its head craned back. He was no match for the current, but this didn't seem to worry him; in the same way we did, he picked out a target on the bank far downstream, slanting across rather than trying anything perpendicular. An eagle followed it across, providing air cover—or was it hoping for a mooseburger?

We couldn't get enough of these islands, particularly the ones separated by narrow bays from their neighbors. The Penobscot tribe still owns every one of these; in Thoreau's day, many Indians had houses here, but were in the process of abandoning them for a less lonely, more sociable life down in Old Town.

Jeff, when he dropped us off at the launch spot, pointed to the middle of the river and one island in particular, or rather two islands in particular: a flat grassy one separated by a watery slot from a forested, humpbacked one.

"Big bass in there?" we asked.

Jeff rolled his eyes. "Oh yeah."

We kept a weather eye on these islands while we tried closer ones, saving it for dessert—and we're glad we did. Never have I fished a prettier place. The small grassy island had trees on its downstream edge, but they were flooded well up their trunks, so there was a swampy, bayou-like quality to the water, while, twenty yards away against the wooded island, the current ran in a deep, mysterious-looking channel right up against the banks. The trees on both islands touched tops, so there was a shady band in the middle—blue, like the shade of February—and that's where we kept the canoe while we cast, me toward the grass, Ray toward the current. A beaver swam by to port, a muskrat to starboard—it felt like we had slipped inside the covers of *Wind in the Willows*. The whole time we were there a word kept trying to form, though it was only later it finally clicked into place. Elysium. We were fishing Elysium.

The Penobscot bass don't usually have access to the flooded trees, and, rooting in and around their trunks, they accessed food they were usually denied. They rose just often enough to let me see where they were, and every time I dropped my bug on the rings they took it, maybe mistaking it for acorns. There was something uncharacteristically feminine about the way they did this (sexist that I am, I almost always think of bass as masculine, as anyone keeping track of the pronouns will have already noticed)—they folded themselves over the fly like girl swimmers making graceful flip turns at the end of a pool, with just the briefest, loveliest view of flank.

There were just as many bass over on Ray's side, and most of the time we were playing two fish at once. I could have stayed there forever, it was so beautiful, secret, and soft—the part of the Penobscot I'll remember longest.

We couldn't help but be wistful when we finally floated down to the cabins and took out. If the Penobscot isn't the best smallmouth river in America, I'd like to see a better—or at least that's what we told ourselves in the giddiness of having fished it. My home river is the Connecticut, but I was thinking, as we packed up, that it was about time I had an adopted river, a foster one I could spend the next few years really getting to know. As hard as we had fished, we had barely scratched the surface; thanks to those islands, there was a lifetime's worth of fishing just within the two miles of river we had floated.

"We'll be back," we told Jeff as they saw us off.

"We'll be here," he said.

Mary emphatically nodded, glanced around at the cabins they were putting so much work into, the assorted vehicles and boats needing mending, the choppy excuse for a lawn they were trying so hard to smooth out, then—sucking in her breath now, squinting in the sunlight—stared out toward the river it was breaking our hearts to leave. What she said surprised us, not by the sentiment, but by its passionate determination.

"We're going to stay here the rest of our lives."

Eleven

Sometimes I get calls about Sheila and occasionally I get questions about the boy, but only once has anyone phoned to ask about the bass.

It was a schoolteacher from Phoenix—an eighth-grade teacher in a neighborhood, she explained, where most of the children live below the federal poverty line. They had read "The Bass, the River, and Sheila Mant" in their English textbook, enjoyed it greatly, though they wondered, not about the ending so much, but what came afterward.

"I don't know," I said honestly. "It's a short story, it's made up. When it reaches the end, it ends."

It was hard to judge—she was in Arizona and I was in New Hampshire—but this seemed to make her frown.

"We think maybe Sheila eventually got more mature and apologized to the boy," she said. "The boy probably found himself another girlfriend. But the character my kids are really curious about is the bass, what happened to him."

While her question was new, her response wasn't. Lots of people think the story must be true, despite the fact the textbook clearly labels it as fiction. And if it *is* true, then clearly the author knew what happened to the characters in later life.

But I'd never really thought about it before, what happened to the bass. When last seen, he's got a treble-hooked Rapala plug in its jaw, and, with the boy deliberately cutting the line, it probably stayed there a good long time. Long enough to kill him? Possibly. On the other hand, without the pressure of the line, maybe he managed to shake it out, and swim on to a ripe old age. Largemouth bass can live sixteen or seventeen years if they're cautious and lucky. Of course, since I had written the story thirty years ago, that meant even under the best of circumstances he was long since defunct.

"It don't know what happened to him," I said weakly.

This didn't seem to satisfy her. "My class is really curious. If you could tell us something about him, anything . . . "

I tried picturing her in that poor-side-of-Phoenix classroom, a teacher giving her heroic all to interest her kids in reading. I pictured her—and said what I had to say.

"The boy went back the following summer in his canoe, saw this lifeless shape floating like a Viking ship in the shallows, found that it was the bass, with the Rapala still hanging from its lower lip. He carefully scooped it up in his net, took it back to his parents' cottage, buried it out on the lawn under a little marker that's still there today."

I paused—was that enough for her?

"Oh, thank you!" she said. "My kids will love that!"

The story the teacher called about is "The Bass, the River, and Sheila Mant," and if you have a son or daughter, there's a reasonably good chance they've had to read it in English class either in middle school, high school, or college. Once a short story appears in one textbook or anthology, it's likely to appear in a dozen more, since the first thing an anthologist does when they compile their book is go and borrow from the other anthologies/textbooks that are already out there. This can mean your story multiplies fast. One recent textbook that includes Sheila, distributed nationally, had a print run of 600,000 copies, and, with it being passed from grade to grade each year, the story gets *read*.

Sheila's "fish story" aspect makes it immediately accessible; the boy character appeals strongly to reluctant readers; the coming-of-age theme, the metaphors, the characterization, are clear enough that they lend themselves to the kind of exposition textbooks engage in. And, not the least of its virtues, it's very short, so teachers don't have to feel guilty in assigning it as homework.

I wrote it in the winter of 1982–83. Celeste and I were renting a house in Lyme village, or at least the back half of the house, and I had the back part of that as my office—a beautiful room, built in the 1800s, though so drafty I often wrote in my parka. I worked hard that winter; Sheila was the fifth or sixth story I had written in a two-month span.

Like many story ideas, it came to me from two different, seemingly unrelated directions. My teenage brother-in-law Peter was having a hard time with his parents' divorce, and, with no better candidate available, he asked me for advice on a vexing problem: he had a crush on a seven-teen-year old girl. The problem was the age difference—Peter was only fourteen—and it made it difficult for him to ascertain, not just whether the girl liked him, but whether she even knew he was alive.

"Forget about it, Peter," I felt like saying. "A crush like that is totally hopeless, although (the good thing!), hopeless crushes are an important part of growing up."

I didn't say this, of course—didn't tell him to forget her. I mumbled the usual platitudes about time healing all things, plenty of nice girls to choose from out there, yadda, yadda, yadda. I hope this helped, and sure enough, he soon had a girlfriend his own age who made him forget all about that stuck-up seventeen-year old.

That formed one side of the nascent idea. Way over on the other side, in broader strokes, was my newfound love for the Connecticut River and its bass fishing. The previous summer was the first time I ever fished it, and now, writing in winter, the delight of this discovery throbbed through my imagination in search of a theme to attach itself to—as for instance, the plight of a young teenager with a crush on the totally wrong girl.

That's how story ideas often come: a scoop of real-life experience, a wedge of psychology, little add-ons of drama, a few slices of theme . . . and then, after you've mixed all the ingredients, let them marinate for a while, you sit down at your desk and write the first words.

The only other out-of-the-way thing I remember about the actual writing was that I did it while suffering the flu. This was still the macho stage of my career, when I was trying to prove to myself I had the guts to pursue it, and my 102-degree fever, rather than smudging up all my characters, made them stand out with preternatural clarity.

Not on the first draft, not even on the second or third, but somewhere after the fourth or fifth I finally had my beginning.

"There was a summer in my life when the only creature that seemed lovelier than a largemouth bass was Sheila Mant. I was fourteen. The Mants had rented the cottage next to ours on the river; with their parties, their frantic games of softball, their constant comings and goings, they appeared to me denizens of a brilliant existence. 'Too noisy by half,' my mother quickly decided, but I would have given anything to be invited to one of their parties, and when my parents went to bed I would sneak through the woods to their hedge and stare enchanted at the candlelit swirl of white dresses and bright, paisley skirts.

"Sheila was the middle daughter—at seventeen, all but out of reach . . . "

The boy (in the first-person telling, we never learn his name), sucking up his courage, approaches her at a softball game and asks if she wants to go with him to a dance at a nearby town. Sheila, who just barely condescends to notice him, asks the obvious question.

"'You have a car?' she said without looking up.

I played my master stroke. 'We'll go by canoe.'"

He spends all the next day polishing it, arranging cushions in the bow for Sheila's comfort, then, automatically, mounts his spinning reel on his Pflueger rod, and sticks it in the stern.

I say automatically, because he's crazy nuts about fishing.

"When I wasn't swimming laps in the river to impress Sheila, I was back in our driveway practicing casts, and when I wasn't practicing casts, I was tying the line to Tosca, our springer spaniel, to test the reel's drag, and when I wasn't doing any of those things, I was fishing the river for bass."

He paddles to the Mants' dock as dusk settles, picks up the very beautiful but reluctant Sheila, who says she can get her dad's car. He lies, tells her it's faster by canoe. There's an extra paddle in the bow, but Sheila is *way* above paddling. She settles back against the cushions, takes her shoes off, dangles her feet over the side.

Ten minutes go by.

"'What kind of band?' she asked.

'It's sort of like folk music. You'll like it.'

'Eric Caswell's going to be there. Dartmouth? He strokes number four.'

'No kidding?' I said. I had no idea who she meant.

'What's that sound?' she said, pointing toward shore.

'Bass. That splashing sound?'

'Over there.'

'Yeah, bass. They come into the shallows at night to chase frogs and things. Big largemouths. *Micropetrus salmonides,*' I added, showing off.

'I think fishing's dumb,' she said, making a face. 'I mean, it's boring and all. Definitely dumb.'"

With that, the boy realizes he's in *big* trouble. If she sees his fishing rod in the stern, the date is ruined, so he decides to push it further back out of sight.

"It must have been just exactly what the bass was waiting for. Fish will trail a lure sometimes, trying to make up their minds whether or not to attack, and the slight pause in the plug's speed caused by my adjustment was tantalizing enough to overcome the bass's inhibitions. My rod, safely out of sight, bent double. The line, tightly coiled, peeled off the spool with the shrill, tearing zip of a high-speed drill.

Four things occurred to me at once. One, that it was a bass. Two, that it was a big bass. Three, that it was the biggest bass I had ever hooked. Four, that Sheila Mant must not know."

That's his terrible dilemma—how to play the bass while keeping Sheila from knowing. She prattles on from her cushioned seat in the bow . . . she skis, she parties, she dates . . . while downstream he sees the bass jump with a concussion heavy enough to ripple the entire river.

"'Eric said I have the figure to model, but I thought I should get an education first. I mean, it might be a while before I get started and all. I was thinking of getting my hair styled, more swept back? I mean, Ann-Margaret? Like hers, only shorter?'

She hesitated. 'Are we going backwards?'

We were. I had managed to keep the bass in the middle of the river away from the rocks, but it had plenty of room there, and for the first time a chance to exert its full strength. I quickly computed the weight necessary to draw a fully loaded canoe backwards—the thought of it made me feel faint."

Torn between longings—for Sheila and all she represents there in front of him; for the bass and all he represents there behind—he's faced with a wrenching decision.

"Twenty yards ahead of us was the road, and once I pulled the canoe up on shore, the bass would be gone, irretrievably gone. If instead I stood up, grabbed the rod, and started pumping, I would have it—as tired as the bass was, there was no chance it could get away. I reached down for the rod, hesitated, looked up to where Sheila was stretching herself lazily toward the sky, her small breasts rising beneath the soft fabric of her dress, and the tug was too much for me, and quicker than it takes to write down, I pulled a penknife from my pocket and cut the line in half.

With a sick, nauseous feeling in my stomach, I saw the rod unbend. 'My legs are sore,' Sheila whined. 'Are we there yet?'"

Somehow he manages to get her to the dance, but it all passes in a blur.

"I may have danced once or twice with her, but all I really remember is her coming over to me once the music was done to explain that she would be going home in Eric Caswell's Corvette.

'Okay,' I mumbled.

For the first time that night she looked at me, really looked at me. 'You're a funny kid, you know that?'"

Only one more paragraph now—and it's a bittersweet one.

"Funny. Different. Dreamy. Odd. How many times was I to hear that in the years to come, all spoken with the same quizzical, half-accusatory tone Sheila used then. Poor Sheila! Before the month was over, the spell she cast over me was gone, but the memory of that lost bass haunted me all summer and haunts me still. There would be other Sheila Mants in my life, other fish, and though I came close once or twice, it was these secret, hidden tuggings in the night that claimed me, and I never made the same mistake again."

So. Finished at last. Now came the usual dilemma of the American short-story writer: where in hell can I get this published? I could try the "little magazines," the literary quarterlies, but while they had helped earlier in my career, I'd found that publishing a story in them was, as far as reaching an audience went, little different from throwing it in the trash. Luckily, I learned of a brand-new program to get short stories published in American newspapers. (This, of course, was revolutionary—newspaper fiction that was actually labeled as such.)

I sent Sheila off to the appropriate address, waited, and then found it had been accepted by the program and offered, along with the others accepted, to the ten participating newspapers so they could choose which ones they wanted. All ten took the story, at $100 per, which represented a big sum of money for us in those days. These were important papers with big readerships—*Chicago Tribune, Washington Post, Boston Globe*—and so the story, rather than reaching the 500 that subscribe to a little magazine, was there with the Sunday paper for many hundreds of thousands.

Once out in the world a story usually expires very quickly—but not this time. My first indication that things would be different with this one was a request from an international aid agency to translate the story into Tamil and publish it in Sri Lanka. Shortly after this, the U. S. Information Agency asked if they could translate it into Russian and publish it in *America,* a magazine distributed in the Soviet Union to encourage the new tentative thawing in the Cold War.

I have it in front of me right now, from May 1985. President Ronald Reagan is on the cover, and it's not a very good photo (or is it?), making him look like a mummified Soviet *apparatchik.* My keyboard doesn't do Cyrillic characters, so I can't reproduce the story's Russian title, except for the words *peka* for bass, and *Maht* for Mant. There seem to be a lot of capital letters in the text, a lot of reversed Rs standing alone, and dashes instead of quotation marks.

The title spreads across two pages, alongside a wonderful water-color that the Information Agency must have commissioned. The boy rows Sheila through a river of aqueous blue shadows; she sits lovely in the bow, dangling her feet in the water, her unused paddle propped across the thwart. Behind the canoe a bass that looks more like a salmon leaps up through the water's surface in a scattering of impressionistic white drops. On the last page there's another illustration: the boy alone this time, guiding the canoe toward a lonely full moon, while below the lily pads the bass broods on his lucky escape.

And that has turned out to be one of the story's great fringe benefits—seeing it interpreted visually in so many ways. Between the bass, the boy, the river, and Sheila, there's a lot for artists and art directors to work with.

I've gone down to the basement and dug some of them out, textbooks where the story has appeared in the thirty years of its existence. In *Glencoe Literature,* there's a shimmery, watery splash of color under the title, then a full-page reproduction of a watercolor called *Country House with Canoe* by Ed Labadie. On the next page, in the lefthand corner, is a small pastel, *The Carnival,* by Fred Wagner, with a romantic looking carousel spinning through a classic summer night. And, since young people expect *lots* of visuals, there's one more: *Trout Fishing Lake St. John 1895* by Winslow Homer, which—though I was never consulted—is one of my favorite paintings.

The Language of Literature starts off with a photo of a big large-mouth swimming behind a trolled spinnerbait just below the surface; this may be Photoshopped, since there's something not quite right about the angle of the bass's attack. The art director makes up for this on the next page, since he or she has found a remarkably evocative painting, an egg tempera called *Early Evening,* by Ken Danby. It shows a wistfully beautiful girl sitting on a rough-hewn wooden bench near a river, mini-skirted, pensive, adorable—a Sheila shorn of her narcissism.

Literature and Language Arts leads with a goofy-looking teenager with goofy baseball cap and goofy smile. Above him is a photo of a bass reproduced five times, so it's like there's a whole school. It's not the sharpest of reproductions, perhaps deliberately, and at first glance the bass looks upside down, as if the art director didn't understand much about fishing. But no—if you look closer, they seem upright all right, but even then they're still a little odd, with a big splash of red on their pectoral fins. On the next page is a drawing of a wood-and-canvas canoe, then another upside-down looking bass, and then, redeeming everything, a reproduction of an "oil, enamel, pencil, and wood fragment on canvas" called *The Heart in Bliss* by Jim Dine—and yes, it's a heart, and the colors and abstract shadings do indeed suggest bliss.

Textbooks being textbooks, these all include sections called "After You Read" or "Vocabulary Workshop" with questions students can take a crack at, as for instance—"Did you find this story to be humorous, serious, or both?"; "The narrator said there would be other Sheila Mants in his life. What does Sheila come to represent for the narrator?"; "In your opinion, is Sheila's comment that the narrator is a 'funny kid' part of the falling action or part of the resolution?"; and, getting at last to the nub of it, "What theme, or overall message about life or human nature do you think this story represents?"

I can find only two questions that relate to the bass: "What could be the deeper meaning of the bass's hold on the line?"; "Why does the narrator call his decision to cut the bass off a mistake?" And I'm not sure I could answer either of them very easily.

Footnotes abound, plus highlighted vocabulary words; with each new edition it seems that more and more has to be explained. Several references have become dated—teenagers can't be expected to know who Ann-Margaret was, and probably not even Jackie Kennedy—and the vocabulary lists I have no quibbles with. In one edition, the following words are explicitly defined at the bottom of each page: *scull, coxswain, epitome, denizens, pensive, chamois, dubious, antipathy, filial, surreptitiously, conspicuous, concussion, paisley, lithe, luminous, quizzical*—not the kinds of words a fourteen-year-old would tap out on their phones.

If you Google on the web, you'll find dozens of assignments posted there by English teachers and professors, and a good number of You Tube videos students have created as their response—most are charming, some are hilarious. A few years ago I got a call from a high school in northern Maine that wanted permission to make a short film of the story, and I told them sure, as long as they sent me the finished product. It's excellent—but Maine lakes are cold in early May, when it was filmed, the blackflies are terrible, so there are more goosebumps and welts than the story calls for, particularly on the otherwise perfect skin of their Sheila. They went and asked a Maine game warden for a bass, and sure enough there he is, making a brief cameo under the final credits—a chunky smallmouth, which is held up for a second, and then gently released.

A Sheila cottage industry has arisen online. A recent search shows that the Oak Park Unified School is reading it, as is the Ionia School eighth grade, Zachary High School, the Windbess School, Lake Oswego High, West Madison Middle School, Mrs. Webb's sophomore English class, and Mr. Mendoza's ninth-grade honors section. Some students have posted their responses online, including Kimberly Gonzalez, Sophia Nguyen, Tracy Bauer, Aaren Nichole, Idameisha Moreland, and Parker Buchanan; another student says on her "You Tube notes" that "this is a project which I failed, not because I got a bad grade but because my computer is stupid." And, for lazier students, there are "enotes" on the story for sale, and even free essays on a site called "AntiEssays."

The story works well read out loud, particularly on a summer evening, and so it's become my party piece, the reading I use before an audience who has no idea who I am. If I read it right, everyone groans when the boy cuts the line. I read it once in Charleston, and heard later than a married couple in attendance had a furious fight on their way home. "I'm not Sheila!" the woman insisted, while her husband kept saying, "Oh yes you are!"

The story has been out in the world thirty years now, and the older I get the more the writer in me identifies with the bass. The story tells us very little about him. He's a largemouth, which means, in a river of smallmouth, he feels like an outsider, though a proud one. He's probably ten years old, to have achieved that kind of heft—mid-sixties in human years. A survivor obviously—he's been hooked many times, but never once landed or subdued. His outstanding attribute is a stubborn refusal to give up, no matter the odds, and as age gradually weakens his other strengths, it's become the only emotion he values, the one that pushes him on. If I were answering a test question about him, I'd say that he represents the overwhelming tug of life's beauty and life's mysteries, ones that are even deeper and more tormenting than the ones posed by a seventeen-year-old girl you have a crush on . . . and so it's no wonder people groan when the boy cuts the line. I groaned, too, when I wrote it. But groaning is what writers do if they're any good.

Sometimes I've wondered if a big trout would have served as well, and decided it wouldn't. Trout don't swim with summer evenings draped over their shoulders they way bass do. And muskie or pike would have severed the line on their own.

I try to explain all this to students, on those rare occasions when someone dares let me near them. My fishing partner Ray Chapin teaches eighth-grade English at Thetford Academy, Vermont's oldest secondary school, and the textbook he uses includes Sheila Mant. He assigns it early in the school year, and then has me come over to speak to his three classes—and speaking in front of a roomful of thirteen-year-olds is as intimidating a public-speaking challenge as life offers.

It's a ten-minute drive from my house, and the closer I get, the more nervous I become. They're waiting for me in the library, and something in their demeanor, their chair posture, reminds me of a skeptical jury predisposed to convict.

Ray is a wonderful teacher, with just the right mix of sensitivity and authority. And he's got them well primed. ("No questions about fishing," he warns them. "Ask Mr. Wetherell about the story or the writing process.") When we're fishing, I only have to share his attention with the trout or bass, but here he's got his students to watch over, and at first that seems strange. Then, too, I like to swear a lot when I'm fishing, so

I have to remember I'm on dry land, monitor my mouth before it gets me into trouble.

I usually start by outlining how the story came to me, much as I've done here, then, twenty minutes in, open it up for questions. They're always shy about this, at least at first, and my favorite prompt is to ask, "All those who thought the boy should have kicked Sheila overboard and kept the bass, raise your hands."

More than half raise them—and that gets a good conversation started. Finally, one girl (it's always a girl) braver than the others will ask a question on her own, and then someone else will, and by the end of the period there are hands up all over the room, and I feel bad I can't stay longer.

Before I've come, Ray has given them an assignment: they have to write a sequel or alternate ending explaining what happened next. He'll have students read out loud some of the better ones, and I'm always amazed at how good they are. One girl stood up and in a soft voice read her response: Sheila's morning-after letter to the boy, apologizing, explaining how her own emotions were just as tormented and confused as his were, and that her sophisticated confidence was just a pose. Another girl read her alternate ending: the boy paddles home alone, brokenhearted, at least until out on the river he spots a girl his age paddling a canoe, casting a Rapala toward the weed beds for bass. Perfect!

There's one question I think is important, and if a student doesn't ask it, Mr. Chapin will step in. "We know you like fishing, so is this story autobiographical?"

"Yes and no," I answer. "Everything is made up, entirely invented. There is nothing in this story that ever happened. But yes, it's autobiographical—the most autobiographical story I ever wrote."

This earns me some puzzled looks. Some obviously don't understand what I mean. Some will eventually puzzle it out. Some . . . and these are the shy, quiet ones sitting way in back . . . already have.

Let me end by quoting the response from one of them, a sequel explaining Sheila's behavior, written as a homework assignment by Kayla Glazer, one of Ray's eighth-graders.

"Dear Boy,

That night when I walked away from you after informing you that I was ditching you for Eric, you may have thought it was because I didn't enjoy hanging out with you. Actually, you probably thought it was because I thought I was too good for you by the way I used to act, and that is not such a bad guess. But in reality, it was because I was ashamed and felt that you were really too good for *me*. Let me explain . . .

I told you I hated fishing—at the time that was true. But after that night, after I watched you trying to catch that bass without me noticing—it was a beautiful bass, by the way—I felt my heart melt a little, not just for you, but also for your passion.

As I watched you sneakily adjust the line and reel him in, I secretly hoped that I would win the battle for your heart between me and that fish. Back then, it was like my ego constantly needed to be stroked. It was just the way I was—a stuck-up cat wanting to be petted NOW. But suddenly, it was as if the other suitors and their niceties didn't matter anymore—this was the final test to see if I was irresistible, to see if I could get all the attention I wanted. Of course I should be able to win against a petty fish! But still I was afraid your true love for fishing would come through, and I resisted the urge to bite my fingernails as you began to reach slowly, once again, for the reel. Finally, when you cut the line, I was elated—I had won, I was beautiful!—until suddenly it all slipped away when I saw the sinking expression on your face. I felt terrible. All I had ever cared about was what other people saw when they looked at me, but when I finally looked at me, I was disgusted.

I wanted to slip away as the fish had done, into the moonlit water. I didn't want to look into your eyes anymore, and see that you had chosen me instead of that fish, when really even a fish would make a better person than me.

Once you made me realize I didn't like myself the way I was, you also got me to want to change. And the first thing I did was to learn to fish, something that has proved to be my new passion. If you can possibly find a way to forgive me, I would like to invite you over to my house for dinner tonight. And if you still can't forgive me, at least you could come over to help me eat the biggest bass I ever caught.

Sincerely,
Sheila."

Twelve

Earlier, I wrote of the Connecticut River near my home, the long productive corridor where the water is backed up by Wilder Dam. Now, as August deepens with day after perfect day, it's time to describe the fishing downstream of the dam, with its entirely different set of conditions and challenges. At its best, it offers the most rewarding fly-fishing in this valley, and the chance to catch some of the biggest smallmouth in New England. It's the place I bring visiting flyfishers whom I want to impress—which means, having come this far with me, you.

Wilder Dam is fifteen miles south of us, and it's another eight or nine miles to Sumner Falls. We leave the canoe locked to a tree near the water's edge, drive south another seven miles to Windsor in two separate cars, cross the covered bridge to New Hampshire, park my car there in a cornfield, load up my friend's car with paddles, life jackets, and fly rods, drive back to Sumner to rejoin the canoe. We float downriver, fishing all the way, then, when we reach the covered bridge, load the canoe on my car, drive back to Sumner to my friend's car, redistribute our gear, then, separately, drive home—and try not to lose anything in all the shuffles.

A strenuous day, not even counting the paddling, wading, and casting—you really have to want to do it. But float fishing . . . letting the river carry you to the fishing . . . is a traditional, much-loved part of the American bass-fishing experience; bass buggers were floating rivers in jonboats long before trout were being caught off driftboats. Ray Bergman's 1945 book on bass has an evocative chapter on floating Arkansas rivers back in the day, and what he says could apply to the Connecticut.

It is my belief that no one sees the real beauty of the Ozarks unless he floats the rivers . . . Although I am a trout angler as well as a bass fisherman and have all the dry fly trout fisherman's prejudices, I forget them all when fishing for bass on moving water . . . Floating means drifting down the river aided by the paddle where the drift isn't fast enough, or where an eddy might keep you from going places . . . Each bend of the river brings forth new beauties of unusual distinction . . . As very few people other than fishermen travel the rivers, I'd say that most tourists miss the best scenery and atmosphere the country has to offer.

All true—and I would add the confident, optimistic surge that comes with floating one-way on a fast-flowing river, with new water constantly under the bow. If we're lucky, the bass will ornament the scenery, add to the surge; there's a good chance for a trophy on this stretch, a smallmouth over twenty inches, and there's no good way to reach them other than by floating. It's been a summer full of bass, I've encountered many hundreds, but I haven't found a really big one yet, and if it's going to happen, it's going to happen here.

Most of our floats start early in the mist. I drive down the New Hampshire side of the river, pass Wilder Dam on my right, check out its flow; there's a number you can call to get this information, but it's not very reliable, and I want to check in person that they're not releasing water big-time. They're not—the water trickling over the concrete lip makes it look like a small country weir, not a big hydroelectric dam—and so I cross over to Vermont on the Route 4 bridge, follow the river downstream past some of the most exuberantly fertile cornfields in New England.

The turn down to Sumner Falls is obscure and easy to miss. A shady dirt road leads past a lonely grave site near where a young riverman from

Quebec died in a log drive back in the 1890s. Beyond it rises another, much more recent stone; fishermen drown here with some regularity, and this marker, with a poem inscribed across the granite ("If tears could build a stairway," it begins) commemorates a bass fisher named Brian who was lost just a few years ago.

Sumner Falls is the only section of wild rapids left on this stretch of the Connecticut, and people are always underestimating them. On a morning like this one, with the dam releasing at 900 cubic feet per second, it looks like a pleasant, greenish-gray causeway of rocks deliberately placed there to allow you to promenade out in the river to picnic or fish. Come back when the release is 10,000 cfs, and it looks like the dangerous trap it is, with the river tripping and falling over itself in angry somersaults that look like they're hoping, just hoping, to find someone to knock down.

I stop above the rapids to check them out—still quiet in the mist. The access road ends on a sandy shelf, and this is where Tom Ciardelli is waiting in his truck. He's one of my oldest fishing buddies, but we don't go out much anymore. He fishes in Quebec for salmon ("Faux largemouth," I tell him), the Caribbean for tarpon ("Poor man's smallmouth"), and less and less near home; it's my job to remind him how much fun fishing local can be.

We're the same age, Tom and I, born four days apart in 1948, and this creates a bond—when the fishing slows, we can talk about Medicare or the sixties. And I realize I've missed something about him—I've missed watching him cast. His style is old-school, economical, wasting no energy, his arm held close to his torso—and yet it's wonderful now easily, how gracefully, the line shoots out.

(*Nota bene:* At times in this narrative, it will seem like Tom has jumped ship and been replaced by another angler. And, thanks to the miracle of postmodernist prose, he has. I fish this stretch with a lot of people, and when anecdotes require it, they'll replace Ciardelli in the bow.)

This early in the morning, with the flow having been low all night, there's a bathtub ring around the shoreline and a tidal kind of smell,

something that combines seaweed with mildew and a hint of wet copper—a smell I associate with big fish. The weather has been settled for
five days straight, a Bermuda high sitting right over us, and bass love that
sunny regularity even more than we do.

"What should I put on?" Tom asks as we string up our fly rods.

"Anything," I tell him. "As long as it's a mouse."

We fish these almost exclusively on the Sumner Float. Sneaky Petes
and the other bug imitations that do so well north of the dam hardly
interest the bass down here. They're meat eaters—they want minnow
imitations, crayfish patterns, or deer-hair mice, with tails long as shoe-
laces. Whether they actually think these *are* mice—that rodents floating
down the Connecticut are a common enough occurrence that they regularly look for them—is unlikely, but not impossible. My own theory is
that their hunched, round-backed silhouettes resemble floating crayfish,
which you see quite a lot of here—but it's more fun to pretend that bass
hunt mammals.

The water floating over the Sumner ledges spread apart from three
separate channels to form a wide bay. I always make sure to fish the
choppy, chocolate-colored edges of these, on the off chance that one of
the river's legendary brown trout is in the mood for a rodent, but, as I'm
just explaining to Tom, I never, ever catch a bass there.

It's always good to say this—"I never, ever catch a bass here"—since
it inevitably results in an immediate strike. Still, thanks to my disclaimer,
Tom isn't ready for the heavy fish that comes up. *Swoosh!*—he hooks
nothing but air. But it's a good sign, since the bass in this stretch are
either really ON or really OFF, and this suggests ON. In the eddy to the
side of the next channel, hard against the exposed ledges, Tom's mouse
elicits another strike, and this time he hooks it, an eighteen-inch smallmouth that runs into the heavy foam, stirs it into frothiness, and then
plunges toward the bottom, reminding Tom—and he need reminding—
what bass are at their best.

Everything that is beautiful and vivid in a small bass is even more
beautiful and vivid in a big bass—the vertical black bars, the flashing red
iris, the bronze color flowing back from the gills, the compact muscu-

larity. Tom holds it up, we both admire it, and then back into the river it goes—and any mouse that swims over it in the future will do so in perfect safety.

(As for those monster browns reputed to live here, but which we never catch, I take solace in the great A. J. McClane's verdict: "The river bass is superior to the brown trout; the smash of a heavy bass at a floating bug is the most tense moment an angler can experience at the end of any search.")

The two heaviest chutes of water find each other and flow westward toward Vermont in a rippling sheet of satiny gray water. Where this nears the bank, turning the gray to a languorous green, is a sunken weed bed, and from the center of this weed bed, casting a Lazy Ike, my wife Celeste once hooked a monster pike. Her excited shouts, as if jumped clear of the water, echo there yet.

No pike today—no bass either. We paddle back to the New Hampshire side and the resumption of the rocky shelf that forms the rapids proper. After this brief westward slant, the river's course is due south. The great pool right below Sumner's seems bottomless, but from now on, with the flow being so low, the riverbed will be visible almost everywhere; I often spend more time staring down at it than I do at the surrounding forest and hills. A jewel case of a bottom— polished cobble and suntanned gravel, with the scoured brightness of an Atlantic salmon river . . . which long ago in the vanished past the Connecticut once was.

And could be again—*not*. In the 1970s, a well-intentioned, well-funded government program attempted to restore the river's salmon run that had been wiped out in the eighteenth century with the construction of the first bank-to-bank dam in Massachusetts. Hopes were that this would be the capstone to the largely successful effort, begun in the 1960s, to clean the river into something more than the "best landscaped sewer in the world." The salmon would add a mascot, a living presence, to make conservation efforts appeal to a large section of the public otherwise indifferent to water quality; salmon would be the Bambi of the Connecticut, the Flipper, the Smoky the Bear.

The effort had its successes—for a time in the 1990s, it seemed like the run was on the point of being restored, with more than 400 adult salmon finding their way back to the river—but gains made on the Connecticut proper were negated by the problems salmon face in the greater world of the ocean, including overfishing and global warming. By the turn of this century, only a lonely handful of salmon, out of all the millions stocked upstream (often by schoolchildren in hands-on science projects) were returning to the river, and many of these met a sorry fate.

Just last year, a fisherman caught and killed a nine-pound brown trout in the White River tributary just upstream of Sumner Falls—a record catch, only it wasn't a brown, but a strictly protected Atlantic salmon. This salmon, spawned at an expensive, state-of-the-art federal hatchery in Bethel, by some miracle making its way as a smolt down the Connecticut to the Atlantic, growing to adulthood there, navigating back again through Long Island Sound, up the Connecticut, up the fish ladders over the dams, back to the White River, back to the pool by the hatchery where it was born, one of only a dozen that made it that year, its eggs, its genetic route-finding ability of incalculable worth to the restoration efforts . . . this million-dollar salmon, this survivor of survivors, was killed by an angler who either didn't know the different between a trout and a salmon or didn't care. A tracking device implanted in the salmon when it was a smolt enabled game wardens to track it to the fisherman's freezer.

That was the second-to-last straw that broke the restoration effort's back; the first came in 2011, when Hurricane Irene severely damaged the federal hatchery.

"So it's over now?" I asked Tom. "They've given up?"

"And over on the Merrimack, too. You and I will never catch a salmon here and our kids won't, either."

In retrospect, the chief beneficiary of the salmon stocking were the river's bass, who grew fat on their diet of smolt and smolt pieces—the dam turbines sliced many of them into sushi.

Tom picks off a bass at the base of the cliff, I miss one where it flattens, and then we need to scoot around a long shallow stretch where the canoe scrapes bottom. When it deepens again, we make a sharp left and paddle like hell to get back upstream, earning ourselves, when we finally stop and turn, a longish drift along a wine-dark slot where the water stays deep right up the bank. The current is quick beneath us, sluggish in close, causing some problems in casting and navigation.

"Let's get out and wade," I suggest, paddling hard on the right to beach us.

"Here, Dad?"

"Watch your step on that clay."

It's daughter Erin in the bow now; she's twenty-six, but only yesterday—yesterday!—she was twelve, in a transformation that bewilders me. She hops out first and drags the canoe high enough that it won't wander off while we're wading. Twenty yards below us the gravel slides into the river as a stubby point.

"Forget about the water," I tell her, in my best coaching voice. "Cast toward the sun on your backcast, toward Vermont on the forward. The line will find the water on its own."

Erin is just learning to fly cast, she hasn't gotten the timing down yet, the muscle memory, but from sheer niceness is able to coax the fly into doing approximately what she wants. Twenty-five feet is her maximum, but it's enough to slide her popper down the frothy quickening where the current is bulged by the gravel hump. She's done her part— and now the bass sheltering there does his, coming up at the very last second before the popper swings back into the bank. A ten-inch fish, but by darting out into the current he doubles the fun factor.

While Erin's dealing with all the splash and fuss, I notice an even bigger commotion in the shallows. A much bigger bass is chasing prey through ten inches of water, so its back juts up like the blunt end of a plow. Chasing crayfish—you see that often, particularly when the crayfish are molting—and it reminds me that when you float this stretch you should always be fishing the skinny water, not just the drop-offs.

For the next 500 yards there isn't much to choose from between the New Hampshire side and the Vermont side, with both banks enjoying their share of bass. If the sun were out, New Hampshire would be shadier and cooler, which might be a reason to stay there—but it's still foggy. And so, as usual, which side we fish depends just as much on cultural-political factors as it does piscatory ones. My liberal friends seem more comfortable drifting along the Vermont side, while my Libertarian friends (well, the one I have) prefer floating down New Hampshire.

Ray Chapin, who's replaced Erin in the bow, is a native Vermonter, so there's no use asking him to vote. I paddle us over to the west bank, but in exchange for that he's got to listen to my spiel.

"It's genius, the way Vermont has branded itself. That image of purity—it's moving the merchandise. Vermont ice cream. Vermont maple syrup. Vermont microbreweries. And now my local hardware store sells Moo Doo fertilizer crapped in Vermont."

Ray nods in satisfaction. "That's what we do all right. But there's no reason your state couldn't do similar."

"Are you kidding me? New Hampshire as a brand? The only thing we're famous for is being a great place to live for rich people with no social conscience."

I like to exaggerate, and like it best when fishing. Actually, floating down from Sumner Falls, not knowing the enormous differences between the two states, an unbiased observer might vote for New Hampshire as being the nicer, more enlightened state. You can't see them from the river, but there are great scars just inland from the Vermont bank, where gravel is being excavated by heavy machinery in ugly open-pit mines. Over on the New Hampshire side, forest extends right down to the water, and you never hear any traffic; the resident eagles, one of which soars over us now, all prefer New Hampshire.

The scarred stretch doesn't last long, but in one of the abandoned pits is a shooting range where Vermonters, the lazy ones who don't like to reload, fire off their Bushmasters and AK-74s. They're doing it now . . . *POP, POP, POW* . . . and we both have to fight down the urge to duck.

"You know what I'm remembering?" I ask Ray.

"I know what you're remembering."

We floated this stretch the morning of the mass shooting near Denver, where twelve people were killed and seventy wounded while watching the latest Batman movie in a multiplex theater. We floated early that day . . . out in Aurora, it wasn't yet dawn . . . but so many guns were being fired off in the gravel pit that it seemed, when we later heard about the body count, that local sociopaths were practicing for the time when it would be their own turn to set records.

There's some generous water here. The bank shelves steeply, and the current sweeps along so smoothly it reminds us of floating the Yellowstone out in Montana. The bass wait in the shallows like hitchhikers begging rides, and we both have ones on simultaneously; one tugs us toward the bank, one tugs us out toward the middle, but they end up compensating for each other and leave us pretty much where the current wants us: floating backward parallel to shore.

We stay that way even after releasing the bass; floating backward gives right-hander Ray the chance to cast naturally, without tossing backhand. I find it disorientating—I've never liked riding backward on a train—but it quickly pays off. Ray's mouse lands in water barely deep enough to float it and is immediately taken by a huge bass that must have been buried in the gravel, since it's otherwise impossible to imagine how we wouldn't have seen its dorsal fin.

It fights Ray hard but futilely—not for nothing is Ray Chapin the best flyfisher in this valley. We measure it at nineteen inches, which makes me jealous, but not as jealous as if it measured one inch more.

The water is so clear it's easy to make out the cribbing of the bridge that once spanned the river here; out in the middle is a rock pile that used to support one of the abutments, and below this the fish like to sunbathe. The river curls to a view of Mount Ascutney, rising in successive terraces to its surprisingly high top. A much painted, much loved mountain, Ascutney—it centers a landscape that seems begging to be framed.

Hart Island swells up on the right, and son Matthew, having replaced Ray, asks for a break so we can eat the blueberry-zucchini bread we baked last night. Hart isn't just any island, but the home to several species of plants and mollusks that are found only in a few other places in the world. The Connecticut River Macrosite, this stretch of river is called, with the highest concentration of globally rare species in either New Hampshire or Vermont. There was talk of building a dam here, but the salmon restoration effort and the presence of these rarities kept it out.

While floating Hart's edges, I like to stare down searching for the rarest of the rare species: cobblestone tiger beetles. They like to "inhabit sandy cobble beaches on the upstream side of islands along the banks of free-flowing rivers"—criteria, which in all fussy particulars, Hart Island meets. New Hampshire's total population hovers around 100 individual beetles, meaning one bad flood could render them extinct, but somehow, year after year, they cobble on. Plainfield has made it their "official town insect," selling T-shirts with their picture.

We wade wet here, enjoying the chill on our legs, knowing the sun will dry us off the minute we step back out. And the sun is out now full strength—really, it's a gorgeous August day, eleven on a scale of ten. Matt, very much the athlete, is casting his Heddon Torpedo with a great deal of *oomph*. He's getting strikes the instant it lands, but only strikes—the bass, as they do sometimes, just slap at the plug, much to Matt's frustration.

There's a steep drop-off toward the edge of the island creating a fishy back eddy we're always careful to search, but then the current quickens to a point I have to concentrate on navigation. Blowdowns become more common now—pine logs slant out into the water like flippers in pinball. The navvies who built the railroad along the bank drilled holes in the rocks when they tamped in their dynamite, and the unnaturally squarish rocks you see here on the bottom all have these holes and half-holes showing where they were split apart.

The bank is sandy here, pocked with swallow holes, and holds, for a surprisingly long distance, the convolute shape of a breaking wave. In a spot where the wave had broken, in the salty-looking clumps of dirt at its base, I once saw something glisten, went over to investigate, found a small glass bottle that was perfectly intact.

I rinsed it in the water, shook the drops off, stared down. *Cabot Sylpho Nathol Chelsea, Mass.* read the raised lettering on the glass. It was slightly larger than a shot bottle, and probably had held only four or five ounces. There was another on the bank, and then, when I kicked at the dirt, dozens more, all with the same label.

Was it patent medicine? *Sylpho Nathol* had a pseudo scientific ring that could have suckered in the rubes. Had they been dropped here by rivermen in the old days? After spending their days immersed in freezing water they would probably be ready for a snort. Or was it something people used to ward off influenza? The bottles were old at any rate. I cleaned two of them off, stowed them in my tackle bag, forgot all about them until weeks later when I was moving fly boxes around.

A quick Internet search solved one of the mysteries. Cabot turns out to be a company that's still in business making wood stains—every hardware store in America sells Cabot stains. Back in the 1890s, the original Mr. Cabot used coal tar to make his *Sylpho Nathol* disinfectant, which is clearly what these bottles held.

Interesting—but why were there so many here, and what had people been trying to disinfect? Their hands? They tools? Their innards?

"Hey, Nick!"

My teenage nephew, concentrating on his casting, only slowly looks around.

"See that yellowish cliff up ahead? Look carefully and you're going to see these cool old-time bottles."

He's impressed—it's not just bass that his Uncle Walter knows about. We stop and pick one up to take home to show his parents.

Nick has replaced Matt in the bow—Matt, who in the space of three seconds has gone home to dry off, gone to Philadelphia to college, gone to Manhattan to work, gone to med school in Boston. I badly need another teenager in the bow to help ballast time, slow it down to reasonable levels, and Nick, my fellow redhead, fills this role nicely.

A season of competitive rowing has broadened Nick's shoulders to the point I can let him do the heavy paddling. He's new to fly-fishing, and since it's hard to learn sitting down, I'm stopping at the sandbars so he can get out and practice.

During one of these wade stops, after he misses a nice strike, I tell him this:

"Hey, listen. There's something you've probably already figured out. I curse a lot when I'm fishing. I don't feel particularly bad about this, but on the other hand, I don't want you telling your parents, they might think I'm a deleterious influence. Cursing isn't a bad thing, if you know when not to. Cursing around old people and girls—bad. Cursing around bass—good. Got that?"

"Kids curse in school."

"I bet they do . . . See that splash? Jesus! I bet that's the same goddam bass that jumped you last time, the greedy fucker!"

Over to Vermont to finer things.

The action has slowed after our fast start, so it's time to give the mice a rest, let them sunbathe on the canoe thwart until needed. I'm trying sinking flies now—rust-colored Clouser minnows, brown wooly buggers, pumpkin-colored wooly grubbers—hoping the bass will mistake them for crayfish. Every thirty casts one does, smaller than the bruisers caught earlier—future bruisers, bruisers in training.

Two hours out now and the current, the downstream impetus, really gets into your bloodstream, so you feel, after years of searching, that you've finally discovered the perfect way to go through life: coasting, the force of the world, for a blessed change, at your back.

Up above the dam with the water being so deep, the current is uniform from bank to bank; floating down it is like striding along a moving walkway at an airport. On this stretch, with the uneven bottom, the effect is more like being in an amusement park where there are tricky variations on the moving walkway theme, with escalators added on, conveyor belts, waterslides, rocky chutes, so the slickness and speed of the ride is always changing. Most of the time this allows you to drift along in a lazy reverie, but sometimes—when a jack-in-the-box of a boulder suddenly jumps up from the bottom—it requires immediate attention so as not to be spilled.

Somewhere along this stretch we've crossed the town line into Cornish, New Hampshire, remembered in American cultural history as the home of the "Cornish Colony" back in the idyllic days before the First World War. Drawn by its natural beauty, its remove from the fashionable tourist haunts, its view of Ascutney across the river, a prominent group of American artists and writers built summer homes here, some quite lavish—even Woodrow Wilson vacationed in Cornish. Most of these homes overlooked the river from a safe distance; these were artists who favored the long view, and the river, in those days, was rowdy with rivermen and dirty with logs.

Winston Churchill, the best-selling American author, not *the* Winston Churchill (who added an S. to his byline in 1904 to avoid confusion), was one of the writers, and though he lived in a Gilded Age mansion, ended up running as a progressive for governor, taking on the railroad interests that controlled the state. Maxfield Parrish lived here, too, the artist whose androgynous models, pseudo-classical themes, and richly saturated hues made him a fortune in advertising before critics began taking his work seriously. His favorite model was Sue Lewin, a local farmgirl, and what the exact nature of their relationship was provides local gossip to this day.

The most talented Cornish colonist was August St. Gaudens, the sculptor, whose home and studio, maintained by the National Park Service, is well worth a visit when you're done fishing. St. Gaudens did the Shaw monument in Boston, General Sherman at Central Park, the "Standing Lincoln" in Chicago, and many other famous works of public art. He loved his studio's setting over the river, loved, most of all, the view of Mount Ascutney.

"It is very beautiful," he said a few days before he died in 1907, as he looked out at a sunset over the mountain. "But I want to go farther away."

Cornish's last artist/writer of note was none other than J. D. Salinger, the infamous hermit of American letters, who came to town in 1953 and never left. In the local paper appeared frequent ads by autograph collectors willing to pay big bucks for any receipt signed by

Salinger, any plumbing or carpentry contract, any bill. When he died in 2010, the same paper ran a series of now-it-can-be-told interviews with the local people who had been so protective of his privacy, but the only thing new they had to say was that he liked to cross the river over to Hartland's famous Saturday night church dinners, and always made sure he got there early so he could be among the first in line for roast beef.

The day, bright already, now develops into something special, as the approach of a weather front brings in melodramatic blue clouds that Maxfield Parrish could have painted, with those luminous tones that were his trademark. From the most luminous part of this luminosity a solitary figure appears, riding down the center of the river on one of those boards, so popular now, that I always want to call waterboards.

"Waterboard?" Celeste says from the bow, with uncharacteristic sarcasm. "That's another part of the American experience altogether."

"I get confused."

"*Paddle*board. Paddleboard yoga is all the rage."

This paddleboarder isn't doing yoga—she's content to scull downriver, taking the occasional languorous stroke. Like a gondolier floating through Iowa, Celeste says, and that's the right analogy, since for the last few hundred yards we've been floating down a river of cornstalks. The farms on either bank enjoy some of the most fertile soil in New England, and, this late in August, a lot of stalks end up in the river, though none seem to have ears of corn attached. Later in the fall they'll be joined by pumpkins—a flood a few Octobers ago filled the river with them, and they floated a surprisingly long distance.

The paddleboarder will be the only person we see on our four-hour float. Summer ends sooner and sooner each year, people's lives are too hectic to let it continue too long, and the kayaks, inner tubes, and inflatables have all been put away until next year. And as good as the fishing is here, the bass boys—victims of their own technology—avoid this stretch altogether, since they can't navigate with their bass boats. Two or three angler paths lead down to the steeper of the rock ledges, and you'll seen bank fishers, but not very often.

The number of bass per square mile probably isn't as high here as it is north of Wilder Dam, but this is more than made up for by the size and strength of the fish. That said, I haven't encountered anything on this float larger than Ray's nineteen-incher, and with the stated intention of catching a twenty-inch fish, I'm beginning to feel antsy. Antsy, not desperate. On this perfect August day, I'm feeling the exact opposite of desperate, and one of the reasons is the water we're now approaching.

In all 400 miles of Connecticut River, this may well be the single best spot to catch smallmouth. A stretch of shallows sweeps past a gravel bar that is dry at low water; a bay is created by its encircling, crab-like arm, and below this the water deepens along the bank into a long narrow aquarium. For 150 yards, conditions are perfect, with an even flow of oxygenated water flowing over a cobbled gravel bottom, deep toward the inside, deep toward the outside, but rising to a sandy ridge in the middle where fish like to hunt. In low-water conditions, it's easy to spot them, especially if you're standing up in the canoe or walking high along the grassy bank.

Today there are a dozen or more bass visible—Celeste, who's scrambled up the bank toward the railroad tracks, sees them before I do and points out which ones I should be trying for. Easier said than done—these bass are as fussy as trout when it comes to taking flies. I have to tie on a finer leader, pay more attention to technical things like drag, presentation, drift—and, when I do, start getting hits. Small ones, not the obese granddads we can see holding a lazy confabulation on the ridge.

Their disdain is palpable. One turns and approaches my crayfish imitation, but then, when he really gets a good look at it, the thickening of lip that passes as his nose turns up like a snob's and he swims away.

I paddle us upstream so we can have one last pass at the aquarium, then, reluctantly, lever us back out into the current.

Until now, we've only seen two houses on the five miles of float, but now the first outliers of Windsor hove into view. There's a path leading up to an outdoor sculpture garden, and if you walk through the meadow behind this you'll end up in the parking lot of the Harpoon

Brewery. We've always been tempted to beach the canoe here, admire the art, then saunter on up for a restorative cold brewski—but we've never actually done it.

Windsor is an interesting place—a river town, set right on the bank. By certain reckonings, it's the oldest town in Vermont, since the meeting that formed the temporarily independent Republic of Vermont in 1777 took place in a tavern on Main Street you can still visit. Vermont's constitution was the first anywhere in the world to prohibit slavery, so that happened on Main Street, too.

It's a town of contradictions. It boasts a dignified, genteel downtown, though many storefronts stand empty. It's got a reputation for scruffiness, a stubborn crime problem, a prison, but it's citizens are among the friendliest in the valley. Tourists will accidentally stumble upon downtown, take pictures of the beautiful churches and gardens, and yet a few yards away down by the railroad tracks, old tenement three-deckers that have been rotting away since the machine tool industry died fifty years ago still house families who can't afford anything better. It's a town for the ninety-nine percent; the one-precenters have their own enclave, their ski homes and horse farms, in West Windsor, a few miles away.

Back over to New Hampshire . . .

The only substantial tributary we'll pass on this float, Blow-Me-Down Brook, flows into the river on the east bank with minimum fuss—an inconspicuous cut in the bank, a triangle-shaped delta of sand, and a flow just substantial enough to trill. A bald eagle sits in the shallows watching the world with the dignified indifference with which eagles always regard things. Seeing us, it calls out an *e-e-e* sound, only we're not the ones it's meant for—its mate slants down in a long slow wheel until it lands on the delta, too.

Blow-Me-Down brings in water fresh off the hills, so it's reasonable to assume there might be bass in the shallows cooling off. I mention this to Celeste, and, cheerleader that she is, she takes it and runs.

"Catch him! Catch him, honey!"

And though I have no faith whatsoever that my cast will produce anything, I double haul my damnedest and manage the longest cast of the day. A few minutes ago I switched over to a Todd's Wiggle Minnow; its humped foam body shimmies alluringly across the surface, suggesting a wounded baitfish or a crayfish with a broken back. It hasn't wiggled very far before an enormous bow wave approaches it from downstream. I don't have time to fuck it up, I don't even have time to yell "Shit!" before I'm attached to what created the wave, and then it's like Earth itself, the whole secret power of it, has taken hold of me and started shaking.

The bass jumps the way heavy ones do, not quite managing to clear the water, wallowing backward in a piggish bath of spray. This wakes him up—in the space of six seconds he becomes the first bass of the summer to strip all my line out and start into my backing. The current helps him, though he doesn't need much help—fighting him is so quantitatively different than playing a smaller fish that it becomes qualitatively differ-ent, too, so I feel like I'm involved in an entirely different enterprise.

And this isn't because he jumps again or wraps the line around a log or tail walks or pulls any of those tricks that are supposed to happen in epic fish-man battles. He tugs a ton, sets the reel spool rattling in its frame, makes my arms ache, gets my heart racing, and somehow this shocks me—that a creature can be so desperate to be rid of me, me who means it no harm, me who, if he treats me respectfully, may write about him in a book.

The fight is so strenuous, lasts so long, that there comes a moment of weakness when I long for someone else to take over and relieve the strain, the way I would if I were carrying the heavy end of a piano; if Celeste were a flyfisher, I would hand her the rod, say "Your fish, dear," sit down and watch. But the faintheartedness soon passes—it's like an invis-ible hand has slapped me bracingly across the cheek, yelled "Be a man!"

I swing my legs over the gunwale, steady myself, clamber out onto the gravel, fight the fish standing up. This is what turns the tide—being able to follow his runs on foot, and then, when the tugs start weakening, coasting him shoreward through the shallows by bending the rod ten or twelve degrees past prudent. Still, I can't manage to lift his head out of the water, and it isn't until I remember the old pump-and-reel tech-nique big-game fishers use that I manage to land him.

Celeste extends the tape measure across the sand. "Twenty inches!" I predicted during the fight, but he's a good inch past that, and if I pulled the tape tight I could coax out a half-inch more. I put both hands under his torso, and, in an evolutionary atavism going back God knows how many thousands of years, lift him up so my wife can admire his heft, proving—if Celeste still needs proof after thirty years of marriage—my prowess as a hunter.

"Good job, honey!"

The fish is not only the biggest of the summer; it's the darkest— probably the darkest bass I've ever seen. It's as though the black striping has leached sideways until his entire flank is that color, with hardly any bronze visible at all. And it's an old bass, to have attained that size here in New England where growth rates are so slow; unlike in our own species, age confers great strength on bass, not decrepitude—no young bass would have pulled with such power.

(We don't know much about the death of bass, except for the ones we kill ourselves. Once every few years I'll see one that size floating belly-up in the shallows, and there's something lonely and poignant about the sight—they look like those decaying schooners you used to see rotting away on the mudflats of coastal Maine.)

I start swimming the bass around to restore its vitality, but he doesn't need that—the moment his tail touches water he's gone. I mop the sweat off my forehead, stagger over to the canoe for lemonade, and, without thinking about it, wanting only to get it out of our way, roll cast my Wiggle Minnow downstream.

It comes tight against the current, sinks a bit from the force, and this brief nodding submersion prompts another bass to strike. It's not quite as big as the first one—twenty inches when I bring him to the still-extended tape—but he fights just as hard. Life doesn't often give you instant replays like this, so I enjoy it to the max, with none of the *will-he-get-away?* angst I suffered the first time.

Twenty-inch bass from successive casts. What a river!

The rest of the float is going to be anticlimatic, though there's still plenty to enjoy. On the New Hampshire side comes a series of ledges that draw the current over with a granite kind of magnetism, and the deep pockets where they release it again is a good spot for pike. Over on the Windsor side, forgotten rowboats lie well up on the bank, making it look like the tide has gone out on Cape Cod.

The dirt landing where we beach the canoe is the one place on the entire float where you can count on encountering your fellow humans. My old pal John Marshall might be there, the only guide who floats the river with a driftboat, or the prim and proper Plainfield woman who brings her poodle down for its daily swim, tying a line to his collar and tossing him in the current until, when the line comes taught, she hauls him back in, or the man who likes bringing his lawn chair down when it's hot like this, immersing it in the shallows, stretching out with a beer. Or, once, Al Gore when he was running for president and wanted to burnish his environmental credentials by taking a canoe ride on the river, accompanied by a flotilla of Secret Service men, reporters, and flunkies—none of whom seemed happy to see me.

Or the friendly young people working for North Star Canoe rentals, who shuttle groups up here so they can float back down to the Taylor Farm. We've done that stretch ourselves, which means another three miles of fishing—but not today. Below us the weathered Cornish-Windsor covered bridge, the longest covered bridge in the country still handling traffic, spans the river, looking as ramshackle and temporary as it probably did in 1866 when it was first constructed—and yet an awful lot of water has flown beneath it since.

If you float under it, you soon come to a soot-stained railroad bridge that is nearly as old. I enjoy looking back upriver here, because you can see both bridges at once, and few other traces of this century. Railroad bridge, covered bridge, islands, cornfields, and river harmoniously blend in an era when hardly anything is harmonious and absolutely nothing blends.

Up near home, I sometimes take the Connecticut for granted, since I can fish it any time I want. Down here, with our visits being rarer, I always feel wistful when I finally tear myself away. I try to extend the day's ritual as long as I can. Lunch at Windsor Diner, with the best mac-

and-cheese in Vermont; a growler of IPA from the Harpoon Brewery to save for dinner; corn and cucumbers from Meacham's farm stand in Hartland—and then the bouncing drive back down the road to Sumner Falls, returning Tom, Ray, Erin, Nick, Celeste, or whoever's been fishing with me to their car.

I drive back north to Lyme, but for most of the trip I can still feel the downriver flow in my shoulders, my chest, my imagination—can feel it now, for that matter, after writing about it here. Time—time as an imperceptibly diminishing bank account—feels that way, too; there's a lot more tugging on my heart than smallmouth. It's been a beautiful day. No, a perfect day. And how many of those can a man my age still expect?

Thirteen

Coming to the end of a long book, for the author, is like entering old age. You take some satisfaction at having come so far, tempered by some mortification for all you haven't accomplished. I've not had time to write about all the subjects I've intended to, but perhaps it's not too late to touch upon several.

It's been fifty years now performing the same trick, and yet when I manage to pull if off it still makes me laugh. I select from my box a tiny bundle of feather and cork, tie it to my leader, toss it out to water where I think bass might lurk, and—like magic!—the fish thinks it's an insect, bites down hard, starts jumping, sends a throb up my wrist through my arm to my funny bone, gets a smile going across my kisser. I always smile when I play a bass, whereas with trout I'm often more pensive. Trout can be ridiculously picky, the wading is difficult, the leader needs tending so as not to snap—and, if you overcome all the challenges, it may well be to capture a wan, spiritless creature that was raised in a tank. You often meet trout like that, fish you don't particularly approve of—but I've never met a bass I didn't like.

Many flyfishers nurse a fantasy that becomes more urgent the nearer to retirement age they come: they want to be able to fish all they want. I am extraordinarily lucky in that respect; for many years, I've ordered my life in precisely that fashion, so, at least theoretically, I can go fishing whenever the mood strikes. In reality, much interferes, starting with a long northern hemisphere winter when—no ice fisher, and without the disposable income to fly south—I end up daydreaming about fishing like so many others.

Even during the season a lot gets in the way, including weather, writing, dam releases, chores, aches, pains, weekend guests—but these only make those moments when I do go out all the sweeter and more precious.

But, leaving aside these grudging compromises with reality, I am indeed one of those fortunate people who can fish any time they want—and yet I have to tell you who dream of this that *fishing any time you want is still not enough.*

I'm writing this last chapter in late November after my own fishing season has ended, though it's still legal on certain lakes. Yesterday, needing some sunshine, I took my bike and rode around Lake Morey over in Vermont, enjoying that summer-resort-out-of-season kind of loneliness I've always found so evocative. Bass season is long finished, the trout have now quit, but out in the middle of the lake in a kayak was a solitary fisherman trying his luck for pickerel or perch. After fishing more than 100 days this season, having experienced enough small adventures to fill a book, I still felt intensely jealous that he was out there and I wasn't.

I remember as a boy driving back to the suburbs with my parents after October weekends at our summer home on Lake Candlewood. The road followed the shoreline for the first half mile, and, peering out from my backseat window, I would often see two fishermen in a boat working the far shore. Seldom in my life have I longed for anything so desperately—to be able to do what they were doing; not be a shy, bookish teenager being dragged against his will back to the city, but a grown man who was master of his fate, a country man, a flyfisher, someone who could spend beautiful October afternoons ensconced as deeply in autumn's beauty as it's possible to be ensconced. Write in the morning, fish in the afternoons—that was my dream.

Fifty years later, looking back, I marvel that I've managed to accomplish this, against all odds—and yet there's a mysterious, not-to-be-entirely-despised kind of greediness in us that makes even a lifetime of fly-fishing turn out to be not enough. Whatever I seek to grasp in fly-fishing—and many times I've tried explaining it—it can't be grasped. Fun, adventure, wonder, enlightenment, companionship, epiphany, solitude, solace. All can be achieved, but what lies beyond these will forever elude us. The secret of life? I can't give a name to it, me who is reasonably good with words. But I do know this. Going fishing, my hands still shake when I string up my rod, my heart is filled with wild excitement, and my boyhood self, every other trace of which the years have smothered, comes flooding back with all its unquenchable longing, all its exuberant strength.

Summer used to quit these hills very suddenly. Clouds in late August would grow bronze around their edges, wind squalls would start harrying girls' hair, and the maples shed early, so anyone taking a late summer nap in the hammock might wake up covered in red and gold leaves. Labor Day, the very thought of it, seemed to hustle the season autumnward, with an early frost acting like a shot across the bow, warning us to get out those sweaters, ready those rakes, harvest that garden.

All this has changed. We used to say that the only problem with living this far north was that summer was too short, and things would be perfect if it would last four months rather than three. Thanks to climate change, we've gotten our wish. Those sharpish winds wait until October now, so we swim in the pond through September. The foliage season peaks later and later. Farmers get in a last crop of hay from fields that, this time of year, used to be brown and shriveled. The flowers in our hanging baskets spend September getting their second wind, and October's blossoms can be as abundant as June's.

Summer's end, so abrupt in the old days, has become as stubbornly prolonged as winter's; just when it feels like it's gone for good, it returns again, with afternoon after afternoon of brilliant sunshine and bluebird blue skies . . . summer taking a curtain call, starting a farewell tour, staging a comeback.

It's people who quit on summer now, not summer that quits on people. We long for it in winter, go semi-crazy when it actually arrives, vow to enjoy it to the max, trying to suck every summery thing right through our suntanned pores . . . and then about August fifteenth, long before Labor Day, throw up our hands, say, okay that's enough now, summer's over, time for all good Americans to go back to working off their asses.

Colleges start earlier and earlier, so there are no young people to staff the resorts and cabins; grade school begins as early as August twentieth, so late-summer family vacations are impossible; preseason sports practices sweep up the stragglers; our local swim beach closes because they can't find lifeguards. Labor Day weekend, when it finally arrives, has a lonely, almost November kind of feel, despite boasting the best weather of the year. Meteorologically, September has replaced August as our new high summer, but there's no one left outside to notice.

The same pattern applies to bass fishing. Even in summer, I never see anyone fly-fishing the river, so it could be an odd activity, a watery yoga or martial art, I've invented on my own. For many locals, fishing is strictly a springtime thing, and when the stocked trout have all been caught, they pack it in. Tourists fish in the summer, but they're gone by September. The fishermen I encounter in autumn on the Connecticut are the hard-core addicts, but they're spinners and trollers, not flyfishers. Some are still looking for bass, but the majority fish for walleye and pike, which come into their own now just as the smallmouth get shyer. I'm not sure why, but these fishermen are notorious hyperbolists, so when they tell me they've been hauling in twenty-pound pike and ten-pound walleyes, I immediately divide by half—and subtract even more if they're sporting B. A. S. S. stickers on their Hummers.

Read any how-to book on bass fishing written in the last hundred years, and you'll be told that bass go on a feeding frenzy in autumn to get ready for the lean days of winter. (Jason Lucas: "A bass's instinct makes him try to fatten up, as a bear does in fall, before his winter of inactivity.") And maybe they do, though in my years of fishing for them I've never encountered this frenzy in action. I'm not sure that bass are quite smart enough to foresee winter, even instinctively, or prudent enough to deliberately pack on the carbs if they do. Me, I'm putting up storm windows, getting in a supply of firewood, weather-stripping the doors, but the bass, I suspect, are living blissfully in the present. That you will catch bigger bass in autumn is a rule that does seem to apply, but the numbers are nowhere near as plentiful as they are in summer.

Bass will sometimes move back into the shallows on particularly warm days, and I can sympathize with their motivation. I swim as late in the autumn as I can, and toward the end, instead of plunging toward the middle of the pond, I stay parallel to shore in the twenty inches of water the sun has had the chance to heat up. Out in the middle of the pond I'd be shivering to the verge of hypothermia, but there in the shallows it's summer again—and surely the bass's inner core responds to this like mine does.

Something like a frenzy can occur, if conditions are perfect. Every September, I keep my antenna aimed toward a unique combination of elements. If there's a frost near the equinox followed by a warmer than usual afternoon, a gentle breeze from the south or southwest, a release of 4,000 cfs from the dam, a late hatch of mayflies, no errands to run or family obligations to keep me at home—if all these stars and ducks are aligned just so (which happens maybe one year out of three), I can look forward to some extraordinary fishing out on the Connecticut, with thirty-fish afternoons a real possibility. Still, even then I don't get the feeling that the bass are feasting to build up body fat, but celebrating a brief return to June.

The frenzy, a legitimate one, happens in late summer. Enormous clouds of flying ants appear on our waters, descending in two or three successive swarms over the course of two weeks. I sometimes think that passenger pigeons must have given this effect, staggering you with their abundance; if I dip a kid's beach bucket in our pond, the number of ants floating inside the rim is too high to count.

I'll grab my four-weight outfit and go out in the canoe to try for trout, but it's next to impossible—with millions of real ones to choose from, the odds of a rainbow mistaking my fly for the real thing is next to zero, particularly when the naturals are so tiny.

Luckily, bass like ants, too. Out on the river they'll be feeding on them all day, with a sipping kind of rise much daintier than their normal grab-and-go. Within all the various threads and swirls that make up a river's surface, one current line, by some trick of hydrography, will carry most of the food, like a narrow moving smorgasbord. (We call this, rather inelegantly, the "scum line.") The ants flow downstream atop this and the bass pluck them off, rising just like trout do and being nearly as picky. *Nearly* as picky—if you put a good ant imitation over them, you can be confident of getting a response. The problem comes after that. The ants are so small that you can only fish them on very fine leaders, so it takes concentration and patience to bring the fish in.

These occasions—the flying ants in late August; the bassy mid-September afternoons—provide some of my happiest fishing of the season, and it takes something special to make me miss either. Last year, just when I should have been concentrating on bass, I went on vacation to the Gaspé Peninsula in September, and spent a day fishing the famous Dartmouth River for Atlantic salmon, the reputed king of gamefish.

It was enjoyable—sort of. My guide, Eli, was a Jew from Casablanca who, having emigrated as a young man, was now French-Canadian as they come. A great mix of personalities as it turns out. He had a brooding way of staring out over the water that seemed wise and ancient, plus the hearty *voyageur* habit of slapping you on the back when you did something right.

I fished hard, but didn't catch anything, despite Eli's coaching. The water was low and the salmon were lazy, though I did get a buzz from seeing twenty-five pounders stare up in boredom at my fly. I was a bit bored myself, truth to tell. Salmon fishing is mechanical, you use the flies and tactics tradition dictates, and there's little room for freelancing or experimentation. Then, too, I had to listen to Eli's sad stories about how good the fishing used to be and how diminished the run now is; it didn't make me particularly eager to catch one. And the expense. This day was costing me serious money ("I could buy a decent bass rod for this," I realized, halfway through), and I knew that when it came to salmon fishing I couldn't afford to get too interested.

I elaborate on this to make a simple point. Fishing a famous salmon river, having huge salmon swim right in front of me, being coached by a wise and experienced salmon guide. It was right out of a fly-fishing fantasy, and yet I spent most of the day thinking about bass—wondering whether I was missing a late flying ant hatch at home, or one of those perfect September afternoons when the smallmouth go wild.

There *is* a fish that gets in the way of my autumn bass fishing: trout. While in the course of these pages I've occasionally dissed trout fishing and its mystique, the truth is I'm nuts about it, though sometimes in summer I forget about it entirely. In autumn, I remember again— remember how much fun it is to hike up a mountain stream casting for brookies, or how much beauty you find on our local ponds fishing for "gulpers." These are rainbows that feed on *subimagos* of the mayfly that haven't escaped to the air, or midge pupae that hang shrimp-like in the surface film—rainbows that you stalk like you're hunting, and are a real challenge to fool. The trout cruise along sipping these flies on the surface, their noses bulging the water like the snouts of submarines, which, after an enemy ship approaches, prudently submerge. Often their fins are visible, too—they cut through the surface film like they're slicing and dicing the water into private soup bowls they can slurp from without using spoons. Tiny flies, gossamer leaders, careful stalking, delicate casting, a precise way of striking if you do raise a fish. It requires a fussy style of fishing that's not for everyone, but I happen to love it.

While the gulpers are gulping on the pond the bass are probably rising to white caddis flies out on the river, so I'm faced with a difficult choice. I'll usually concentrate on bass for most of September, and then switch over to mostly trout when October comes. Actually, one of the pleasures of autumn fishing is how many species you can catch at one go. I went out on Lake Fairlee on my birthday, October fifth, and in the course of two hours caught (on the same soft-hackled fly) bluegill, chub, pickerel, brown trout, rainbow trout, largemouth bass, smallmouth bass, yellow perch, and a rock bass—nine species, without moving my canoe from the spot where I first anchored.

Some autumnal quality to the sunlight, absorbed by the water, made these the most vibrantly colored fish I caught all year. The bass in particular. Never do I see largemouth that lemony; never have I seen smallmouth so bronze. The bars on their flanks could have been splashed with paint seconds before I caught them, so fresh and vividly did they shine; after releasing them, I was surprised to find that my hand wasn't black.

The politics of bass fishing—that's something that could be written about by a George Orwell of a bass writer, since we live in an age when everything has become bitterly political. Sometimes, sipping bourbon, I decide that when, as now seems inevitable, America breaks into two separate countries (which, for lack of better terms, we'll call the Union and the Confederacy), and we begin divvying up the country's most precious assets, my half will have to relinquish the largemouth, but—the good news!—the smallmouth stays ours. If this creates a problem, we'll throw in the catfish, but in return they have to leave us the trout.

Bass art is something I'd like to delve into someday. And when I say bass "art," I don't mean Winslow Homer's largemouth watercolors from the 1890s, timeless art, collectible art, but the kind of art that illustrated calendars, postcards, and tackle catalogs back in the 1940s and 1950s— illustrative art, commercial art, art for the moment that ages quite well.

You sometimes come upon these old sporting calendars in used bookstores or antique shops; if you turn to *May* or *June*, you'll often find a bass jumping at the end of a line, and, off in the background, the pipe-smoking fisherman who's attached to it. The pictures have an appealing old-time patina, not just because the colors have faded, but because they're so redolent of an era when sportsmen were just sportsmen and not professional "bassmasters," and bass were just bass, not corporate playthings. The angler will be wearing a red shirt, suspenders, a battered porkpie hat—he'll have a pal in the bow readying the landing net—and the bass will be cartwheeling over a log or rock with the streamer or bug very prominent in its lip. *MAY 1944* it will say somewhere over the water, and you wonder how anyone could make May 1944 seem so innocent and appealing.

Many old bass books have great illustrations—the illustrations are probably the only reason to still collect them. Photography in the 1930s was still somewhat primitive, at least when it came to capturing fish in motion, so publishers planning a bass book would commission illustrators to decorate the chapter heads with pen-and-ink drawings, and possibly add three or four full-color plates. The bass are either leaping at the end of a fisherman's line in these, or jumping to snare a moth out of midair, and you seldom see them depicted underwater.

Some of my favorite illustrations are in Ray Bergman's *Fresh-Water Bass*, published in 1945. Fred Hildebrandt illustrated it "in color and line," and he has a real knack for capturing the bass's exuberance and strength, plus the rarer ability to show quieter moments when they feed beneath the surface with not a fisherman in sight.

One color plate shows a bass leaping to catch big mayflies, backlit by a huge yellow moon, and I'd give a lot to own the original just for the way Hildebrandt captures its eye. One of the line drawings I like even better. A bass has risen toward a dragon fly, missed, and is now falling back down into a bed of jet-black ink strokes, which his weight shoots to all sides.

An earlier book, *Black Bass Lore* by Wallace W. Gallaher, published in 1937, is illustrated by the author's son, Paul Gallaher—and no bass book was ever decorated better. These are pen-and-ink drawings, more delicate and less brash than most bass illustrations, and they show a real appreciation, not just of bass, but of bass fishing—the quiet moments of anticipation when the bass is nothing more than a subtle swirl under the surface; the solitary moments in the reeds after he's been captured and released.

The real test of a bass illustrator is what they do with the fish's extravagant mouth; many seek to deemphasize it, making it smaller and less greedy than it really is, but Gallaher gets it just about right—"the mouth that swims." The other criterion of a good bass illustrator is that they make you feel wistfully nostalgic, and, looking at Gallaher's illustrations, I really pine for the 1930s, a decade I'd not otherwise care to visit.

There's another subject I've deliberately stayed away from so far—bass fly rods, what makes a good one and how it can enhance and subtly shape the whole fishing experience. I'm a rod freak, always have been since the first time I held one in my hand, and all I can say in my defense is that the fly rod is the one and only tool I've ever learned to wield properly; it's my saw, my screwdriver, my hammer, my—for that matter—violin, piano, and guitar. I made the mistake in an earlier book of calling fly rods "an epistemological tool," and was accused of being highfalutin, but there you are—I understand the world, the natural world, a lot better when I have a fly rod in my hand then when I don't.

But there's this funny thing about bass fly rods. Fly rods for trout can often approach perfection, blending extraordinary delicacy and great reserves of power, but bass rods, even the best of them, are inherently clumsy—and, what's more, *should* be clumsy, since they're tasked with delivering a fly, a bug, that is so much heavier and air resistant than a trout fly. They get tossed around boats a lot, which also argues against delicacy; they need "lifting power" unless you want the bass to push you around, so that bulks them up, too. I've had lots of good bass rods, but I've never had a great one (well, maybe once), and I've come to believe that great bass rods don't exist.

My first bass fly rod was my first fly rod, period. My father was legally blind, and couldn't even spin fish without my help, but for a reason I will never understand, showed up at our summer house once with a Heddon fiberglass fly rod he had just purchased at the Abraham & Strauss department store on Long Island. I'm not sure he even knew it was a fly rod, and not just a long brown pole; the salesman's pitch I would give a lot to travel back in time to overhear. At fourteen, I was already hooked on fishing, so it might have been a not-so-subtle ploy to introduce me to fly-fishing, but my father didn't operate that way—if I wanted a fly rod, he would have made sure it showed up at Christmas.

He never used it, so it quickly became mine; it was the rod I learned casting on, entirely on my own out in the yard, practice cast after practice cast, until I slowly began understanding its peculiarly fascinating rhythm. My arm ached after these sessions; it was a canon of a rod, weighing close to six ounces, or double the weight of a modern fly rod. I caught my first fly-rod bass on it (and, for that matter, my first fly-rod trout), and it was a sad day when, ten years after my father bought it, it died the classic fly rod death: smashed in a car door, the fiberglass shattering into shards.

My second bass rod was a Vince Cummings fiberglass I bought in 1976 with the $35 I'd received for selling my first short story. "Chowder" it was called, and Cummings—a respected rod builder—was nice enough to inscribe the title on the shaft. This had a slower action than the Heddon, and while slower is often better while bass bugging, it was a bit underpowered for what I asked of it. Its death was better—broken in hand by a good largemouth who plunged toward the bottom just when I had it to the net.

My favorite all-time bass rod came next, and, again, it's a sad story about its end. (I don't seem to have many sad stories about *trout* rods dying; must think about this further!) In 1985, I fished the Connecticut in southern Vermont with Tom Rosenbauer, the fishing writer and tackle guru. After a good day on the water, I handed him back the fly rod he had loaned me, an Orvis B&B, as in "Bonefish & Bass." It was an excellent smallmouth rod, slower and more forgiving than the rockets they make now, and, unlike most eight-weights, came unencumbered with a fighting butt that frequently gets in the way.

"Oh, that's for you," Tom said, handing it back. "And here, take this box of poppers, too."

That's what brought me back to bass fishing after years when I just chased trout—Tom's generous gesture.

Fast forward twenty-five years. I've caught hundreds, maybe thousands of bass on the B&B, like it so much I have never bought another bug rod, though I'm spending plenty on trout models. I have a friend, Chatsworth, who's retired CIA or military intelligence (he's a bit coy on which), and, while he's a spin fisher, we sometimes forget our differences and go out.

One August night we canoed across the Connecticut to the railroad tracks, started casting, and immediately got into fish. They crowded the shallows, feeding, it seemed, on the chokecherries overhanging the water or the lichen covering the rocks. Dessert after a main course of crayfish? I'd never seen anything quite like it.

I picked up the paddle to get Chatsworth into a good casting position for his plug, thought I was putting my fly rod across the edge of the canoe seat like I have a zillion times . . . laid it instead right in the river.

No problem. I've dropped fly rods from canoes plenty of times, and they always float thanks to the cork grip; or, if they start sinking, you can always grab the floating line and pull them back in. But I had a new reel on the rod, a large arbor that I had already decided was way too heavy—heavy enough, I now realized in horror, to make the rod sink and the line with it.

I grabbed for the bobbing tip and missed, tried turning the canoe so I could reach again, but with a passenger in the bow I couldn't lever it around quickly enough. My next thought was to jump overboard for it, but I knew that would capsize us, and I wasn't positive Chatsworth could swim. I had one more chance—I saw my Sneaky Pete drowning, its chartreuse face wearing a look of tremulous despair—but when I grabbed for it, I came up empty and the rod was gone.

I haven't given up hope that I'll recover it someday—that, fishing deep, my fly will snag it and bring it to the surface, weed covered and slimy, with a skeleton bass attached to a petrified fly.

It drowned five years ago, and I'm still looking for a rod that is its equal; most rods advertised as "bass action" are far too stiff and fast, so you might as well be spin fishing. Instead, I'm fishing by committee, alternating four or five fly rods that all have their virtues, without any having them all. Perhaps it's my age, but I've been in a retro mood lately, and have gone back to the fiberglass rods I first learned on, or at least their modern equivalent, which often has a small amount of graphite mixed in the rod's layup. Glass shapes itself to the fishing experience, yields to it, cushions it, while graphite often dominates. Why catching a bass on a fly rod that flexes down toward the butt is more satisfying than catching a bass on a rod that flexes only halfway down is a puzzling thing to a non-fisher, but to an old gearhead like me it makes perfect sense.

And before you criticize me for owning twenty-seven fly rods, ask yourself this: How many golf clubs do I own? How many tools?

I learn something about bass fishing every time I go out, but some of these observations are going to need another season or two before I understand them well enough to write about them. The sound a bass makes when it jumps is one of these. Until this summer, if you asked me to describe the sound a bass makes clearing the water, I would have talked about watery sounds, the cannonball *whoomph* when it hits the fly or the fluid whisking it makes as it churns the water into spray. Between the wind, the buzz of the reel, and shouted advice from whomever you're fishing with, it's hard to hear much more than splashes.

But a few times this summer, fishing alone in perfect silence, I noticed another sound quite independent of what the bass was doing to the water: a dry, distinct and vaguely prehistoric-sounding rattle. Whether it's the gill plates clicking against each other, or some unexpected crinkliness in the flesh, the bass I caught that morning all made a rattle when they cleared the water, like wooden beads shaking against each other on a string. You don't get much time to listen to this . . . watery splashings almost immediately drown it out . . . so I'll need to spend the next few seasons listening harder if I'm going to describe it right.

There are subjects I haven't written about because absolutely no one will believe me. Miracle lures is one of these. All my fishing life, I've read about miracle lures that will catch fish when everything else fails, of such potency that you have to be careful tying it on, or else be swarmed by voracious fish racing each other to devour it first. Most of these are spinning lures—we bass buggers don't do miracle lures.

And so, until this year, I never expected to find a fly that works under every circumstance. Now, to my utter amazement, I have. I'll call it the X, so as to (1) prevent people thinking I'm on the take, (2) avoid a run on the tackle stores, and (3) keep from jinxing it.

It's a simple enough design, having the shape and thickness of a floating twig. Made of foam, it's easy to cast, and the sloping lip pulls it under when you twitch it back. It has two white eyes, some decorative spotting over a pure white belly, a short tail of Flashabou or some other wispy synthetic flash material, a business-like hook, the barb of which I always pinch down—but the real key is the slightly humped way it's mounted on the hook, which gives an irresistible wiggle even when it's just floating, and increases in sexiness when you strip it back. It looks and acts something like the old Lazy Ike plug, which old-timers will remember from their youth.

I've used it before this summer, and had good results, but for some reason I was slow to appreciate its extraordinary fish-taking qualities. On our trip to the Penobscot I whimsically tied it on, and the bass, which were hitting regularly before this, went absolutely nuts. I brought it home to the Connecticut, and if anything it did even better; I would fish a hundred-yard stretch of shoreline with my usual favorites, catch nothing, go back and start over with X, and catch eight or nine bass. Again and again it did this—I was catching twice as many bass as before, and from spots where

I'd never had even a bite; often when fish missed it, they came up on the next cast to wallop it again, which is very rare. What's more, the X works just as well fished deep as it does fished on the surface. Canoeing between spots, I let whatever fly I have on troll out the back, and with normal bass bugs this will produce a hit maybe once every three trips. With the X, trolling near shore, I was getting strikes every thirty yards; for the first time in my life, I had a lure that fish were racing each other to attack.

Miracles being miracles, it's hard to account for X's potency. Like all classic lures, it has the ability to mimic several kinds of baits simultaneously, so the bass may be taking it for a moth, a minnow, a dragonfly, a crayfish—or maybe it's just that shape and the way it undulates, which speaks the language bass understand.

So, after years of searching and despite being previously a skeptic, I've found that they really exist after all, miracle lures. Great news? Partly. But since, on pragmatic grounds, there is absolutely no reason to put on another fly, it's taken the fun out of going through my box wondering which one to try.

Every fly fisher has a list of places they'd like to fish before they can't. *Someday* we say, until the years mount up and we begin to worry that means *Never*. I'm still on the *Someday* side of things, but not for much longer. If health, energy, and bank account hold out, there is a long list of bass waters I'd like to fish and write about, including . . . .

The upper Mississippi in Minnesota and the state's St. Croix. Smallmouth bass in their ancestral heartland. Use the same trip to head over to the Menominee on the Michigan/Wisconsin border, said to be one of the best bass rivers on the planet. And Georgian Bay in Lake Huron— big water, but there is no place on the continent bassier than that. On the way home I'd try the Erie Canal, catch descendants of those bold pioneering bass who left the Great Lake state to colonize New York and New England.

In late March, when there's no fishing to be had around here, I'd like to go down and fish Okefenokee Swamp in Georgia, do some red state fishing for largemouth, maybe with a good ol' boy guide who calls me Bubba. Okefenokee is where Pogo lived, and I've always been a big fan of Walt Kelly. Pogo fished a lot (for a possum), usually with Albert the Alligator in the bow, and I like how Kelly always inscribed the jonboat they fished from with the names of his friends. That's what I'd like to do, fishing Okefenokee. Lean over the side and scribble the names of my pals. *The Terry Boone. The Karen Kayen. The Gary Waelik. The Jane Curtis. The Nick Lyons.*

May would be the time to drive down to Virginia. The Shenandoah is worth fishing for the beauty of its name alone, and the James is said to be full of bass. Over on the western side of the state, the New River, geologically speaking, is one of the oldest rivers on the continent, and I'm at an age where that might be soothing. Rebel territory, of course—I'd have to keep my blue-state attitudes to myself.

I've fished the White River in Arkansas, which has gone from being one of the best bass rivers in the country to being one of the best trout rivers, but I'd like to explore the lower reaches for bass, or maybe the Buffalo, since so many old-time bass writers loved these Ozarks rivers best of all.

And then, come summer, I'd love to canoe the lakes of Quetico/Superior or Lake in the Woods, every inch of which is classic bass water. I'd like to fish Lake Mead in Nevada, which I used to read about as a kid. And, since I'm really fantasizing now, I'd like to try the Zapata Swamp in Cuba, especially Treasure Lake in the middle, *El Tesoro,* where's it said you can catch 150 largemouth a day, with a real chance for a world record. Or how about trying something truly *outré,* smallmouth fishing in South Africa, preferably on a river where I can view wildebeest and lions at the same time.

And I'll say this, to any readers who live on these waters or have a magic spot of their own they might like to share: I keep my travel rod packed at all times, and I'm perfectly comfortable sleeping on floors.

It's tempting to say that summer ends the moment I catch my last bass, but the truth is I'm still finding them on Halloween and even past Election Day. By then, I'll be concentrating on the brown trout that run up tributaries to our lakes; out in the delta where they gather, a lonely bass will sometimes come up to take my streamer, not like it's hungry, but like it wants to be saved from the mean-looking, hook-jawed browns it's gotten itself mixed up with. This will inevitably be a largemouth. Counterintuitively, smallmouth quit first, at least around here, when you think the cold water would chill out the largemouth much earlier.

It won't fight hard, this last bass of the season. Even bass, looking at their calendar, know when it's time to quit.

Or do they? In New England, the largest bass of the year are caught through the ice, so clearly they continue feeding through the winter; New Hampshire's length limits are intended to protect winter bass, not summer ones. This would surprise the old-timers who thought bass hibernated down in the mud. Dr. Henshall, writing on this in 1881, is as dogmatic as ever. "Bass undoubtedly hibernate in colder waters of the north, since it's proven in numerous instances that they bury themselves in the mud and remain dormant until spring." W. J. Loudon, writing in 1910, held the same opinion. "That they hibernate seems to be proved by the fact that when they reach their spawning beds in the early spring they are covered with snail-shells, leeches, slime and mud."

By the 1930s, opinion was beginning to change, so someone like Wallace Gallaher could tentatively suggest, "I realize this is heresy and contrary to men whose business it is to know about such things, but the fact remains that there is a strong likelihood that all bass do not hibernate."

And no one really believes this now, that bass hibernate in the mud like a bear in its cave. Hibernation has taken on a looser definition; bass are cold-blooded creatures, so their metabolism slows in winter, their feeding is sporadic, but they don't spend winter sleeping. They seem to find sheltered resting places near the bottom—and Henshall tells of occasions when loggers, drawing sunken logs from a river, found sluggish bass living in the hollows.

The exact moment in the autumn that I stop going out for bass and switch over to trout depends, like the start of bass fishing does in May, on events/milestones/turning points that seemingly have nothing to do with fishing. And it's not the very first signs of fall that signal the change, the crisp little frissons of coolness so welcome after summer's heat, but the second, more serious wave that comes past the equinox and is tinged unmistakably with winter.

And so, judging by that more impressionistic calendar, bass fishing ends when girls begin wearing wool sweaters and scarves, not just cotton ones; when the hardwoods shed their colors and the larch turn yellow; when the phone never stops ringing with politicians soliciting your vote; when the first oil delivery of the season lumbers up the driveway; when the sun is low and blinding through the windshield even at noon; when the tomatoes in the garden turn brown and the kale finally quits; when there's snow on New Hampshire's White Mountains summits; when the World Series goes to game six; when even a small country store in a rural New England village advertises the arrival of *Beaujolais Nouveau;* when Christmas catalogs begin filling the mailbox; when Orion rises in the east sideways, as if the hunter is still sleeping; when the trees are so bare it's impossible to imagine them ever having had leaves.

When those things happen, it's time to stop fishing for bass.

I become nostalgic for it almost immediately, the summer that's ended. Already, though only weeks have passed, it seems like it all happened in another era, to another person, a "he" not a "me"—which brings me to the moment I'll finish my book with, with gratitude for your having stayed with me so long, and hope that—one day!—we get to go out after bass together. "Next year in Jerusalem!" the faithful used to promise when saying farewell. And in the same spirit I extend my own vow to you. Next year on the Connecticut! Next year on the Shenandoah! Next year on the Mississippi!

A perfect summer day in late August. A flyfisher parks his car in a clearing in a cornfield on the east bank of the region's largest river. He's not young anymore, not in most aspects of his life, not while he's driving, cursing under his breath at the news, and worrying about his latest mysterious ache or pain—and certainly not when he slides the canoe down from the roof, banging his shoulder as he tries to cushion its landing. But once it's loaded and he pushes off from the bank, the years slip away, so if you want to know what's going on inside his heart as he paddles upriver, replace dullness with ardency, stiffness with flexibility, crankiness with hope.

He's been fly-fishing this stretch for a long time, so he knows where the bass hold—immediately he begins catching them. The current is strong enough that he has to really dig in and paddle in order to make any headway, and when he does play a bass, he loses twenty or thirty yards of river, and has to start upstream all over again. Tiring of this, he puts down the rod and just paddles until he's as far upriver as his muscles can take him, and then turns the canoe around and floats down again, knowing he has a mile of water he can fish in comfort.

He's casting a deer-hair mouse imitation, and, landing near a log, it's engulfed by a wave so greedy and imperious it's like a river god is sucking down a sacrifice made to appease him. It's a bass and a big one . . . this stretch is famous for four-pounders . . . and the man laughs out loud when it jumps, since whatever else happens, this one single moment has made the long drive, the hard paddle, worthwhile.

While he's playing it, a shadow crosses his head—it's like some kindly person has interposed an umbrella between him and the hot sun—and when he looks up he sees an eagle, a bald eagle, gliding from the pines on the near bank toward the maples on the far shore. He's seen young eagles here all summer, but this one is beautifully mature, the smooth white curve of its neck matched by the somewhat ragged white fan of his tail.

He knows it's a big moment even while it's happening. A bass tugging on the line, an eagle tugging on his heart. Two American symbols, their stories complementing each other perfectly, the eagle coming back from the brink of extinction, the bass representing one of the few precious corners of the natural world that man hasn't yet messed up.

Airy meanings versus deeper ones—they represent these, too. The eagle is what Americans like to think of themselves as in their best moments—lofty, noble, glorious, exceptional—while the bass probably comes closer to who we are in fact: strong, pragmatic, bigmouthed, opportunistic, turbulent, something of a bruiser but a creature who doesn't quit.

Bald eagle, smallmouth bass. That leaves the man in the middle to account for. He's probably as atypical an American as is out fishing anywhere today (and nowhere more atypical than in his style of bass fishing), and yet, even with that, he shares many of the classic American values. Belief that he's as good as anyone and anyone is as good as he. A love for the American landscape, its mountains, rivers, lakes, and hills, matched by an even stronger love for the stories of its people, where they came from, who they are. An optimism that, even with all the battering it has taken lately, refuses to give up.

Usually when he lands a bass, he's content to release it quickly and quietly, with a minimum of fuss, but he can't let a symbolic moment like this go past without at least acknowledging it with a gesture. As it turns out, it's a simple one. He puts his hands under the smallmouth's middle like a proud poppa cradling a baby, and then lifts it high in the air to show the eagle what a great American symbol looks like in its prime.